TRAVELLERS IN EUROPE

J. G. LINKS

TRAVELLERS IN EUROPE

Private Records of Journeys by the Great and the Forgotten

From Horace to Pepys

THE BODLEY HEAD
LONDON SYDNEY
TORONTO

British Library Cataloguing
in Publication Data
Links, J. G.
Travellers in Europe.
1. Europe—Description and travel—To 1600
2. Europe—Description and travel—17th–18th centuries
3. Europe—History—Sources
I. Title
914'.04'1   D907
ISBN 0-370-30202-8

© J. G. Links 1980
Printed in Great Britain for
The Bodley Head Ltd
9 Bow Street, London WC2E 7AL
by BAS Printers Limited, Over Wallop, Hampshire
Set in Monophoto Imprint
First published 1980

CONTENTS

PART THREE
Sixteenth-century Travellers

PART FOUR
Seventeenth-century Travellers

List of Illustrations

Grateful acknowledgement to the museums, galleries and photographic archives for permission to reproduce illustrations, as listed above.

Maps

Maps drawn by Ken Jordan.

AUTHOR'S PREFACE

Montaigne said that he took such pleasure in travelling that he hated the very approach to the place where he was to rest. In this he stood almost alone. Until a century or two ago hardly anyone left home voluntarily unless it was to improve his lot. One travelled for spiritual refreshment or to improve one's mind by study; some went in furtherance of their trade or profession, others to seek a cure for their ailments (this was the ostensible reason for Montaigne's travels, however much he may have enjoyed them). No one went just for pleasure, to bask in the sun, or because his neighbours had been.

A few told the story of their travels and, since they were not tourists and for the most part had no thought of publication in mind, they also told much about themselves and the usages of their time; some of them even lit up a page or two of history without knowing it. I have chosen twenty-two of these travellers and allowed them to tell these stories as far as possible in their own words. Because of their widely differing character, position and period, a general picture of early European travel seems to have emerged. This, though, is incidental. The tales have been chosen first for the freshness of the traveller's response to the events of his journey and to what he found on arrival.

I have defined 'travel' as the kind of journey the reader might see himself as undertaking—might, indeed, in a number of cases, have already undertaken himself. It is in travels of this kind that the story-teller, seldom practised in the art of descriptive writing, can best hope to carry his reader with him all the way. Explorers who set off for unmapped territory have therefore not been included, nor have those who went to conquer (Robert of Clari was first a pilgrim, unwillingly made a conqueror by chicanery). Those who become giddy if they stand on tiptoe, or who value their lives more than they value glory, may delight in reading about the ascent of the north face of the Eiger or Caesar's conquest of Gaul, but they will hardly be able to see themselves in the traveller's shoes. For much the same reasons I have confined the territory covered to the frontiers of Europe. This provided a quite large enough field for adventure and its travellers' tales carry a sense of conviction often lacking in, say, those of Marco Polo.

The period chosen begins with classical times and ends with the transformation of the land-traveller from a rider to a passenger. The later traveller in a wheeled vehicle may have much of interest to tell but his experiences do not belong to the same book as those whose vantage point was the ground or the saddle or the deck of a sailing boat. There is, of course, no day or year when driving began and riding or walking ended, but Pepys's purchase of a coach was symbolic of the end of an era even though it may not have coincided exactly with the end.

Two more self-imposed restrictions should be mentioned. The voluntary factor has been taken as essential since the unwilling traveller will see little worth recording. This does not exclude those who respond to the call of duty : her voice is seldom heard except by those who are listening for it. A home to return to is also a prerequisite. The settler's flight from poverty, persecution or high taxes might well be the subject of a book, but not this book.

The documents used were for the most part private documents—diaries, despatches and personal letters not intended for publication. In a few cases a short extract has been taken from a published source in which travel was quite incidental (Horace, de Comines or Cellini, for example) but only in two cases did the traveller leave home in order to write a book. The reader will have no difficulty in recognizing Fynes Moryson and Coryat as travellers of a different stamp from all the others, the first professional travel writers. It is an honourable profession, if a little over-crowded, but I must make an editorial confession: whereas the problem generally has been one of deciding what nuggets of gold must be sacrificed in the cause of manageability, in these two cases it has not been easy to select a few thousand from the hundreds of thousands of words each wrote.

The privacy of the documents has raised certain problems of its own. Diaries and letters are seldom works of art (although there are enough exceptions, even in this book, to prove the rule). The writers are apt to use ceremonial addresses to their superiors, to moralize to their inferiors and to repeat themselves to both. Generally, if they are writing for a reader at all, it is for a reader who knows as much of the background as they do. It would therefore not do to leave them entirely to themselves. As well as an introduction, they need a helping hand, sometimes to look up a date for them, sometimes to lead them back to their paths, sometimes just held over their mouths. This has been done as unobtrusively as possible and it has not been thought necessary to indicate where words or longer passages have been omitted. The reader should understand that he has a book of extracts in his hand and if there is too little of any traveller to his taste he will find, on reference to the bibliography, that plenty more awaits him.

The English came late to recording their travel experiences (although they soon made up for their tardiness) so that rather more than the first half of the book consists of translations. In all these cases the writers speak in the modern English of their translators: no one would attempt to translate Robert of Clari into the language of Chaucer, or Montaigne into Elizabethan English. The English writers, on the other hand, are reproduced more or less in the language they used themselves, archaic though some of it may sound. To do otherwise would be an affront to any lover of the language, who is more likely to question such tampering as has taken place. The consequence is that the style changes from modern English in the first part to seventeenth-century English in the second. This is of course anomalous but for the reader unversed in ancient European languages there is no real alternative.

My debt to the translators is acknowledged with gratitude; their learning has been plundered for the entertainment of the present reader. However, I have not felt inhibited from using more than one translation or transcription of a text, turning occasionally from one to another to find a happier word or phrase. No good scholar claims omniscience and I am confident of forbearance on this score.

J. G. LINKS
London 1979

PART ONE

Roman and Medieval Travellers

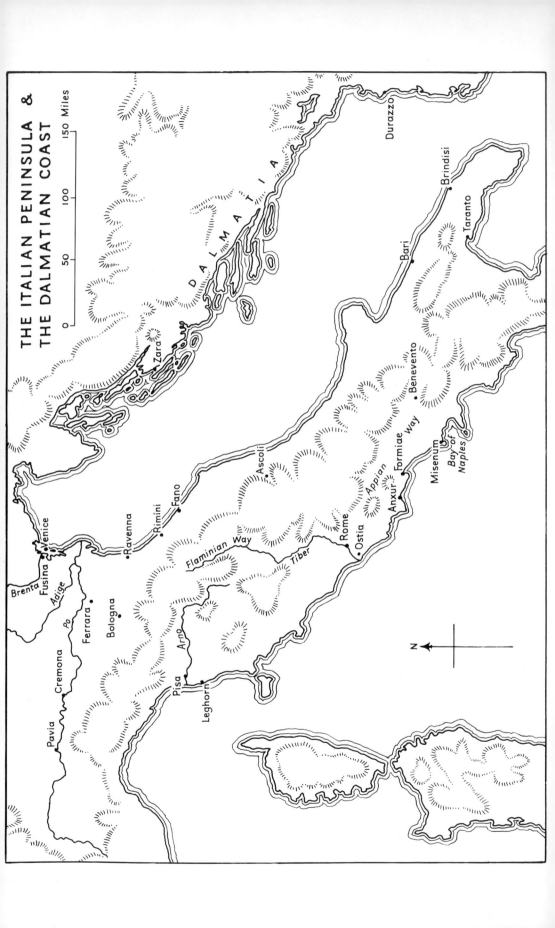

THE ITALIAN PENINSULA &
THE DALMATIAN COAST

150 Miles
100
50
0

DALMATIA

Durazzo
Brindisi
Taranto
Bari

Zara

Ascoli
Benevento
Formiae Way
Misenum
Appian
Anxur
Bay of
Naples

Rimini
Fano
Ravenna

Flaminian Way
Rome
Ostia
Tiber

Venice
Fusina
Brenta
Adige
Arno
Po
Ferrara
Bologna
Cremona
Pisa
Pavia
Leghorn

N

Horace

'Like the great fool I was'

Rome to Brindisi, 37 B.C.

(Map on p. 14)

During 38 and 37 B.C. the diplomat Maecenas was negotiating between his master Octavian (Augustus) in Rome and Octavian's fellow triumvir, Mark Antony in Athens. His task was to avoid a clash between the two triumvirs in the face of a threat from Sextus Pompeius, and he more than once found himself travelling on the Appian Way which led from Rome to Taranto and Brindisi. On one such journey Maecenas and his party were joined by his close friends, Horace and Virgil, and Horace later told of their travels in a poem which was included in his miscellany called *Satires*.

In some respects it is a model traveller's tale. It is short, indeed only six hundred words, perhaps too short. It is topographically accurate, with the scenic descriptions rigidly controlled, and lacks few of the elements expected from a traveller. The account of delay and discomfort, of bad food and mosquitoes, warms the heart of the reader as he sits in his comfortable armchair, and the contrasting luxury and gaiety of the party at Cocceius's house brings a sense of intimacy with the great and the gifted. There is adventure in the account of a fire and even some sex, sadly frustrated.

For a time, at the end of the last century, classical scholars tended to suggest that Horace's *Journey to Brundisium*, as the poem came to be called, was not a true account. The need for a wood fire, they argued, indicates a journey in the autumn whereas the frogs' chorus shows that it must have been spring; in any case, said some, Horace was merely following Lucilius, who had described a journey to Sicily almost a century earlier in similar terms, even to the erotic dream. But naturalists and historians have since been able to reconcile apparent conflicts and too little survives of

1. 'The Appian Way is less tiring to those who travel slowly'.

Lucilius's work to prove anything. The best modern opinion accepts Horace as a good witness. Moreover, a man is not upon oath, Dr. Johnson reminded Boswell, in lapidary inscriptions; nor, he might have added, in travellers' tales.

'After leaving mighty Rome I was received in a modest inn in Aricia [sixteen miles away]: my companion was Heliodorus, a most learned Greek. We then went on to Forum Appii, a town crammed full of boatmen and extortionate innkeepers. This journey we were lazy enough to do in two stages: it is only one to the more energetic. The Appian Way is less tiring to those who travel slowly.'

It is unlikely that Horace and his companion were on foot and, whether they were carried in litters or being jolted in springless carriages, the Appian Way must have been tiring, however slowly one travelled. The road had long been completed right down to Brindisi, and was for the most part paved, but it was often eroded by water from the Apennines. On reaching Forum Appii most travellers therefore preferred to use a canal which took them through the Pomptine marshes as far as Anxur, nineteen miles farther on. This was Horace's choice in spite of the drawbacks.

'Here, by reason of the dreadful drinking water, my stomach and I were on hostile terms and I waited for my companion, and the others who were taking dinner, with some impatience.

'Now the night began to dot the sky with stars. The slaves jested with the boatmen and the boatmen with the slaves. Whilst the fare is being demanded, and the mule fastened, a whole hour is gone. Accursed mosquitoes and marsh frogs keep sleep from our eyes. The boatman, drenched with much sour wine, sings of his absent mistress and a passenger rivals his song; when at last the weary passenger drops asleep the boatman ties the halter of the mule to a stone, turns it out to graze and himself lies on his back, snoring.

'So now day is dawning and we find the boat is not yet under way. Up springs a choleric fellow and belabours the mule and the boatman with a cudgel of willow. At last, late in the morning, we come ashore. We bathe our faces and hands in fair water and after breakfast re-embark and crawl along. Now we go under the gate of Anxur, a town built on rocks that shine white from afar.'

This was Terracina, where a headland fell sheer into the sea, forcing the Appian Way to go over the hill and past the temple of

2. 'The boatman, drenched with much sour wine'. A Roman decorates his wine-cellar with a portrayal of the wine being towed in a barge manned by a mellow boatman.

Jupiter Anxur. Trajan later built a cutting to enable the road to follow the coast. The travellers now disembarked. 'Here good Maecenas and Cocceius were to meet us, both sent as envoys on important matters, and old hands at reconciling estranged friends. My concern was to put black ointment on my sore eyes.'

After the arrival of the diplomats, and some jesting, the party went on by road to Formiae, near Mola di Gaeta, where they had been lent a house for the night and were entertained to dinner.

'The following day shines upon us as much the pleasantest day in our journey for we were joined by Plotius, Virgil and Varius, all devoted friends to me. A little villa next to the bridge over the River Savo gave us a roof over our heads and the [Government-appointed] commissaries all the necessaries they are bound to supply. After the next stage our mules are eased of their pack-saddles early in the day at Capua. Maecenas goes to play at ball, Virgil and I to sleep, for it is bad for the dyspeptic and sore-eyed to play ball. At the end of the next stage we are received in Cocceius's well-stored villa above the taverns at Caudium.'

Here there was much recondite banter and 'we were so diverted that we continued supper to an unusual length'. The next day's stage was of twelve miles and took the party to Benevento (Horace's own birthplace).

'Here our bustling landlord nearly burnt his house down while roasting some skinny thrushes, for the flames quickly licked the top of the roof. Hungry guests and frightened slaves were to be seen snatching the supper out of the flames and trying to extinguish the fire.

'From this point Apulia begins to show the outlines of its familiar hills, scorched by the sirocco. We should never have got over these mountains had not the owner of a villa near Trivicum welcomed us, but his fire drew tears from my eyes as the wood was still green with the leaves on. Here, like the great fool I was, I wait till midnight for a deceitful mistress; sleep however overcomes me while meditating love, and disagreeable dreams make me ashamed of myself and everything about me.'[1]

Next morning, Horace goes out of his way to record, the party were 'whirled in carriages [*redis*] twenty-four miles', implying perhaps that they had not hitherto been travelling by *reda*. This was a four-wheeled carriage, generally drawn by mules, as opposed to *cisium*, a two-wheeled carriage often drawn by one horse. Private vehicles are very seldom seen in the sculpture, and never in the painting, that has survived from Roman times but there are

3. 'Brindisi is the end of my long journey and of my long story'. Remains of two columns erected by Trajan to mark the terminus of the Appian Way at Brindisi (Brundisium).

enough references to make it certain that they played a part in the citizen's life. The journey was nearing its end. At night they reached a place that the poet 'could not speak in verse' (because it would not scan), so providing classical scholars with a subject for a great deal of learned controversy; Ascoli seems to meet most requirements—but for the fact that there would be little difficulty in making it scan.

'However,' continues Horace, leaving his readers to argue the matter for two thousand years, 'I can very easily describe it. Here the commonest of all things, water, is *sold*; but the bread is excellent so that the traveller who knows the road loads it on his slaves' shoulders a stage further, the gritty bread at Canosa being hard as a stone and the water no more plentiful.

'Thence we arrived at Rubi, quite fatigued as was to be expected, the stage being long and the road broken up by rain. Next day's weather was better but the road still worse, even to the walls of Bari, a fishing town; then Egnatia, a place built when the water-nymphs were angry [i.e. the water was poor or scarce]. Brindisi is the end of my long journey and of my long story.'

Here the Appian Way came to an end and Durazzo (Dyrrachium), the Calais of Greece, lay forty miles from the Dover of Italy. It may be taken that Maecenas and Cocceius went on to conduct their state business, leaving the poets to return to Rome, some 370 miles away. More than one of Horace's readers have been tempted to retrace his route, stopping where he stopped or may, from the length of the stage, be assumed to have stayed. The consensus is that the journey took fifteen days but Edward Gibbon, who thought the poem betrayed a lack of taste on the part of Horace but was nevertheless constrained to follow in his footsteps, managed it in twelve.

---

[1]*Hic ego mendacem stultissimus usque puellam/ ad mediam noctem expecto : somnus tamen aufert/ intentum Veneri : tum immundo somnia visu/ nocturnam vestem maculant ventremque supinum.*

Victorian schoolmasters in England were spared the embarrassment of dealing with awkward questions from their pupils over the passage. Not only was the tactful translation generally omitted: line 81 of the original text was often followed by line 86.

2

Pliny The Younger

'Leave the road at the fourteenth milestone'

Rome to Laurentum, c. A.D. 100

(Map on p. 14)

One day, at the turn of the first century, a Roman called Gallus received an invitation to visit a friend who has since become known as Pliny the Younger. No record exists of Gallus's journey, which was only eighteen miles in length; indeed, there is no absolute certainty that he ever accepted the invitation or, for that matter, who Gallus was. However, the invitation was so attractive a one that it is hard to believe that Gallus refused it, and Pliny's description of the road and what awaited the traveller at its end is so specific that only pedantry would exclude it from these records merely on the grounds that it preceded the journey and was told by the host rather than by the guest. Laurentum was a few miles south-east of Ostia, then at the mouth of the Tiber; Pliny himself can be relied upon for more detailed instructions.

'You may wonder why my Laurentine place is such a joy to me, but once you realize the attractions of the house itself, the amenities of its situation, and its extensive seafront, you will have your answer. It is seventeen miles from Rome, so that it is possible to spend the night there after necessary business is done, without having cut short or hurried the day's work, and it can be approached by more than one route; the roads to Laurentum and Ostia both lead in that direction, but you must leave the one at the fourteenth milestone and the other at the eleventh. Whichever way you go, the side road you take is sandy for some distance and rather heavy and slow-going if you drive[1] but soft and easily covered on horseback. The view on either side is full of variety, for sometimes the road narrows as it passes through the woods, and then it broadens and opens out through wide meadows where there are

4. 'The house is large enough for my needs but not expensive to keep up'.
A model of Pliny's house, based on his description.

many flocks of sheep and herds of horses and cattle driven down
from the mountains in winter to grow sleek on the pastures in the
springlike climate.

'The house is large enough for my needs but not expensive to
keep up. It opens into a hall, unpretentious but not without
dignity, and then there are two colonnades, rounded like the letter
D, which enclose a small but pleasant courtyard. This makes a
splendid retreat in bad weather, being protected by windows and
still more by the overhanging roof.'

Out of the courtyard led a hall and then a dining-room which
looked out on to the sea towards the west. Four bedrooms
succeeded one another off the south side of the dining-room. The
second and third of these had windows facing east, to receive the
morning sun, and the fourth, which was fitted with bookshelves,
had a bow window towards the south so that it received the sun all
day. One of these rooms had a 'a floor raised and fitted with pipes to
receive hot steam and circulate it at a regulated temperature'. On
the west side of the first three bedrooms was a gymnasium, used as
winter-quarters, and on the east side of the first one, instead of a
window, were the staff quarters; these were 'kept for the use of my
slaves and freedmen, but most of them are quite presentable
enough to receive guests'.

Another bedroom and a room which could 'either be a bedroom
or moderate-sized dining-room' led off the other, north, side of the

main dining-room, the bedroom particularly being very elegant [*politissimum*]. On the landward side of these two rooms were a series of baths and recreation rooms.

'The cooling-room of the bath is large and spacious and has two curved baths built out of opposite walls; these are quite large enough if you consider that the sea is so near. Next comes the oiling-room, the furnace-room, and the ante-chamber to the bath, and then two rest-rooms, beautifully decorated in a simple style, leading to the heated swimming-bath which is much admired and from which swimmers can see the sea. Close by is the ball-court which receives the full warmth of the setting sun. Here there is a second storey with living-rooms and a dining-room which command the whole expanse of sea and stretch of shore with all its lovely houses.'

5. 'A stretch of shore with all its lovely houses'. A wall-painting from Pompeii.

The garden had box and rosemary hedges and a vine pergola, and was thickly planted with mulberries and figs; there was also a kitchen-garden. There was a huge covered arcade on the north side of the house and, at the end of this, a small private suite for Pliny when on his own, 'really and truly my favourites, for I had them built myself'.

'When I retire to this suite I feel as if I have left my house altogether and much enjoy the sensation; especially during the Saturnalia [the week starting on 17 December] for I am not disturbing my household's merrymaking nor they my work.

'Only one thing is needed to complete the amenities of the house—running water [*aqua salienti*]; but there are wells, or rather springs, for they are very near the surface. Wherever you dig you come upon water which is pure, although the sea is so near. The woods close by provide plenty of firewood, and the little town of Ostia supplies us with everything else. There is also a village, just beyond the next house, which can satisfy anyone's modest needs, and here there are three baths for hire, a great convenience if a sudden arrival or too short a stay makes us reluctant to heat up the bath at home. The sea-front gains much from the variety of the houses; from the sea these look like a number of cities. The sea has admittedly few fish of any value, but it gives us excellent soles and prawns, and all inland produce is provided by the house.

'You are too wedded to the city[2] if you don't covet this retreat— but I hope you will, for then the many attractions of my treasured house will have another strong recommendation in your company.'

---

[1] *. . . iunctis paulo gravius et longius.* All authorities translate *iunctis* (which means 'harness') in the same sense; 'if you travel in a coach', 'in a wheel carriage' and 'with a pair' are some of the alternatives to 'if you drive'. Compare Horace p. 18.

  With the fall of the Roman empire the carriage, or its equivalent, disappears for many centuries.

[2] *. . . quem tu nimis urbanus es nisi concupiscis.* Translators have had many tries, including 'too polite a townsman' and 'perfect cockney'.

3

Pliny The Younger

'The terrors I had to face'

From Misenum and back, A.D. 79

(Map on p. 14)

Pliny, as may be gathered from the description of his villa, was by that time a rich man and before his death a much richer one. He had been born at Como in 61 or 62, the son of Lucius Caecilius and Plinia, whose brother we know as Pliny the Elder. His father died young and Pliny went to Rome at the age of fourteen to finish his education. Here he came into closer contact with his uncle who, at various times, was a soldier, admiral and lawyer but, above all, a scholar who published 102 volumes including an encyclopedia called *Natural History*. On his uncle's death the young man inherited the estate and adopted the uncle's name instead of his father's. Pliny became a highly successful lawyer and official and hoped to retire to one of his two country houses. Instead, not long after his letter to Gallus was written, he accepted a post as representative of the Emperor Trajan in Bithynia on the Black Sea and there he died in about 113 after only three years' service.

In the letter that follows Pliny is describing events that had taken place many years earlier, in 79, when he was seventeen years old. He is writing to the historian Tacitus, who had evidently asked for an account of the elder Pliny's death. This had occurred while the nephew had been staying at Misenum, on the bay of Naples, where his uncle was in command of the fleet. A cloud of unusual appearance had been seen above a mountain, later known to be Vesuvius, and the elder Pliny determined to order a boat and proceed to the spot.

Pliny never saw his uncle alive again but he gave Tacitus a vivid account of the incident based on the evidence of witnesses he questioned immediately after the event. The elder Pliny had soon realized that there were many people to be rescued and ordered his warships to the danger zone. He himself had landed in the face of the hot, falling ashes and joined friends at Stabiae. When it became impossible to remain in the swaying buildings, and as many as possible had been embarked, the whole party had put pillows on their heads, tied down with cloths, and made for the sea again, but by this time the old man had breathed too much of the dense fumes; his windpipe was blocked and he choked to death.

Meanwhile the younger Pliny remained with his mother at Misenum and, after a letter to Tacitus describing his uncle's death, he proceeded with an account of his own adventures.

'So the letter which you asked me to write on my uncle's death has made you eager to hear about the terrors and hazards I had to face when I left Misenum, for I broke off at the beginning of this part of my story.

'After my uncle's departure I spent the rest of the day with my books, as this was the reason for my staying behind. Then I took a bath, dined, and then dozed fitfully for a while. For several days past there had been earth tremors which were not particularly alarming because they are frequent in Campania: but that night the shocks were so violent that everything felt as if it were not only shaken but overturned. My mother hurried into my room and found me already getting up to wake her if she were still asleep. We sat down in the forecourt of the house, between the buildings and the sea close by. I don't know whether I should call this courage or folly on my part (I was only seventeen at the time) but I called for a volume of Livy and went on reading as if I had nothing else to do. I even went on with the extracts I had been making. Up came a friend of my uncle's who had just come from Spain to join him. When he saw us sitting there and me actually reading, he scolded us both—me for my foolhardiness and my mother for allowing it. Nevertheless I remained absorbed in my book.

'By now it was dawn, but the light was still dim and faint. The buildings round us were already tottering, and the open space we were in was too small for us not to be in real and imminent danger if the house collapsed. This finally decided us to leave the town. We were followed by a panic-stricken mob of people wanting to act on someone else's decision in preference to their own, who hurried us on our way by pressing hard behind in a dense crowd. Once beyond the buildings we stopped, and there we had some extraordinary experiences which thoroughly alarmed us. The carriages [*vehicula*] we had ordered to be brought out began to run

6. 'I called for a volume of Livy'. Pliny the Younger: fifteenth-century
sculpture on the porch of Como Cathedral.

in different directions although the ground was quite level, and would not remain stationary even when wedged with stones. We also saw the sea sucked away and apparently forced back by the earthquake: at any rate it receded from the shore so that quantities of sea creatures were left stranded on dry land. On the landward side a fearful black cloud was rent by forked and quivering bursts of flame, and parted to reveal great tongues of fire, like flashes of lightning magnified in size.

'At this point my uncle's friend from Spain spoke up still more urgently: "If your brother, if your uncle is still alive, he will want you both to be saved; if he is dead he would want you to survive him—why put off your escape?" We replied that we would not think of considering our own safety as long as we were uncertain of his. Without waiting any longer, our friend rushed off and hurried out of danger as fast as he could.

'Soon afterwards the cloud sank down to earth and covered the sea; it had already blotted out Capri and hidden the promontory of Misenum from sight. Then my mother implored, entreated and commanded me to escape as best I could—a young man might escape whereas she was old and slow and could die in peace as long as she had not been the cause of my death too. I refused to save myself without her, and grasping her hand, forced her to quicken her pace. She gave in reluctantly, blaming herself for delaying me. Ashes were already falling, not as yet very thickly. I looked round: a dense black cloud was coming up behind us, spreading over the earth like a flood. "Let us leave the road while we can still see," I said, "or we shall be knocked down and trampled underfoot by the crowd behind." We had scarcely sat down to rest when darkness fell, not the dark of a moonless or cloudy night, but as if the lamp had been put out in a closed room. You could hear the shrieks of women, the wailing of infants, and the shouting of men; some were calling their parents, others their children or their wives, trying to recognize them by their voices. People bewailed their own fate or that of their relatives, and there were some who prayed for death in their terror of dying. Many besought the aid of the gods, but still more imagined there were no gods left, and that the universe was plunged into eternal darkness for evermore. There were people, too, who added to the real perils by inventing fictitious dangers; some reported that part of Misenum had collapsed, or another part was on fire, and though their tales were false they found others to believe them. A gleam of light returned but we took this to be a warning of the approaching flames rather than daylight. However, the flame remained some distance off; then darkness came on once more and ashes began to fall again, this time in heavy showers. We rose from time to time and shook them off, otherwise we should have been buried and crushed beneath their weight.

'At last the darkness thinned and dispersed into smoke or cloud; then there was genuine daylight, and the sun actually shone out, but yellowish as it is during an eclipse. We were terrified to see everything changed, buried deep in ashes like snowdrifts. We returned to Misenum where we attended to our physical needs as best we could, and then spent an anxious night alternating between hope and fear. Fear predominated, for the earthquakes went on, and several hysterical individuals made their own and other people's calamities seem ludicrous in comparison with their frightful predictions. But even then, in spite of the dangers we had been through and were still expecting, my mother and I had no intention of leaving until we had news of my uncle.

'Of course these details are not important enough for history, and you will read them without any idea of recording them; if they seem scarcely worth putting in a letter, you have only yourself to blame for asking for them.'

4

Sidonius Apollinaris

'You ask what route I took'

Down the River Po, 467

(Map on p. 14)

In 467 the Roman Empire in the West was within a few years of its end. Sidonius Apollinaris was approaching forty and living a life of retirement in the Roman province of Lyons. He had had his day, during which he had been married to the Emperor's daughter; he had played backgammon, or a game very like it, with the Visigoth Theodoric II and known everyone of consequence in the dying Roman civilization. He was primarily a poet but it is hard to believe that anyone could have read or listened to his poetry even when he was alive.

Suddenly the situation in Rome changed. There was a *rapprochement* with the court of Constantinople, and the Byzantine Emperor, at the request of the Senate in Rome, had not only sent a distinguished and noble soldier, Anthemius, to be the new Western Emperor but had given his own daughter in marriage to Ricimer, the most powerful man in Rome. There was a new hope in Italy that the barbarians might be held back after all. There was also a new hope in the mind of Sidonius that his career might not after all be ended, and he decided to cross the Alps with a letter for the new Emperor from the people of Lyons. Expecting to find the Emperor at Ravenna he journeyed down the river Po and then, finding the Emperor had gone to Rome for the wedding of his daughter, Sidonius turned on to the Flaminian Way.

On arrival at Rome Sidonius wrote to his friend Herenius at Lyons describing his journey. His letter gives no hint of the momentous events that were taking place around him but it gives a rare picture of how a civilian travelled as the shadows lengthened just before the Dark Age fell upon Europe.

'I received your letter after I had settled down at Rome. You ask whether the affairs which brought me here are prospering as we hoped. You also ask what route I took and how I fared on it, what rivers celebrated in song I saw, what towns famed for their situation, what mountains, what battlefields; for, having read of these things, you want to compare the descriptions with the account of an eye-witness. Well then, though some things went wrong, I will begin with my good news, for our ancestors used so to begin, even for a tale of their misfortunes.

'As the bearer of an imperial letter I found the state post at my disposal when I left our native Lyons; moreover the homes of intimate friends and relations lined the route. Delays on my journey were due not to scarcity of post-horses but to multiplicity of friends, so closely did everyone cling about me and wish me well. In this way I drew near the Alps, which I ascended easily and without delay; formidable precipices rose on either side but the snow was hollowed into a track and the way thus smoothed before me. Such rivers, too, as could not be crossed in boats had convenient fords or traversable bridges which our forefathers had built on vaulted arches. At Pavia on the Ticino I boarded a packet-boat and travelled quickly downstream to the Po; be sure I laughed over those songs we have often sung about Phaeton's sisters and their tears of amber gum.' Phaeton's sisters, according to Ovid, mourned so bitterly upon his death that they were changed into poplars and their tears into amber-coloured gum. The so-called Lombardy poplars evidently lined the banks of the Po long before the arrival of the Lombards.

'I passed the mouths of many tributaries, the sedgy Lambro, the Blue Adda, the swift Adige and the slow Mincio which have sources in the Ligurian or Euganean mountains.' It was at the junction with the Mincio that, only fifteen years earlier, Pope Leo the Great had met Attila the Hun and persuaded him to turn away from Rome.

'I cruised a little way upstream from the point of confluence so as to see each actually in its own waters. Their banks and knolls were everywhere clad with groves of oak and maple. A concert of birds filled the air with sweet sounds; their nests swayed on the hollow reeds or amid the prickly rushes or the smooth reed-grass luxuriantly flourishing in the moisture of this springy soil. The way led past Cremona and then we entered Brescello just long enough to take on Emilian boatmen in place of our Venetian oarsmen.' The Veneti were an ancient tribe who had probably founded Padua and who had been citizens of Rome since 49 B.C. Their country was soon to be devastated by the Huns under Attila but refugees from the barbarian invasions were already inhabiting the islands of the Venetian lagoon and became the forerunners of the Venetian Republic.

'A little later, bearing to the right, we reached Ravenna where Caesar's road runs between the old town and the new harbour; one could scarcely say whether it joins or parts them. The Po divides above the city, part flowing through, part round it; it is diverted from its main bed by the city embankments along whose course are branch channels which draw off more and more of the stream. The effect of this division is that the waters which encircle the walls provide protection while those which flow into the town bring commerce. But the drawback is that, with water all about us, we could not quench our thirst; there was neither pure-flowing aqueduct nor filtered reservoir. On one side the salt tides rushed up to the gates and elsewhere the sewer-like filth of the canals, churned up by the boat-traffic and the bargemen's poles boring into the slime at the bottom, fouled the current, sluggish at the best.'

Ravenna, now six miles from the sea, had been a seaport on a branch of the Po. The 'new harbour' was at Classis, three miles away, and under Augustus it could contain two hundred and fifty ships. The sea had long since retreated but Ravenna had been the chief residence of the Roman emperors since 404 when Honorius, alarmed by the progress of the barbarians, had transferred his Court there. The town held this position until the fall of the Western empire in 476. Water was proverbially dearer than wine there until Theodoric, who took Ravenna in 492, restored an aqueduct which had been built by Trajan.

Sidonius found the Emperor had left the city and he followed the Flaminian Way down the coast to Fano, then turning inland for Rome. 'From Ravenna we came to the Rubicon; the name is derived from the red tint of its gravel. This used to be the dividing line between Cisalpine Gaul and the old Italy, the towns on the Adriatic coast being divided between the two peoples. Thence I went on to Rimini and Fano, the first celebrated through the rebellion of Caesar.' By crossing the Rubicon and occupying Rimini Caesar had taken the momentous step of entering 'the old Italy'.

'As for the other towns of the Flaminian Way, I just passed through them—in at one gate, out at the other. But then my exhausted system succumbed either to the Atabulus [sirocco] from

Calabria or to the insalubrious air of the Tuscan region which brought on sweats and chills alternately. Fever and thirst ravaged my very marrow; in vain I promised it the deliciousness of springs and hidden wells, water of Velino, clear as glass, or of Clitunno, ice-cold—I longed to drink but prudence stayed the craving. Then Rome burst upon my sight and I thought I could drink dry not only its aqueducts but all its ponds. I sank on my knees at the triumphal threshold of the Apostles [St. Peter's, founded in A.D. 326 and St. Paul's in A.D. 386, both still outside the city walls] and straightway I felt that all the sickness had been driven from my enfeebled limbs; after which proof of heavenly protection, I alighted at the inn of which I have engaged a part and here I am trying to get a little rest, writing as I lie upon my couch.'

Sidonius went on to describe the general rejoicing in the city at the wedding celebrations. The schools were closed, no business doing and the Court was unapproachable. 'When this merry-making has run its course,' he ended, 'you shall hear what remains to tell, if indeed the idleness to which the whole State seems now surrendered is ever to end.' Eventually Sidonius's hopes were realized and he was given a position of high honour and small responsibility for which he was well suited. It did not last long, though, and he was soon back in Lyons, enjoying the wealth and prestige of appointment to the Bishopric of Clermont and the leisure to spend his remaining twenty years sorting out his correspondence and writing his execrable poetry.

5

Robert of Clari

'We have a good excuse'

France to Constantinople, 1202–4

(Map on p. 44)

'Here begins', wrote Robert of Clari, 'the history of those who conquered Constantinople and afterwards we shall tell you for what reason they went there.'

He was a simple and pious knight of Picardy who played an active role in what was perhaps the greatest crime in history, the Fourth Crusade, the crusade against Christians. Had he set out to conquer Constantinople, his tale would have had no place among those of our travellers, who do not include conquerors. But Robert began his journey as a pilgrim—the crusaders saw themselves as pilgrims—and it was only as the dupe of Doge Enrico Dandolo that he and his fellow pilgrims found themselves abandoning their holy motives and becoming conquerors.

The crusaders, as we shall call them here, had been left 50,000 livres by Count Thibaud who had received the blessing of the Pope for the fourth attempt to recover the holy city of Jerusalem from the Turks, but who had died before his preparations were complete. Their new leader was Boniface, Marquis of Montferrat, and their first task was to find vessels able to transport 4,500 knights and their horses, 9,000 squires and 20,000 foot-soldiers to the Holy Land. The Genoese said they could not help them at all and the Pisans did not have enough vessels, but the Doge of Venice, when he learnt how much money they already had, promised that if they paid him half of it as a deposit he would build a fleet big enough for the purpose. A further payment would be necessary when the crusaders arrived in Venice but more than enough were expected to take the Cross to cover this requirement. Nor was Enrico Dandolo's other condition expected to raise difficulties; he and the Venetians would go along with the crusaders and, if there were any gains, the Venetians should take half of them.

A year later the crusaders arrived in Venice and set up their tents on the island of St. Nicholas (now the Lido) which had been allocated to them. They were delighted to see the rich navy which had been built to carry them and were disappointed only in the numbers who had rallied to the Cross; many, moreover, had made their way direct to Syria, leaving too few to foot the Doge's bill.

For Dandolo everything had turned out as planned. He was extremely old and half-blind as a result of a brawl in Constantinople thirty years earlier, but this did nothing to quench his energy or his ambition. He now had a large army on the Lido entirely at his mercy, for there was no possibility that the crusaders would be able to fulfil their contract.

They had done him ill, Dandolo told them, in that they had demanded a navy for 4,500 knights but not more than a thousand had put in an appearance. Those who were present need not expect to depart from the island before the agreed price had been paid, nor would they find anyone to bring them anything to eat or drink. A collection was made and the Doge was given everything the crusaders had brought with them, but it was not enough. Fortunately, Robert of Clari wrote, the Doge now relented and made them a generous offer: the rest of their debt could be paid out of the first gains they should make for themselves once the Venetians had taken them overseas. There was much rejoicing that night. The Doge and the Venetians were to be trusted after all.

However, Dandolo told them next morning, it was now winter and too late to make for Egypt. 'The fault cannot be laid on me,' he went on, 'for I would have had you make the crossing long ago. But let us make the best of it. There is a city near here, Zara is its name. They have done us much harm and I and my men want to be avenged on them. If you trust me we will go there and stay this winter and then go oversea to the service of God.' So they all got ready their gear and put to sea, continued Robert. 'Each of the high men had his own ship for himself and his people and his transport to carry his horses and the Doge had with him fifty galleys all at his own cost. His galley was all vermilion and there were four silver trumpets trumpeting before him and drums making a great noise. Everyone wept with emotion and for the great joy they had.'

The crusaders now had to choose between the Doge, who made it perfectly clear that they were expected to recover Zara (which the Venetians had recently lost to the King of Hungary), and the Pope,

7. 'Each of the high men had his own ship'. A thirteenth-century mosaic
from St. Mark's showing a Venetian ship. The mosaic was destroyed in the
seventeenth century, but it is shown in Gentile Bellini's painting of *c.* 1500.

who had threatened them with excommunication if they allowed
themselves to be deflected into an attack on other Christians. But
the Pope was not their creditor. Zara was taken and pillaged; the
whole expedition was excommunicated, the crusaders later
forgiven, although not the Venetians, and everyone settled down
for the winter.

When the morale of the crusaders had reached its nadir the voice
of the serpent spoke again. 'In Greece', said the Doge, 'there is a
land that is very rich and plenteous in all good things. If we could
have a reasonable excuse for going there and taking provisions and
other things until we were well restored it would seem to be a good
plan. Then we should be able to go oversea.' As if by a miracle the
excuse appeared in the form of a youth named Alexius. Not only
had he a claim to the imperial throne of Constantinople, but he was
willing to promise that, if the Venetians and crusaders were able to
restore him as Emperor, he would provide money and supplies for
the conquest of Egypt and 10,000 men—from the Byzantine army.
Alexius even had the support of his brother-in-law, Philip of
Swabia, who was expecting soon to become Western Emperor and
would welcome a close relation on the Eastern throne. As for the

Pope, he distrusted all concerned but if the diversion was to achieve the union of the churches and Byzantine help against the infidel he could not resist. The cards were falling into Dandolo's hand and Robert explains how he played them.

'All the barons of the host were summoned and the Venetians. And when they were all assembled the Doge rose and spoke to them. "Lords," said the Doge, "now we have a good excuse for going to Constantinople if you approve of it for we have the rightful heir." Now there were some who did not at all approve of going to Constantinople. Instead they said: "Bah! what shall we be doing in Constantinople? We have our pilgrimage to make, and also our plan of going to Egypt. Moreover our navy is to follow us for only a year, and half of the year is already past." And the others said in answer: "What shall we do in Egypt when we have neither provisions nor money to enable us to go there? Better for us before we go there to secure provisions and money by some good excuse than to go there and die of hunger. Then we shall be able to accomplish something."

'After the Doge had said that now they had a good excuse for going to Constantinople and that he was in favour if it, then all the barons agreed to it. Then the bishops were asked if it would be a sin to go there and the bishops answered that it would not be a sin but rather a righteous deed.

'Then all the pilgrims and the Venetians agreed to go there and they got ready their fleet and their gear and put to sea.'

In fact, by no means all the crusaders agreed to go on the diversion. Some left on their own for the Holy Land or deserted and tried to make their way home, many being drowned on the voyage. Those whose moral scruples were overcome by the prospect of loot, and the reassurances of the bishops, were still, together with the Venetians, a powerful force and on 24 June 1203 they arrived before the imperial capital. They were surprised to find the city gates closed against them, and soldiers manning the walls, since young Alexius had assured them he would be welcomed by all Byzantium. His claim to the throne was based on the fact that his father, Isaac, had been Emperor, incompetent though he was, until ousted by his brother, also named Alexius. The Emperor Alexius III, as he now was, had blinded Isaac and thrown both him and his son into prison from which young Alexius had later escaped to Germany.

The Byzantine leaders really wanted neither the youth nor his uncle, whom they regarded as a usurper, and once the invading force had breached the walls and entered the Golden Horn, these leaders made a subtle move. They allowed the Emperor to escape through the land walls, with his favourite daughter and a bag of precious stones, and they brought the blind ex-Emperor Isaac out of prison. With the rightful Emperor restored to the throne the invaders no longer had any ostensible justification for being there, but they agreed to call off the attack only on condition the young Alexius was made co-Emperor with his father, and this was accepted. On 1 August the coronation took place, the invaders remaining in the city to await their payment. Several demands were made for it.

'Alexius said he would gladly pay them as much as he could and he paid them 100,000 marks. Of this, the Venetians received half, for they were to have half of the gains, and they were also paid the 36,000 marks which the French still owed them for their navy. From what remained to them the pilgrims paid back those who had loaned money to pay for the passage.'

Soon the new Emperor found that it was going to be impossible to keep both his promises and his throne. He asked for a respite which he was given, then another and another.

'In the meantime his followers and people came to him and said: "Sire, you have already paid them too much. Do not pay them any more. You have mortgaged everything. Make them go away and dismiss them from your land." When the French saw the Emperor was not going to pay them anything the barons told him that if he did not pay them they would seize enough of his possessions to pay themselves.

'When the Doge saw the Emperor he said to him: "Alexius, what dost thou mean? We rescued thee from great wretchedness and have made thee a lord and had thee crowned Emperor. Wilt thou not keep thy covenant with us?" "Nay," said the Emperor, "I will not do any more than I have done." "No?" said the Doge. "Wretched boy, we dragged thee out of the filth and into the filth we will cast thee again."[1]

It was not difficult to find those who would carry out the threat. One of the Emperor's cousins was encouraged to invade the palace and Alexius was thrown into prison and strangled there, unlamented by anyone; a few days later his father Isaac died, allegedly of grief but probably of ill-treatment. But the new Emperor was no more welcoming to the invaders in his city than his predecesssors. Indeed, 'he sent word to all the barons telling them to go away and vacate his land, and letting them know he was

Emperor and that if he came on them a week from then he would slay them all.' On this, the crusaders and the Venetians came to the conclusion that the city must be taken and divided between them, leaving the question of who was to be Emperor for later. 'Thus it came about on a Friday that the pilgrims and the Venetians got their ships and their engines ready and prepared for the assault.' Robert still used the word 'pilgrims' but he well knew the truth : all pretence that the expedition was ever to go on to fight the infidel had been abandoned.

Success did not come immediately. Murzuphlus, the new Emperor, set up his vermilion tents on a hill 'and he had his silver trumpets sounded and his timbrels and made a great din.' The Venetian ships drew close to the walls and the French prepared to land.

'When the Greeks saw the French attacking them thus, they set to hurling huge blocks of stone and they began to crush and break to pieces the engines [with which they intended to land] so that no one dared to remain inside them. And the Venetians on their part were not able to reach the walls or the towers, they were so high. When they saw that they could not do anything they were greatly disheartened and drew off. When the Greeks saw them withdrawing they began to hoot and to call out lustily. Murzuphlus began to have his trumpets sounded and his timbrels and to make a din and he sent for his people and began to say : "See, lords, am I not a good Emperor? Never did you have so good an Emperor! Have I not done well? We need fear them no longer. I will have them all hanged and dishonoured."

'When the pilgrims saw this, they were very angry and sorrowful, and they returned to their quarters. When the barons returned they met together and they said it was for their sins that they were not able to succeed better at the city. Finally the bishops and clergy of the host consulted together and gave judgment that the battle was a righteous one for they of the city were disobedient to the law of Rome and said that all who believed in it were dogs. On this account they were right to attack them and it was not at all a sin, but a righteous deed. The bishops commanded the pilgrims to confess themselves well and to take communion and not to be afraid of attacking the Greeks. And it was commanded that all the light women of the camp be sought out and sent far away and so they put them in a ship and sent them away from the camp.

'So they all confessed themselves and were given communion. When it came to Monday morning, the pilgrims all made themselves ready, and the Venetians also. They drew up as close as they could to the walls and cast anchor. Then they began to attack vigorously and to shoot and hurl stones and throw fire on the towers but the fire could not take hold because of the hides with which they were covered. And those within the city defended themselves right hardily.'

In the end it was the ship belonging to the Bishop of Soissons, tied to that of the Bishop of Troyes, which was able to come alongside and land a Frenchman. Exhortation was only a part of a bishop's duty. The Frenchman got inside one of the towers and single-handed drove out the English, Danes and Greeks who were defending it. Soon another tower was taken but greater prowess was needed to leave the towers and attack those who were defending the walls below them. One Frenchman noticed that there was a space in the wall where a door had been removed and replaced by stones. He and Robert's brother Aleaumes attacked this weak point and were soon joined by others. 'So they picked away at this postern with axes and with good swords, with bars and with picks until they made a great hole in it. And when it was pierced they looked through it and saw so many people that they did not dare risk entering in.

'When Aleaumes saw that no one dared enter he pushed forward and said that he would enter. Now there was a brother of his, Robert of Clari was his name, who withstood him and said he should not enter. Aleaumes said he would and got down on his hands and knees. His brother seized him by the foot and began to pull at him but finally, in spite of his brother, Aleaumes got through.'

8. 'Then they began to attack'. An illustration from Villehardouin's manuscript describing the attack on Constantinople.

This was the turning point. Other knights and their men followed through the breach and then, either by accident or treachery, a fire broke out in the city behind the defenders and trapped them. The defence collapsed; the French and Venetians poured into the city. 'When the French were inside all mounted and the Emperor Murzuphlus, the traitor, saw them he had so great a fear that he left his tents and his treasures and fled away. Thus was the city taken.'

Only once had Robert referred to his own part in the proceedings and that was to his attempt to hold back his brother. Nor does he write as anything but an observer throughout his story.

By next morning the Doge and the leading Crusaders were established in the Great Palace and their soldiers were told that they might spend the next three days in pillage. Robert complained that 'the high men, the rich men, came together and agreed among themselves to take the best without the common people or the poor knights knowing anything about it' but there was more than enough for everybody. 'When the poor people were aware of what was happening they went each one as best he could and took what they could get.'

9. 'They took what they could get'. Selection from the loot taken back to Venice after the sack of Constantinople, including the four bronze horses, and the reliquary of Christ's blood.

Constantinople was filled with works of art that had survived from ancient Greece, and masterpieces of its own artists and craftsmen as befitted the city that had been the capital of Christian civilization for nine centuries. Robert and the drunken Frenchmen and Flemings knew nothing of this and were concerned only with the gold and silver and jewels for they had been told that 'two thirds of the wealth of this world is in Constantinople and the other third scattered throughout the world'. But the Venetians knew the true value of the treasures and carried off the pick of them to adorn the churches and palaces of their own city. For three days the pillage and bloodshed continued until Constantinople was a shambles. Eventually order was restored and the booty that had been neither destroyed nor concealed was gathered together and divided up. Three-eighths went to the Venetians, three-eighths to the Crusaders and a quarter was reserved for the future Emperor. When one was found who would prove tractable enough for the Venetians he was denied three-eighths of his own city which the Venetians claimed as their right and all those parts of the Empire that would aid their maritime supremacy. Thus they became the 'Lords and Masters of a Quarter and a Half Quarter of the Roman Empire', as they claimed. Dandolo remained in Constantinople until he died a year later at the age, it was said, of ninety-seven.

In the long run the only gainers were the Turks. The defence of Christendom had been destroyed by this great crime against humanity and the Latin and Greek churches were farther removed than ever from one another. Robert went home to write his story which he ended with the words: 'Now you have heard the truth how Constantinople was conquered, as he bears witness who was there and saw it and heard it, Robert of Clari, knight. And though he has not told the conquest as finely as many a good teller would have told it, none the less he has told the very truth, and there are so many things that he cannot remember them all.'

---

[1]Garchons malvais; nous t'avons', fist li dux, 'geté de la merde et en la merde te remeterons.'

PART TWO

Fifteenth-century Travellers

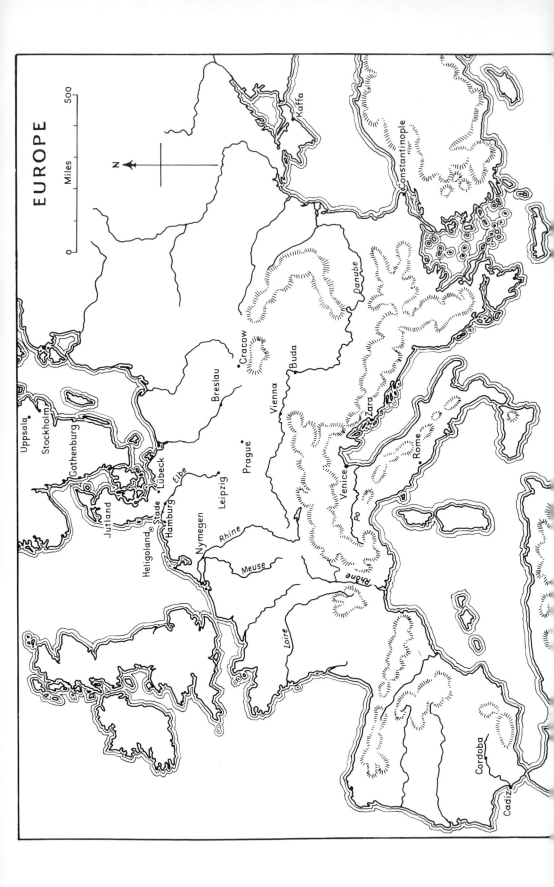

6

Pero Tafur

'I passed my time pleasantly'

A tour of Europe, 1435–9

(Maps on pp. 14, 44, 92, 154)

Pero Tafur was a Spaniard of some wealth and some rank, although no excess of either, who spent four years travelling to the East and through Europe from 1435, when he was twenty-five years of age. He could write with reasonable fluency and seems to have had contacts wherever he went on whom he could rely to provide money or entertainment. He was clearly a man of affairs in spite of his comparative youth and his claims to nobility; his family had no doubt prospered in the world and provided him with a well-rounded training. For all these reasons there is a temptation, when reading the memoirs he wrote some years after his return home, to forget that he was really a product of the Middle Ages and that he was writing in an age when printing was unknown in Europe, barely four years after Joan of Arc had been burnt, and before Leonardo or Erasmus or Columbus had been born.

Tafur set out from Spain towards the end of 1435 and landed at Leghorn after getting involved in the bewildering wars of the time. After some adventures he made his way to Pisa by the River Arno and then by land through Florence and over the mountains to Bologna. There he found Pope Eugenius IV who had fled from Rome the previous year after a dispute with the Council of Basle. Tafur was to become involved again with the Pope, and the Pope's troubles, at the very end of the long journey which lay before him, but at this stage he wanted only a licence from the Pope to go to Jerusalem, which was granted to him.

Of Bologna he wrote: 'A small river runs through the city which improves it very much and there are a hundred sluices with mills; some grind wheat, others spices, some scour arms, others make paper, saw wood and spin silk. While at Bologna I sold my horses and placed myself and my goods and people on board a boat, and travelled to Ferrara, all the way by that river.'

He had set out with two companions, or squires, and there must have been servants, but Tafur rarely mentions how many 'people' were travelling with him. The river was the Reno which, since Roman times, had flowed from Bologna into the Po near Ferrara— it now flows directly into the Adriatic.

Of this river Tafur continues: 'It is very narrow so that only one boat can travel at a time, and if two boats meet one of them has to be hauled ashore. The river freezes each night and the villagers have boats, the keels of which are shod with iron, and at night they go up and down the river, breaking the ice with poles which are pointed with iron, and thus they make a waterway for the travellers. The children go about singing "good sport" which is to say "May there be a good frost". By this river we reached the Po, one of the greatest rivers in the world, and travelling along the Po we came to the city of Ferrara. I there presented myself to the Marquis, lord of the city, and remained three days. I then left by the river and came to Francolino and, continuing still by the river, I arrived at the place where it enters the sea.

'I reached Venice at Vespers, leaving on the right hand and on the left many churches and monasteries and inns, all placed in the sea as Venice itself, and as soon as I landed I went to see the church of St. Mark, which is on the water's edge, and worshipped there, after which we went to an inn called the *Sturgeon*, a very notable hostelry, where we lodged the day and night following.'

There were indeed at the time many islands in the lagoon, each with its church or monastery, most of them now abandoned; that there were also inns is more surprising. The *Sturgeon* was by the Rialto Bridge, on the west side of the Grand Canal; its sign is clearly visible in Carpaccio's *Miracle of the Holy Cross at the Rialto Bridge*, painted sixty-five years later. Next morning, after Mass, Tafur enquired for one of the Morosini family, on whom he held bills, having paid money to the Morosini's agent in Spain and received bills in exchange.

'I found him speedily and he accepted the bills and paid me the money. This is a matter in which nothing on earth will make them delay, for though all merchants in every part of the world make use of bills of exchange they [the Venetians] are more eager than any for fair dealing.'

It was still only February and Tafur learnt that he would not be able to leave for the East until Ascension Day in May, when the

10. 'We went to an inn called the *Sturgeon*'. The Rialto Bridge in *c.* 1500, showing the *Sturgeon* inn with its sign. Detail from Carpaccio's *Miracle of the Holy Cross*

pilgrim boats set forth. Instead of waiting in Venice he decided to spend the time touring Italy, beginning with Rome, where he spent Lent. The 'grandeur and magnificence of Rome' which he had looked forward to was noticeably absent, not only in the inhabited parts of the city but among the ancient monuments themselves. This was the explanation: 'Pope St. Gregory, seeing how the faithful flocked to Rome for the salvation of their souls, but that they were so astounded at the magnificence of the ancient buildings that they spent much time in admiring them and neglected the sacred objects of their visit, the Pope sent orders to destroy all or the majority of the antiquities which had survived from ancient times.'

In Old St. Peter's Tafur saw, as well as the bodies of St. Peter and St. Paul, the rope with which Judas hanged himself 'which is as thick as a man's arm or thicker' and St. Luke's portrait of Our Lord in a chapel from which women were barred 'for the reason, as they say, that a woman once uttered such things that she burst asunder', whatever that may have meant. As for the Romans themselves, 'I found no one in Rome who could give me any account of those ancient things concerning which I enquired, but they could, without doubt, have informed me fully as to the taverns and places of ill-fame. It is said that people never dine in their houses even by a miracle, and, indeed, their dress and bearing, both indoors and out, show clearly what they are. I say this of the majority, for doubtless in such a multitude there must be some who are virtuous. It is said, further, that Rome, though depopulated, has more inhabitants than any Christian city in the world, but there are parts within the walls which look like thick woods, and wild beasts, hares, foxes, wolves, deer and even, so it is said, porcupines breed in the caves.'

The words of an earlier traveller are curiously echoed by Tafur. Adam of Usk, a Welsh clergyman of standing, had found it desirable to leave England for some years after being convicted of stealing a horse and some money in 1400. He later wrote: 'O God! how much is Rome to be pitied. For, once thronged with princes and their palaces, now a place of hovels, thieves, wolves, worms, full of desert places, how pitifully is she laid waste by her own citizens who rend each other in pieces.'

Despite the number of its inhabitants, Rome was 'very sparsely populated considering its size', with thinly-scattered houses and narrow, litter-filled streets. Tafur cannot have been sorry to resume his journey back to Venice, which he reached travelling overland through Perugia, Assisi, Gubbio and Rimini and thence by a ship which had been lent to him, together with a squire, by the Count of Urbino. On arrival at Venice the squire said, 'Sir knight, the Count, my Master, ordered me to give you a hundred ducats: see, here they are,' but Tafur assured him he had sufficient for his present needs.

As he expected, Morosini had safeguarded the money left in his charge and was willing to accommodate Tafur for the month until his ship was due to leave for Jerusalem on 17 May 1436. The contract with the galley-master provided that Tafur and the two squires he still had with him (or two new ones) should be conveyed at a cost of sixty ducats, about £9 each, including three meals a day. For the return journey the cost would have been thirty-five ducats:

fewer pilgrims returned from the Holy Land than went there, presumably, so the demand for space was less.

'I passed my time at Venice very pleasantly and restfully,' Tafur wrote, 'at small expense, and each day I went about seeing many remarkable and delightful things.' Then: 'On Ascension Day, after receiving the blessing, we departed and set sail at noon, and took the left side of the gulf towards Esclavonia [Dalmatia], the greater part of which is Venetian, and all along the coast there are many safe harbours and islands and ports for taking in provisions. The next day we came to a town called Parenzo, and from there we sailed for Zara, a town of the Venetians.'

It was all very different in May 1436 from those November days of 1202 when Robert of Clari and his fellow crusaders were being turned into mercenaries by Doge Enrico Dandolo and forced to take Zara from the King of Hungary to pay their debts to the Venetians. Nor, now, was there any question of Tafur and the other pilgrims being diverted from the Holy Land they had set their hearts on seeing.

When Tafur disembarked at Jaffa he was no longer a traveller in Europe and his adventures are outside our present province. It had been an adventurous eighteen months that he looked back on when, on the return journey in November, 1437, he reached Constantinople. He immediately sought an audience with the Emperor, John VIII Palaeologus, whom he claimed as a distant relation. The Emperor received him cordially, although less concerned with the family tree than Tafur was. He was about to set out for Italy in an attempt to unite his Church with the West and, perhaps even more urgently, to obtain support for his resistance to the Turks. He would gladly have taken Tafur with him but Tafur was a traveller and there was much that he wanted to see while he was so close to the Black Sea.

There was, for example, Kaffa in the Crimea (now Theodosia) where 'they sell more slaves than anywhere else in the world'. There Tafur went shopping. 'I bought two female slaves and a male', he recorded later, 'and I still have them in Cordova with their children.' He learnt something of the Tartars and their customs and was told 'that when they are moving about, or at war, they carry their meat between the horse's side and the seat of the saddle, and they do not cook it any more than it is cooked by that process.' He would have liked to have stayed longer, but 'the people were bestial and the food did not agree with' him.

Eventually he returned to Constantinople, a miserable city.

'The Emperor's Palace must have been very magnificent but now it is in such state that both it and the city show well the evils which the people have suffered and still endure. The city is sparsely populated. The inhabitants are not well clad, but sad and poor, showing the hardship of their lot which is, however, not so bad as they deserve, for they are a vicious people, steeped in sin. I remained two months in Constantinople and I then departed in a ship of Ancona, carrying with me my slaves and the other things I had purchased in Kaffa.'

Passing through the Dardanelles, they saw some Christian captives on the shore and, after a fight with some Turks in which Tafur was wounded in the foot by an arrow, they rescued them and eventually docked in Venice. It was Ascension Day and a galley was about to set sail for the Holy Sepulchre. Tafur met some of his fellow Castilians among the pilgrims and joined them at Mass in St. Mark's. After Tafur had 'told them what they had to do and how much the journey would cost', they dined together and Tafur returned only to find that all his goods, 'including the slaves and the other things', had been seized by Customs. He appealed immediately to the Doge, Francesco Foscari, then at the height of his power, and was given, as well as his goods, a 'licence to transport them whither you desire, a privilege which is not commonly given to any, since nothing which enters Venice can be taken out.'

By this Tafur must have meant that nothing could be taken out of Venice without payment of tax, since almost everything that entered the city was intended to be taken out and sold elsewhere. Slaves were an important part of this entrepot trade, ten thousand of them having been sold between 1414 and 1423, each bearing a head tax of five ducats. Most of them went to Spain and the other cities of Italy; the well-to-do householders of Florence were among the best customers, at least one slave being employed by almost all of them. The Genoese for the most part by-passed Venice and imported their slaves direct. The price varied between twenty-five and sixty-five ducats but it went up after the fall of Constantinople to the Turks in 1453, when the supply from the Black Sea towns was almost cut off. In Venice itself slavery had nearly, but not quite, disappeared as it had in the north of Europe. Nevertheless, two men are recorded in the Venetian archives of the fifteenth century as having received short prison sentences for amusing themselves 'by pricking with a long pin the slaves who passed by on their way to Vespers at St. Mark's'.

Tafur was now at last free to explore the city. By 1438 the Piazza San Marco had already been enlarged to its present size. It was tiled and colonnaded but there were still trees and vines growing. The Piazzetta façade of the Doge's Palace was on the point of completion, so that the palace looked much as it does today. Almost all the great Gothic palaces on the Grand Canal were finished; the gilding and painting of the façade of the Cà d'Oro was done and the palace lacked only its last two chimneys. One or two Gothic Palaces, including Doge Foscari's own at the turn of the Canal and the little Palazzo Dario, had not yet been built. Gentile and Giovanni Bellini had been born but were not ten years old. Tafur came to Venice when the Republic's wealth and influence was past its peak but before its artistic achievement had begun.

On his first day, since it was Ascension Day, Tafur saw the procession of the Ducal Barge, the Bucintoro, to the Lido where the Doge throws a ring into the sea, already 'an ancient ceremony for wedding the sea to the land to placate its fury, since their city is founded in the sea, and from the sea they draw all that they have'. He then set out on the round of sight-seeing visits which had already become familiar to crusaders and pilgrims. Naturally, the city's unique situation impressed him.

'The city is built on the sea, and there are artificial canals along which boats can pass, and in some parts there are streets where people can go on foot. Elsewhere, in places where the canals are too narrow for ships, there are bridges, and as everyone in Castile has a beast to ride, so here they all have boats and pages to row and attend to them. And as we pride ourselves on a fine horse and a pretty well-dressed page, so they set great store by their boats, which are kept very properly. The exits from the city to the mainland are made artifically, and only small boats can go there, since the water is not sufficient for large craft, and the canals are narrow and sandy. The boats go to the mainland for all necessaries, and also for drinking-water. They take large boats and fill them with sand and in the bottom is a hole with a plug. When the boat enters a river of fresh water they open the plug and fill the boats and replace the plug; thus they carry the water for their needs.'

Tafur soon fell in love with Venice and could see no fault in her customs. The price of necessities was strictly controlled and they were plentiful. 'The fruit which comes from Spain is to be had at Venice as fresh and as cheap as in our own country.' Ships, great and small, were moored to the doors of their owners' houses.

'The city is as clean for walking in as a gracious chamber, so well paved and bricked is it. No beast on four legs can enter it, and in winter there is no water in the streets. There is therefore no mud and in summer no dust. The sea rises and falls there, although not so much as in the West, and cleans out the filth from the secret places, otherwise it would not be possible to live for the stench.'

Tafur's description of the Arsenal was one of the earliest, yet later visitors were able to add little, however high their expressions of wonder were pitched.

'As one enters the gate there is a great street on either hand with the sea in the middle, and on one side are windows opening out of the houses of the arsenal, and the same on the other side, and out came a galley towed by a boat, and from the windows they handed out to them, from one the cordage, from another the bread, from another the arms, and from another the balistas [catapults] and mortars, and when the galley had reached the end of the street all the men required were on board, together with the oars, and she was equipped from end to end.'

He went on to tell of the founding of Santa Maria della Pietà (later to be so closely associated with Antonio Vivaldi). 'In time past there were few weeks, or even days, when the fishermen did not take dead babies from their nets, and this, they say, came from the fact that the merchants were so long separated from their wives. These, urged by their fleshly lusts, gave way to them and became pregnant, and to save their reputations threw the offspring out of the window into the sea as soon as they were delivered. The rulers took counsel together and founded a great and rich hospital and placed in it a hundred wet-nurses to suckle the babes, and now those who would hide their shame take their children there to be reared.'

When he had seen enough of the splendours of Venice, Tafur decided to make an extensive tour of Europe. After leaving his spare cash, slaves and 'goods' with Morosini, he sailed to Chioggia where he saw the Genoese ships destroyed by the Venetians in the critical battle sixty years earlier. His boat then went up the Po to Ferrara where he disembarked. The Emperor of Constantinople, or of the Greeks, as he was known in Europe, had arrived for his meeting with the Pope in the hope of reaching agreement on union with Rome. As he well knew, he would then have the task of inducing his own people to accept the agreement and this, in the event, he failed to do. Tafur was welcomed as a traveller with news.

'The second day I went to see Pope Eugenius who received me very graciously. He desired to know particulars of my journey to Jerusalem and about the Grand Turk, also concerning the Emperor himself and what power he had and I satisfied him to the best of my knowledge. In the evening I went to wait upon the Emperor of the Greeks and give him letters from his consort. He received me gladly and made me sit there beside him, asking for news of his country. Thus we were very familiar together.'

Next morning the Emperor, unable to walk by reason of gout, was carried in a chair to his meeting with the Pope. Tafur joined the 'great company of people, all of whom went in long robes and with great beards, showing themselves to be grave and serious persons; it was indeed a goodly company.' There were chairs for all the kings and princes of Christendom, including one for the 'Emperor of Germany'. This was Albert of Habsburg, King of Hungary, but not yet in fact elected King of Germany or Emperor of the Romans, the title which went with it; Tafur was to meet him again later and he was at present so fully occupied that he is unlikely to have occupied the chair reserved for him at Ferrara.

After leaving the distinguished company at Ferrara Tafur set out for Milan and the Alps. He crossed by the St. Gotthard Pass, being drawn on a trailer by an ox, holding his horse behind him by the reins 'if anything untoward occurs, only the ox is imperilled.' At Basle the wound in his foot, which he had received when rescuing the Christian slaves, was troublesome and he had to stay for three weeks for treatment. There he 'met a lady who was on a pilgrimage for her brother who had been taken prisoner in Turkey' and they spent six days together before setting off, still together, for Cologne 'where she had her estates'.

Under the spell, perhaps, of love, Tafur saw only beauty: 'In truth, the Rhine is so lovely that the world cannot show the like. On one hand and on the other are such stately towns and so many castles and so much beauty that a man can hardly describe what he sees. Towns and castles are all crowded closely together and the towers are adorned with lofty crosses and gilded weather-vanes. So by this river we arrived at a city called Coblenz, a notable place.'

Eight more entrancing days followed in Cologne where 'that lady had her dwelling and she invited me to her house and showed me much honour all the time I was there.' The houses were beautiful, both within the city and on the outskirts and even the inns were excellent, 'worthy to entertain a king if needs be. It is customary for a number of gentlemen to bind themselves together to found an inn, each one putting down a sum of money. They then choose as host a man of parts and of noble birth, for they say that a good host befits good guests. It happens not infrequently that a gentleman, desiring through age to retire from the world, comes to an innkeeper and bargains with him for the rest of his life. He has a room, two large and two small meals, and money for Mass, and having paid his due, he lives without care for the rest of his days.'

As usual, Tafur mixed in the best company and was shown round by the Archbishop, Dietrich II, a powerful prince of the Church who 'did not wholly disdain the ladies'. The Cathedral was still unfinished after two hundred years' work and everyone was talking of a miracle which had taken place a few days earlier: the shrine of the chapel of the Three Kings had 'moved itself as much as one pace to the side' in order to avoid a great stone which leapt from the ropes being used to place it in position and which would otherwise have fallen upon the bodies of the Kings.

'I remained in this city of Cologne,' wrote Tafur, 'in great contentment, and replaced my beasts since those I brought with me were fatigued.' He had bought them in Ferrara. He now travelled down the Rhine, passing Nijmegen, which he rather surprisingly found 'in every way the most beautiful' he had seen, and on to Bois-le-duc where he bought another horse 'for sixteen ducats which would without doubt have fetched a hundred at home'. He saw an odd sight here. 'The people are accustomed to travel in carts, but I could not suffer it, for I would rather be at sea. I continued to ride while my people followed in the carts.' His journey 'down the Rhine' seems to have been down the Rhine valley rather than on the river.

So on to Brussels where he was received graciously by the Duke of Burgundy himself, Philip the Good, and his Duchess who was cousin to Tafur's own King Juan II of Castile. He could have stayed at Court but preferred to go on and was provided with a knight for company. His destination was Bruges, already, like Venice, past its prime, although there could have been little sign of this. In Venice the great age of painting had not yet begun whereas in Bruges Robert Campin, Roger van der Weyden and Jan van Eyck were all active. The people were still suffering grievously from the collapse of their revolt against the Duke of Burgundy the previous year.

'This city of Bruges', Tafur wrote, 'is one of the greatest markets of the world. It seems to me that there is much more commercial activity here than in Venice. The reason is as follows. In the whole of the West there is no other great mercantile centre except Bruges, although England does some trade, and thither repair all the nations of the world; they say that at times the number of ships sailing from the harbour of Bruges exceeds seven hundred a day. In Venice, on the contrary, be it never so rich, the only persons engaged in trade are the inhabitants.

'The city of Bruges is well-peopled, with fine houses and streets, which are all inhabited by work-people, very beautiful churches and excellent inns. The inhabitants are extraordinarily industrious, possibly on account of the barrenness of the soil, since very little corn is grown, and no wine, nor is there any water fit for drinking, nor any fruit. On this account the products of the whole world are brought here, so that they have abundance of everything in exchange for the work of their hands.

11. 'Beautiful churches and excellent inns'. Detail from Campin's *Annunciation*.

'There is a large building above a great tract of water which comes from the sea at Sluys, which is called *La Hala* [or *Waterhalle*]. Here all the goods are unloaded in the following manner. In these parts of the West the sea rises and falls greatly and between Bruges and Sluys there is a great canal; at different places sluice-gates, as of water mills, are set up which when opened admit the water, and on being closed the water cannot escape. When the tide rises the ships are laden and travel with their cargoes from Sluys on the tide. When the water has reached its highest point they lock it up, and those ships which have been unloaded and filled with fresh cargoes return with the same water which carried them up-stream, travelling down again with the falling tide. If the people had to use beasts for this transport it would be exceedingly costly and troublesome.

'Recently the people rebelled against the Duke, at a time when he was in the city, so that he had to flee with his wife and attendants. He then armed himself and made war against the city and took it by force, and took great vengeance upon it, both in lives and property. I myself saw many high gallows around Bruges and Sluys upon which were fixed the heads of dead men.

'This is not a place for poor men, who would be badly received, but anyone who has money will find in this town alone everything which the whole world produces. I saw there oranges and lemons from Castile which seemed only just to have been gathered from the trees, fruits and wine from Greece, as abundant as in that country. I saw also confections and spices from Alexandria and all the Levant, furs from the Black Sea. Here was all Italy with its brocades, silks and armour; indeed there is no part of the world whose products are not found here at their best.

'There was a great famine in the year of my visit. As I was in a church hearing Mass a woman approached me and said that she had something to say to me in private to my advantage. She took me to her home close by and she there showed me two young girls and offered me the one who should please me most. Astounded, I enquired how she could bring herself to behave thus, whereupon she told me that she was almost dead with hunger and that the two girls were like to die of starvation, having had nothing to eat for many days except a few small fish, and that they were virgins. I extracted from the woman and the girls a solemn oath that they would never again attempt such traffic with anyone. The new year, I said, would bring an improvement in their fortunes and I gave the woman six Venetian ducats and departed. The famine was the worst which has ever been known and it was followed by a dreadful plague.'

Tafur now took a circuitous route back to Basle where, instead of continuing on to Italy, he decided to go to Prague in order to see Albert of Habsburg, now elected Emperor of the Romans. This was a formidable journey but on reaching Prague he learnt that 'the Emperor had departed for Silesia on the confines of Poland where he was waging war with the Polish King'. Another long journey, including the crossing of the Giant Mountains, took Tafur to Breslau, 'on the very outskirts of Germany', where he found the Emperor and was soon involved in the festivities which the fighting had done nothing to hinder. Representatives from all the Italian states, and from the Pope, were assembled.

'Many brought presents, especially the Venetians and Florentines, those from Venice being specially noteworthy. The Emperor received them all very graciously, but those from Venice he would not accept, saying that it was not fitting for him to take presents from a people upon whom he intended to make war. He said further, in the presence of all, that he had made a solemn vow not to accept the Imperial crown, nor even to enjoy its revenues, until that which the Venetians had filched was restored to the Empire [Friuli and the territory north-west to the Carnic Alps]. Then, having re-taken the Holy Sepulchre, he would be crowned there. All who heard this vow were very glad, except the Venetians who straightway departed.'

It was perfectly true that Albert had vowed not to accept the imperial title. This had been a condition of his acceptance as King of Hungary but it had not prevented him from being crowned Emperor at Aix the previous May. So far from achieving his ambition of driving the Turks out of the Holy Land, he could not even remove their threat to Hungary and within a year of Tafur meeting him Albert died of dysentery while fighting them.

Meanwhile there were banquets and dances at Breslau and Tafur enjoyed himself, in spite of the intense cold.

'The chimneys and stoves do not give sufficient warmth but there is another kind of stove for heating which they use. They make a fire beneath an upstairs room, and in the floor are covered holes, and they place seats above, also with holes in them. The people then sit down on those seats and unstop the holes and the heat rises between the legs to each one.

'So cold is the city that the Emperor and his courtiers go about the streets seated in wooden vehicles which are drawn by horses shod with iron and so dragged through the streets. Others go in carriages drawn by eight or ten horses. These carriages are entirely closed with awnings and they fix braziers to them. Thus they go from their houses to the palace whenever they wish. No one with any money rides on horseback for fear of falling, for the streets are like glass owing to the continual frosts, and many go on foot. They fortify themselves by taking great quantities of food and drink, a custom which to us seems stranger than anything else. I believe that more money is expended here upon furs and spices than in half the world besides. The people are very wealthy, having much silver and as they do not keep many servants they live very well.'

At last Tafur asked the Emperor if it would please him to grant a licence to depart; two of the Emperor's knights were travelling with an escort of two hundred horsemen to Vienna and Tafur was allowed to join them. The journey took twelve days and for once Tafur found travelling tiresome. 'It was so cold that my teeth almost fell out of my mouth. Without doubt, it is a terrible business to travel through such country in winter.' Two leagues outside the city, Tafur was shown the way and left to proceed without the knights, who were staying in a house belonging to one of them. Within a short time Tafur was attacked by some unmounted noblemen with intent to rob, but escaped and reached his inn in Vienna.

'No sooner had I sat down to eat than those very noblemen appeared who had attacked me. I asked them how they could behave thus and they told me they were poor noblemen and had to rob for a living. I replied that I also was noble and poor, and moreover a stranger in their midst, and that my needs were equally great. Then they craved pardon and offered to go and seek for money so that they could give me entertainment. But I thanked them and made them sit down with me, and gave them money with which they were greatly pleased and they accompanied me on most of the days that I was in the city.'

Thus some other fortunate traveller was spared being robbed to provide Tafur's entertainment and instead he paid for his own and that of his attackers.

Although Tafur frequently made the excuse to his hosts that he must press on as he was needed at home by his King to join in the war against the Moors, he was in fact in no great hurry. He called on Albert's wife, the Empress Elizabeth, daughter of Albert's predecessor, Emperor Sigismund, and, after being well entertained, he proceeded down the Danube to Buda. He found the

Hungarians 'somewhat gross, which comes, they say, from their plenty' and, after a pleasant week at Neustadt with Frederick Habsburg, Duke of Austria (later to become Emperor, on Albert's death), Tafur turned south-west and made for Venice. In spite of his admiration for Albert, and the Emperor's cordiality to him, Tafur had to admit that wherever the Venetians had taken land from the Empire they had brought prosperity and plenty to the inhabitants. He was in no doubt that the Venetians would 'compass the Emperor's death with poison, having been apprised of the oath he swore that they should be dispossessed of what they had taken by violence' and Tafur had himself heard the Emperor 'apprising' the Venetian ambassadors of his intentions. As it happened, poisoning became unnecessary and Friuli remained, and remains, a province of Venetia.

Instead of completing the short journey from Treviso to Venice, as he had intended, Tafur decided to make for Ferrara when he learnt that the Pope was proposing to leave for Florence. On the way he stopped for three days' sight-seeing at Padua.

'I left Padua and travelled along the canals and since that country is very close to Venice they collect the water into lakes, some of fresh and some of salt water, but these lakes have a very evil smell, and they call them marshes, and when in speaking the Italians wish to refer to anything as noxious or stinking they liken it to those marshes.'

Tafur had already travelled twice along the intricate canal system which linked the Brenta, Adige and Po Rivers. Most of the journey must have been over desolate country. There had been canals and water-courses throughout the area since at least the ninth century and the old Brenta had been a thoroughfare for flourishing trade, with the woods and marshes filled with game and fish. But from the thirteenth century there had been continual outbreaks of fighting in the district between the Venetians and their neighbours. Control of the marshes weakened, bringing malaria. The Abbey, where four of the earliest doges had been buried, was gradually abandoned, together with the great Castle and the church. In 1443, only five years after Tafur passed through, Marco Cornaro, the 'Magistrate of the Waters', was writing that everything had been destroyed and everyone had deserted the area. Rehabilitation began in 1452 with the first diversion of the Brenta River to take it into the Lagoon farther south, and farther from Venice itself, than before. The control of this complex water system has ever since been a major pre-occupation of the Venetians who by 1610 had diverted most of the water into the sea at Chioggia, leaving a canal in place of the river itself, and this work was to continue for another three centuries. However, Tafur was more concerned with present celebrations than past disasters or future possibilities and there was much to see.

'On drawing near to Ferrara they told me that the Pope was wishful to depart, and it was so, and on arrival I found the Pope preparing to set out for Florence. As soon as I arrived I waited on the Emperor of the Greeks who rejoiced greatly to see me again, and I also saw the Pope's progress which was in this wise. All the archbishops, bishops, and other prelates and clergy went on foot in procession with the crosses. Then followed the cardinals on horseback, staffs in hand, in order of precedence, and after them came twelve horses with crimson trappings, one bearing the umbrella, one the chair and another the cushion, and so on until the end. The last horse was covered with brocade, and on a rich silver saddle was a casket containing the Blessed Sacrament. This horse had a silver bell, and two prelates led it by the reins. Then came the Pope himself, upon a horse with crimson trappings. He was vested as for Mass, wearing a bishop's mitre and giving his blessing on one side and the other, while men cast coins into the street, so that those who picked them up might gain pardons. This was done to prevent the crowds from pressing upon the Pope, whose horse was led by the Marquis of Ferrara and the Count of Urbino.'

Was the nineteen-year-old Benozzo Gozzoli in Ferrara, or more probably, in Florence to see the Emperor's procession? Twenty years later, in 1459, Piero de' Medici commissioned him to decorate the chapel of his Florentine palace and, in this little jewel-casket which has become one of the best-loved of all minor masterpieces, Gozzoli showed the Emperor and his Patriarch as the second and third of the Kings, or Wise Men, from the East bringing their gifts to the stable at Bethlehem. But Gozzoli was no historian: the men from the East had come, not to pay tribute, but to seek aid in their troubles.

The Emperor had invited Tafur to join the cavalcade to Florence but Tafur had business to complete before he could go on to Florence, where he stayed eight days, 'marvelling at the city with its government which could not be bettered' and its hospitals 'to which a king or prince would straightway go if he fell sick, just as anyone else'.

The first complete tour of Europe, or at any rate the first to be

12. 'The last horse was covered with brocade'. The Emperor John VIII
Paleologus as one of the Wise Men in Benozzo Gozzoli's fresco, based on
the Council of Florence of 1439.

recorded, was now almost over. Tafur went back to Ferrara to recover his horses, which 'had grown very fat', sold them and returned to Venice. 'Here I stayed a month waiting for a ship, and finally I found one which was bound for Sicily, and I collected all that I had and went on board.'

By the spring of 1439 Tafur was home after almost four years of travel. He does not seem to have begun his narrative immediately and was at work on it still as late as 1457. The original manuscript was lost but an eighteenth-century writer had copied it, apparently accurately, to judge from the authenticity of the mid-fifteenth-century phrasing.

With very few exceptions, wherever Tafur's story can be checked he was telling the truth. The movements of the Pope and the Greek Emperor were as he describes them. Albert was at war with the Poles in December 1438 when Tafur was in Breslau and there are a number of other incidents which are known to have occurred just when Tafur writes that he saw them happening.

Only the date of his arrival in Breslau is in doubt. He arrived in Ferrara in time to see the Pope before 16 January and he himself accounts for thirty-three days travelling and being entertained after leaving Breslau. Yet he claims quite specifically to have arrived in Breslau three days before Christmas (*tres dias ántes de Navidad*).

Apart from this, Tafur must be believed and no other European traveller's tale can compare with his for a picture of what land travel was like at a time when few of those who undertook a journey could write at all and still fewer had anything of interest to say.

7

Santo Brasca

'One right full of patience'

Advice to pilgrims, 1480

'In the first place,' wrote the Milanese Santo Brasca, in his instructions to anyone who desired to take the Holy Voyage he had himself just returned from in 1480, 'a man should go solely with the intention of visiting, contemplating and adoring the most Holy Mysteries, with great effusion of tears in order that his sins may be pardoned and not with the intention of seeing the world.' Even less must he boast 'I have been there' or 'I have seen that.' Unfortunately for later readers, the advice was generally heeded and few of the ever-increasing trail of pilgrims who passed through Venice between the thirteenth and sixteenth centuries told anything afterwards except of their spiritual experiences. Santo Brasca also gave some more practical advice which is worth repeating.

'The traveller should carry with him two bags, one right full of patience, the other containing two hundred Venetian ducats [about £90 sterling] or at least one hundred and fifty, namely one hundred which each person needs for the voyage, and then nothing will be lacking to the man who loves his life and is accustomed to live delicately at home; the other fifty for illness or any other circumstances that may arise. Also let him take with him a warm long upper garment to wear on the return journey, a good many shirts, so as to avoid lice and other unclean things as much as possible; and also tablecoths, towels, sheets, pillow cases and such like.

'Then he should go to Venice, because from there he can take his passage more conveniently than from any other city in the world. Every year one galley is deputed solely for this service and although he may find it cheaper to go on a sailing ship he should on no account choose this instead of a galley.

'Further, let him take a supply of good Lombard cheese and sausages and other salt meats, white biscuits, some loaves of sugar and several kinds of preserved sweetmeats, but not a great quantity of these last because they go bad. Above all he should have with him a great deal of fruit syrup because that is what keeps a man alive in the great heat; and also syrup of ginger to settle his stomach if it should be upset by excessive vomiting, but the ginger should be used sparingly, because it is very heating. Likewise he should take some quince without spice, some aromatics flavoured with rose and carnation and some good milk products [*qualchi boni lactuarii*]. When he goes ashore in any place he should furnish himself with eggs, fowls, bread, sweetmeats and fruit, and not count what he has paid the captain [fifty to sixty ducats, including meals] because this is a voyage on which the purse must not be kept shut.

'Finally, it is necessary that the gold and silver money taken should be fresh from the Venetian mint, otherwise the Moors will not accept the coins, even if they were ten grains overweight; and the captain must be paid in the same money because he is obliged to pay the same to the Moors.'

8

Felix Fabri

'I simply answered that I had'

Ulm to Venice, 1480–3

(Map on p. 92)

Two pilgrims who may well have undertaken the journey for the pardon of their sins, but who were nevertheless determined to see the world too, were Felix Fabri and Pietro Casola. Neither were travellers in the sense that Tafur was a traveller: having completed the usual round from Venice to Rhodes and Jaffa and thence to Jerusalem, Bethlehem and the other holy places, they returned to Venice and made their way home as quickly as they could. However, both add something to our knowledge of fifteenth-century Venice and even saw some things that Tafur himself had missed.

Felix Fabri was actually with Santo Brasca on his 1480 pilgrimage and enjoyed himself enough, or was sufficiently moved, to set off again three years later. He was a genial, fun-loving Dominican Friar, not yet forty, who had been born in Zürich but in the 1480s was a preacher in Ulm; a thorough-going German, his greatest interest after his spiritual duties seems to have been good food and good wine. He insisted that his book should not be called a 'Pilgrimage', doubtless with Santo Brasca's warning in mind, but rather the 'Evagatorium' of Brother Felix, as one might say the 'Wandering' or 'Rambling'. It was to be read 'with pleasure and amusement in the intervals of more fruitful studies', and he insisted it was but a 'little book' although it was some half-million words in length.

Fabri was far from satisfied with his first pilgrimage. 'It was exceeding short and hurried and we ran round the holy places without understanding and feeling what they were.' There was much, too, that they did not see at all, and much that he had seen was quickly forgotten. When, therefore, his friends asked him whether he had any wish to go back again, 'I simply answered that I had.' Venice had passed completely from his mind on that first journey and he does not mention it at all. By 1483 he had succeeded in getting a licence from the Pope for a second pilgrimage and the permission of his Prior, as well as an invitation to act as chaplain to a party of German nobles, and on 14 April he started out again from Ulm. They went through Innsbruck and over the Brenner Pass to Trent. On the way they had passed through a village called Tramin and this struck a chord in Fabri's mind since 'near it grows a noble wine which is imported into Swabia and is known as Traminer': the Traminer grape was later to find its way into many vineyards on the Rhine and Moselle. At Trent they stayed the night and were entertained by a minstrel and his wife. 'The foolery made us laugh heartily' but when it came to paying for the entertainment, one of the noblemen insisted that this would be sinful on a holy pilgrimage and that he would rather give money to the poor. The unfortunate Fabri was called upon by the others to adjudicate and decided that a present should be given, but he was far from sure he had done right. 'After I had returned home I searched the writings of learned casuists to see whether I had decided rightly' and discovered to his relief that 'flute-players and jugglers are not in a state of damnation provided they practise for their own sustenance and profit and in order to afford recreation to Princes and nobles when they are oppressed by care.'

13. Trent, where they were entertained by a minstrel, shortly after Brother Fabri's visit. Water-colour by Dürer, 1495.

The next night they stopped at Feltre and were delayed by rain. Soon after they were able to saddle their horses and proceed, they came to a hill at which Fabri exclaimed, 'See, if a man were on the brow of that hill he would be able to see the Mediterranean.' 'Let us climb up thither and see the sea which perchance will be our tomb,' was the gloomy reply and five of them climbed the hill, which was much higher than they thought, and reflected on the dangers which awaited them. The sea seemed in the rain-washed air to be very close. 'The setting sun shone upon the part which was nearest to us and the rest, the end of which no one could see, seemed to be a lofty, thick black cloud; it had a terrible appearance.'

Next day they reached Treviso where it was customary for pilgrims either to sell their horses or leave them in charge of one of the innkeepers for the return journey. 'Many Italians came to our inn who wanted to see our horses and buy them and while we were selling them the Italians squabbled among themselves in a wondrous fashion. They ran up to us, each trying to outstrip the other and each interfering with the other's bargain, and they poured abuse one on another, all alike, even old, rich and respectable men fighting with one another like children, each offering more than the horses were worth to spite the others and each outbidding the other purposely. While this squabbling was going on we stood still and held our peace, and we sold our horses well.'

One more day took them to Mestre and Marghera, on the shores of the Lagoon, and there they were met by a German who took them to an inn and showed them a table spread with food and drink which had been ordered for them by a friend of one of the travellers. A boat had also been ordered for them and, after dinner, they embarked, singing hymns. They were rather over-laden and as they were passing the Torre del Marghera 'a boat which some strong young men were rowing very furiously' collided with them. They hit a post which stood in the water and 'it did very nearly overset with all the people and things in it, so that we were sore afraid. The sailors of each ship abused those of the other, and so we went on our way.

'After a while there met us another boat with people on board, one of whom asked us what inn we meant to put up at in Venice. When we told him St. George's, where Lord John von Cymbern had taken rooms for us, he began to abuse that inn and its landlord, and stood on the prow of his boat, trying to prevent our going there, and pointing out some other inn to us. As he stood there and noisily tried to persuade us, he suddenly met with an accident and fell from the prow of his boat into the sea, from which he was with much trouble dragged out by his comrades and saved from death. He was dressed in new silk clothes which received baptism together with him: this caused great laughter on board our boat.

'As we sailed further on we found before our eyes the famous, wealthy and noble city of Venice, mistress of the Mediterranean, standing in wondrous fashion in the midst of the waters, with lofty towers, great churches, splendid houses and palaces. We were astonished to see such weighty and such tall structures with their foundations in the water.

'Presently we sailed into the city and went along the Grand Canal as far as the Rialto, where on each side of us we saw buildings of wonderful height and beauty. Below the Rialto we turned out of the Grand Canal into another canal, on the right bank of which stands the Fondaco dei Tedeschi, by which we proceeded among houses right up to the door of our inn, which was called the inn of St. George, and in German commonly known as "Zu der Fleuten".'

14. 'Right up to the door of our inn'. The inn of St. George or of the Flute in Felix Fabri's time. (It is the building with 'Fontico Dalamani' inscribed on it, although the inscription indicates the Fondaco dei Tedeschi, which is the building below.) Detail from the woodcut of c. 1500 attributed to Jacopo de' Barbari.

The Inn of St. George, or of the Flute, was on the Rio del Fontego, opposite the north entrance to the Fondaco dei Tedeschi; the rio enters the Grand Canal just north of the Rialto Bridge. The inn belonged to Peter Ugelheimer, a successful business man from Frankfurt, for whom 'Master John' and his wife managed it. The Fondaco dei Tedeschi was the headquarters of the German merchants in Venice. It was provided and equipped by the Venetian authorities, for whom the business brought by the Germans was highly profitable, and supervised by them. The Germans did their own catering and the Venetians often commented on their huge meals of highly spiced meat.

The Fondaco as it was in Fabri's time can be seen in the detail from de' Barbari's bird's-eye view opposite. It is below the words *Fontico Dalamani* which are in fact inscribed on the Inn of St. George or of the Flute. In 1505, soon after this view was published, the Fondaco was burnt down and the present building, now the General Post Office, was erected for the Germans as a replacement. Its façades were decorated by Titian and Giorgione with frescoes which have long disappeared.

'Here we disembarked,' continued Fabri, 'walked up about sixty stone steps from the sea to the rooms which were prepared for us, and carried all our things into them. Here Master John, the landlord and Mistress Margaret, his wife, received us with great good humour, and greeted me with especial friendliness because I was the only one of us they knew, through my former pilgrimage during which I had been a guest in their house for many days. The rest of the household also met us, greeting us and showing their eagerness to wait on us.

'The entire household, the landlord and all the servants, were of the German nationality and speech and no word of Italian was to be heard in the house which was a great comfort to us, for it is very distressing to live with people without being able to converse with them. Last of all, as we entered, the dog who guards the house came to meet us, a big black dog who showed how pleased he was by wagging his tail and jumped upon us as dogs do upon those they know.

'This dog receives all Germans with the like joy from whatever part of Germany they come, but when Italians or men of any country except Germany come into the house he becomes so angry that you would think he had gone mad, runs at them, barking loudly, leaps furiously upon them, and will not cease from troubling them till someone quiets him. He has not grown accustomed even to the Italians who dwell in the neighbouring houses and obstinately remains their implacable foe. Moreover, he will not on any terms allow their dogs to enter the house although he does not interfere with German dogs. He does not attack German beggars who ask for alms but falls upon poor Italians who beg for charity and drives them away. I have often rescued poor men from this dog's teeth.

'The Germans say that this dog is a proof that, as he is the enemy of the Italians, so Germans and Italians can never agree because each nation has a hatred of the other rooted in its very nature. The animal, governed only by its passions, quarrels with the Italians because its nature bids it do so, but human beings restrain their feelings by the aid of reason and keep down the hatred which is engrained in their nature.'

There were four lords in the party, as well as Fabri himself, and seven servants, including one who combined the duties of barber and musician, a steward, a cook and one who had 'undergone much misery as a galley-slave and was their lordships' interpreter'.

The Venetians had been controlling the passage of pilgrims by means of statutes since 1227 when they realized that the crusaders would need to be replaced by other visitors for their inns and passengers for their galleys. They were therefore well versed in ensuring the safety and comfort of those who chose to rely on them for the means of travel and who were able to provide a highly lucrative form of trade. Nor was it ever their intention to hurry visitors away from their marvellous city with all that it had to offer the curious and devout—so long as they could be relied on to pay their bills. Licensed guides found them lodgings and took them shopping and were forbidden to accept any commission from the shopkeepers. As for the shipowners themselves, these were controlled down to the minutest detail, in spite of the fact that some of the greatest names of Venetian families are to be found among them—Gritti, Loredan, Venier, Trevisan and Contarini, for example, all of whom were to provide doges at one time or another.

Fabri and his friends made a contract with Pietro Lando who promised to embark at the first fair wind after twenty-six days had elapsed. They therefore had nearly a month (in the event, just over a month) to see the usual sights and festivities and, to them, mandatory arms, head, bones and teeth of an endless succession of saints. They also saw the models of horses submitted by sculptors who hoped to be chosen for the statue of Bartolomeo Colleone opposite the Scuola di San Marco, where the Venetians had decided to put it, rather than in the Piazza San Marco as Colleone had stipulated in his will. An 'exquisitely-shaped' wax horse had been chosen, but Fabri foresaw the problems. 'As for what will be done about casting it,' he wrote, 'I have not heard; perhaps they will give the matter up.' The matter had still not been decided when the sculptor, Andrea Verrochio, died five years later, and Alessandro Leopardi eventually had to be brought back from his exile for fraud and entrusted with the formidable task.

Finally the party went to S. Cristoforo, the church of the travellers' patron saint, and begged him to bear them safely across the sea, and, for good measure, to the church of St. Martha with the prayer that she 'would take good care to provide us with good and honourable inns, or at all events provide us with patience to bear their shortcomings.' The galley was at last ready. They paid their bills, took their purges and, 'entrusting those things which are useless at sea to the charge of a German who was the cellarer of the inn', they embarked on their great adventure. On the whole, it was a success although when Fabri arrived back in Venice seven months later some of his friends from Ulm did not recognize the lean, pale, weatherbeaten pilgrim. Back at Ulm it was quite different: the convent dog knew his step immediately and set up such a barking and scratching at the door that it was soon opened and all the brethren welcomed him as one come back from the dead.

9

Pietro Casola

'I never saw a fine fish'

Venice, 1494

The last of our pilgrims is the sixty-seven year old Pietro Casola
who 'had often been on the point of setting out on the Holy Voyage
but not until God had freed' him in his old age from every
impediment did it seem good for him to renew the determination.
Even then he was disappointed because the large and agreeable
company of monks and fellow countrymen who agreed to join him
became indifferent as the time of departure grew near. 'Although',
he writes, 'I spoke much every day about my departure, because of
my age I was not believed,' and in the end he set off alone on 14
May 1494, ten years after Brother Fabri had returned home. The
full, terrible significance of the Portuguese discoveries of a sea
route to India would be just sinking into the consciousness of the
Venetians.

Casola was comfortably off, enjoying a benefice and three
canonries in Milan, as well as other posts in Rome, all carrying
emoluments. He was therefore in a position to take Santo Brasca's
advice to travel with an open purse which did much to lessen the
rigours of the journey for a man of his age. He was cultured and
sophisticated but he had a prejudice against those who lived north
of the Alps. 'I always let the Ultramontanes, who trod on each
other's heels in their haste to leave, rush in front,' he wrote of the
disembarkation at Jaffa and he followed this practice everywhere:
he would not have found Brother Fabri's German lords congenial.

The Canon rode from Milan to Venice and put his name down
to be carried on the galley of Agostino Contarini, who had taken
Felix Fabri on his first pilgrimage with Santo Brasca in 1480; he
then settled down for the usual waiting period. Although it is five
hundred years ago since Casola recorded what he saw in Venice his

diary begins on a note of dismay which has been often echoed since: 'I determined to examine carefully the city of Venice, about which so much has been said and written that it appears to me there is nothing left to say.'

Like others, he soon found that there was a good deal to say but he used his own eyes and ears and kept his head well out of his guide-book. He also used his legs, a practice which few visitors to Venice followed until quite recent times. 'Although this city is built entirely in the water and the marshes, yet it appears to me that whoever desires to do so can go everywhere on foot, as it is well kept and clean. Anyone, however, who does not want to endure the fatigue can go by water, and will be entreated to do so, and it will cost him less than he would spend elsewhere for the hire of a horse.'

It had been the banking and commercial system of Venice that had most impressed Pero Tafur in 1436: he was a business man himself. Brother Fabri had really enjoyed the round of relic hunting. The cleanliness, the absence of mud, and the colours in which every building was clothed, had impressed both: gold and blue and marble everywhere, as Tafur had written. For Pietro Casola it was the merchandise in the shops, particularly the food, that dazzled.

'Who could count the shops so well furnished that they also seem warehouses, with so many cloths of every make—tapestry, brocades and hangings of every design, carpets and fabrics of every colour and texture, silks of every kind; and so many warehouses full of spices, groceries and drugs—and so much beautiful white wax! These things stupefy the beholder.

'As for the abundance of victuals, I do not believe there is a city in Italy better supplied than this. I went to the place where the flour is sold wholesale; the world at present does not contain such a remarkable thing.' The Granaries occupied the site of the present gardens between the Molo and the Correr Museum. The sales took place in the Fonteghetto della Farina, the first building on the Grand Canal, later the home of the Academy of Fine Arts, and now the offices of the Port of Venice Authority. 'The bakers' shops', he continued, 'are countless, especially in the Piazza San Marco, and there is bread the sight of which tempts a man who is surfeited to eat again.'

Not everything was perfect. 'With the meat they give a great piece of bone. When I saw the place where the meat is sold [then, as now and since 1339, by the Rialto Bridge], I thought I had never seen such a miserable place in any city, or more wretched meat to look at. It drives away the wish to buy. I do not know the reason for this, unless it be that the Venetians are so occupied with their merchandise that they do not trouble about what meat they eat. You could not have a good and fine-looking piece of meat whatever you were willing to pay.

'There is never a dearth of fish, though in truth its quality is not on a level with that of other cities. All the time I was there I never saw a fine fish and never ate a good one, although my hosts took great trouble to procure good fish.

'Another thing appears to me hard in this city; that is, that although the people are placed in the water up to the mouth they often suffer from thirst, and they have to beg good water for drinking and for cooking, especially in the summer time. It is true that there are many cisterns for collecting the rain water [the *pozzi*] and also water is sold in large boatloads—water from the river called the Brenta, which flows near Padua. In this way they provide for their needs, but with difficulty and expense, and the people cannot wash clothes with fresh water as is done elsewhere.'

The shortage and cost of water was a recurrent theme among visitors to Venice. Tafur had described how it was brought from the Brenta (p. 51), and when Fabri was in Venice in May the wells had already dried up and 'fresh water became very dear, for there was no drinkable water to be had except what was brought in ships from the River Brenta and this was sold very dear.'

Casola's enthusiasm returned when he went to the Rialto markets early in the morning to watch the unloading of the boats.

'There were so many boats full of big beans, peas and cherries— not indeed of every kind, as at Milan, but every day and in such quantity that it seemed as if all the gardens of the world must be there. There is an abundant supply of good vegetables and they are cheaper than in any place I ever visited. I went several times in the morning to watch the unloading of the boats and the vegetables looked as if just taken from the gardens and very fresh.'

As for the colour, 'it is hard of belief for anyone who has not seen such a quantity of marble of every kind and colour, and so well carved.' This was Venice almost at the beginning of the sixteenth century, yet much of the Byzantine city, Ruskin's 'gleaming walls, veined with azure and warm with gold', must have been still standing among the Gothic palaces.

Casola was of course shown the working of the Arsenal, and the main walls of the new buildings which were to replace it, and he was taken to see the glass factories at Murano. But he was also

15. 'A long garment . . . for the most part black'. Venetian dress of Casola's time. Detail from Gentile Bellini's *Procession of the Holy Cross*.

concerned with the Venetians themselves.

'As the day of our departure was drawing near, I determined to leave everything else and study the owners of the beautiful things I have noted—that is, the Venetian gentleman.' (There were no titles or orders of nobility in Venice until the Austrians offered them to patricians in the nineteenth century. A patrician was referred to as 'noble man'.) 'For the most part they are tall, handsome men, astute and very subtle in their dealings, and whoever has to do business with them must keep his eyes and ears well open. They are very proud—I think this is on account of their great dominions—and when a son is born to a Venetian gentleman they say themselves, "A Lord is born into the world." They are frugal and very modest in their manner of living at home; outside the house they are very liberal.

'The city of Venice preserves its ancient fashion of dress which never changes, that is, a long garment of any colour that is preferred, but for the most part black. The individuals of every nation which has a settlement in Venice all adopt this style from the greatest to the least. Certainly it is a dress which inspires confidence and is very dignified; the wearers all seem to be doctors in law. In Milan, if a lark should come from the ends of the earth and bring some new fashion in dress, those who can afford it and those who cannot would want to follow the fashion. I need say no more.

'Their women appear to be small because if they were not, they would not wear their shoes, called *pianelle*, as high as they do. I saw some pairs of them sold that were at least half a Milanese braccio [30 cm. or 12 inches] in height. When they wear them some women appear giants and also are not safe from falling as they walk, unless they are well supported by their slaves. They wear their hair so much curled over their eyes that they appear rather men than women. The great part is false hair, and this I know because I saw quantities of it on poles sold in the Piazza.

'These Venetian women, especially the pretty ones, try as much as possible in public to show their breasts and shoulders, so much so that I marvelled that their clothes did not fall off their backs.'

These, Casola adds, were not the general run of Venetian women, who 'go out well covered up'. Anyway, he concludes, 'I am a priest in the way of saints and had no wish to enquire further into their lives.'

Eventually the galley was ready and the pilgrims boarded it—not in the lagoon but outside, off the Lido. Casola boarded it and prepared to pass through his share of 'the tribulation of the sea'. They returned safely five months later and Casola went into the city by tender. Next day the galley entered the lagoon and moored outside the Custom House, which remained closed so that no baggage could be retrieved. Casola, the seasoned traveller, now came into his own. He had read Santo Brasca's advice to take a sack filled with patience and another with money. He had himself found a third sack necessary: one filled with faith, but he was in no doubt which to use in the presence of the Venetian Customs officers. 'My experience proved that it helped matters greatly to shake one of the three sacks I had carried with me—I mean that of the money.'

Casola stayed in Venice a week, anxious though he was to be home. There was no more sight-seeing to be done—he had covered the vast assemblage of human parts before leaving—but there were several social occasions. The Duke of Milan had recently appointed an ambassador to the Venetian Republic and Casola, as a respected Milanese citizen, was invited to dine with him. After dinner the Ambassador took Casola, the French Ambassador and the Pope's representative in his boat to 'visit the wife of a gentleman who was in childbed'.

'I think this visit had been arranged', Casola wrote, 'to show the ambassadors, and especially the Ambassador of the King of France, the splendour and magnificence of the Venetian gentleman. The King's Ambassador said that truly neither the Queen of France nor any French noble would have displayed so much pomp and our Ambassador said the same and declared that our Duchess [Beatrice d'Este, now married to Lodovico Sforza, the new Duke of Milan] would not have such ornamentation.

'As the room was not capable of holding many persons our Ambassador chose me specially to enter with him and he asked my opinion several times. I could only reply with a shrug of the shoulders for it was clear that the ornamentation of the room where we were with the invalid had cost two thousand ducats and more, although quite a small room. The fireplace was all of Carrara marble, shining like gold, and subtly carved with figures and foliage. The ceiling was so richly decorated with gold and ultramarine, and the walls so well adorned, that my pen cannot describe them. There was so much gold everywhere, such an abundance displayed in the ornaments of the bed and the lady, the coverings and the cushions, that I had better not try to describe them.

'I must tell about one other thing. In the chamber there were twenty-five Venetian damsels, one more beautiful than another, who had come to visit the invalid. They did not show less than four fingers' width of bare skin below their shoulders and had so many jewels on the head, neck and hands that these must have been worth a hundred thousand ducats.

'After staying a good while and contemplating the room and the people in it, every man departed fasting; the custom in this respect differing from that observed in Milan, where at similar visits a magnificent refection is provided. I think the Venetians consider the refreshment of the eyes is enough and I like the idea because the refections at Milan on such occasions are a great expense and those at Venice cost nothing.'

Casola now took leave of those who had been kind to him, including the three ambassadors he had met, and on Friday 7 November he was ready for the last stage of his journey. 'I went on board a boat near the Rialto in company with two Milanese merchants and at seven o'clock we left Venice and set out for Padua, where we arrived very late. We had a great deal of difficulty in entering the city. Finally, after mingling entreaties and gratuities, we were admitted by a postern gate and went to lodge at the Sun Inn, where, because the inn was full and we were late, we fared as the proverb says: "He who comes late has a poor supper and a worse bed".'

It was not until the following Friday that they reached Milan. Casola entered the city in pilgrim's dress and alone, although friends had gone out to meet him. Needless to say, his first act was to visit the Duomo and give thanks for the help vouchsafed to him in the many perils he had passed through.

10

Philip de Comines

'The day that I made my entry'

Venice, 1494

The French Ambassador who was with Casola on his strange visit
to the Venetian lady was Philip de Comines, the statesman and
historian who later described his embassy to Venice in his
Mémoires. He had been sent to the Venetians by Charles VIII at
the beginning of his Italian war 'to return them thanks', in
Comines's words, 'for the civil and obliging answers they had
given to two former ambassadors from His Majesty'. But, far
more important, he had also 'to endeavour, if possible, to continue
them in this friendship; for he saw their power, wisdom and
conduct was more likely to disturb him than any other state in Italy.'
At this moment, November 1494, the French King was having
phenomenal success in his adventure and the Venetians had not yet
decided which of their enemies among the Italian princes would
suffer most from his further success and which might benefit; there
could not yet, therefore, be any question of intervention on either
side. There was no question, either, of supporting friends in Italy,
for Venice had none. 'If you only knew how everyone hates you,'
the Duke of Milan had told his Ambassador from the Republic not
many years earlier, 'your hair would stand on end and you would
let other people alone.'

Venice was at the zenith of her outward splendour and had made
a deep impression on Comines when he had arrived a few months
earlier. 'In my journey thither I passed by several of their cities,
Brescia, Verona, Vicenza, Padua and other places. I was treated
very civilly wherever I came, in honour to the monarch who sent
me, and the people came out to meet me in great bodies, with their
Podestà [civil governor] or captain [military commander]; both of
them never came out together, but the captain met me at the gate.

When I had entered the town I was conducted to my lodging; the master of the house was commanded that I should want nothing and my whole charges were born—and mighty good words given me into the bargain. Yet, if you compute what must necessarily be given to the drums, trumpets and officers in those ceremonies, an ambassador will be found to save but little; however, my reception was most honourable.

'The day that I made my entry into Venice they sent to meet me as far as Fusina, which is five miles from Venice. There you leave the boats which bring you down the river from Padua and get into little boats covered with tapestry and very neat, with fair carpets within and velvet cushions to sit upon. To this place you come from Venice by sea as it is the next place to Venice upon *terra firma*; but the sea (unless agitated by some storm) is very calm, which is the reason for the great abundance of all sorts of fish.

'I was extremely surprised at the situation of this city, to see so many churches, monasteries and houses, and all in the water. The people have no other passage up and down the streets but in boats, of which, I believe, they have near thirty thousand, but they are very small.

16. 'So many churches, monasteries and houses, and all in the water'. The Palazzo Dario, Venice, newly built in Comines's time.

17. 'The fairest and best built street in the world'. The Grand Canal as
seen by Comines. Detail from de' Barbari's woodcut.

'I was conducted to the church of S. Andrea, where other
gentlemen met me, and then, in two larger boats, we went through
the principal street, which they call the Grand Canal. It is the
fairest and best built street, I think, in the world and goes quite
through the city which is the most triumphant city that I have ever
seen.'

But this was not a triumphant moment for the Venetians. The
Ambassador from their old enemy, the Duke of Milan, persuaded
them to join in the effort to get the French King out of Italy. They
dismissed Comines politely and, with their new ally, set upon the
King's army at Fornovo, near Parma. The King escaped, although
his army was defeated. Events now started to move towards that
climax of a few years later when Europe was to unite for the first
time as the League of Cambrai to bring sense to the Venetians. But
meanwhile there was a breathing space. In April 1498, in a journey
unequalled by any recorded in this book, a courier rode the seven
hundred and fifty miles from Amboise on the Loire to Mestre on
the Venetian Lagoon in seven days with the news that Charles
VIII was dead. He had ridden thirteen horses to death on the way.

Andrea Trevisano

'I believe they enjoy their comforts'

Venice to London, 1496–8

Two years after the Venetians' polite dismissal of Philip de Comines, that is on 29 November 1496, the Senate decreed:

'That an ambassador be elected to the King of England [Henry VII]; the person elected not to refuse to serve, under penalty of 500 ducats and other penalties.

'He is to take with him twelve horses and two running footmen [*stapherios*], a notary of our chancery, and his servant.

'Elected: Ser Andrea Trevisano.'

The Trevisano family had been members of the Great Council of the Republic long before its closing, in 1297, to all but the families of existing members. Andrea was now to be the first representative of ambassadorial rank to the English Court since 1319, when a delegate had been sent to settle some disputes arising out of an act of piracy. He and the Ambassador elect to Milan were 'to sit in the Senate until their departure that they may be duly instructed'.

His instruction was evidently thorough since on 22 March 1497 the Senate were told of a letter from Henry VII saying he was anxiously expecting the Ambassador's arrival. A hint must have been given that the King expected an ambassador ranking more than twelve horses and it was accordingly decreed:

'As the Ambassador should journey honourably to the said King, to whom no Ambassador of ours has been sent for a very long while; the English nation moreover requiring what follows: our Ambassador shall be allowed four horses besides the horses and retinue which he was already desired to take, so that he may have 16 horses and two running footmen, and go more honourably, as becomes the dignity of our State.'

In June Andrea Trevisano was given his commission, together with four hundred ducats in silver. His instructions were precise. He was to express the love borne for his Majesty personally and congratulate him on his own well-being, and that of the Queen and his children and (perhaps above all) on his very great successes (such, presumably, as the collapse of Perkin Warbeck's supporters). He was to give the King the latest news of events in northern Italy, working at all times with the Milanese Ambassador, and making it clear that Venice and Milan together were fully able to deal with any further interference in Italian affairs such as the recent presumption of Charles VIII. He was told just who had the greatest influence with the King, with whom to ingratiate himself, and how he was 'to visit such other persons of note in England as he may think fit, addressing them in language becoming their station'. Finally, of course, he was to ensure that the Republic should 'be acquainted with everything' that went on in England.

Trevisano had still not arrived in England by 15 July, when news reached Italy that the King was having difficulties with insurgents from the north and that 'the island was in commotion'. The Senate's official diarist, Marin Sanuto, noted that 'our Ambassador Andrea Trevisano was on the road: nothing had been heard of his arrival, and it was believed that owing to these disturbances on the island he would not cross, but remain at Bruges in the territories of the Archduke Philip of Burgundy'

On 21 August Sanuto reported that Trevisano had still been in Bruges on the 5th and that letters from him had been received recounting his adventures on the journey through Germany. Certain Frenchmen were on the road between Bruges and Calais and in view of the danger he had asked for an escort to be sent him from England. The King was 'in the field, against the King of Scotland and the Duke of York' but on being approached he said he was very anxious for the coming of the two Ambassadors, 'most especially the Venetian' and he sent the escort required. Trevisano was accordingly about to 'get on horseback for Calais and would subsequently cross over to the island.'

At last, on 24 August, Trevisano made the crossing and at Dover found the gentlemen sent by the King to do him honour. Twenty miles from London he was met by other knights and gentlemen and, riding on, was joined by other parties so that he entered London on 26 August with 200 horse and great honour was done him. He was invited by the King to join him at Woodstock where

18. 'His Majesty wore . . . a collar of many jewels'. Henry VII in 1505.

he arrived at the royal palace on 3 September. Sanuto wrote:

'The King received him in a small hall, hung with very handsome tapestry, leaning against a tall gilt [gold-brocaded] chair, covered with cloth of gold. His Majesty wore a violet-coloured gown, lined with cloth of gold, and a collar of many jewels, and on his cap was a large diamond and a most beautiful pearl.'

The Ambassador made his speech in Latin, the King remaining standing throughout, and, 'having discussed his reply, caused him to be answered' by the Cardinal-Archbishop John Morton, the King's principal adviser. Dinner and a visit to the Queen followed and Trevisano returned to London. On 17 September he sent his first despatch to Venice which recounted the latest escapade of Perkin Warbeck; it arrived on 9 October, two to four weeks being the average time for letters between London and Venice. More news followed, including an account of Perkin Warbeck's admission that he was an impostor and the King's kindly treatment of him. However, there was a limit to his kindness; on 31 December Trevisano saw Perkin: 'He was in a chamber of the King's palace and habitation. He is a well favoured young man, 23 years old, and his wife a very handsome woman; the King treats them well, but did not allow them to sleep together.'

And then, a surprising end. Trevisano, after only four months in England, 'asks leave to return home, perceiving that his stay in England is of no importance.' The official excuse was that both Trevisano's parents had recently died and he was instructed to tell the King of his misfortune. He was to tell the King 'that for such business as it may be necessary to transact, the State will employ the Venetian consul in England, and that his Majesty may do the likewise.' The true reason was that there was no cause to fear any injurious action towards Venice on the part of the King who was fully occupied at home. Nevertheless, it was not until March 1498 that Trevisano was able to get away. In April Sanuto noted that a letter had been received from him at Dover telling 'How he quitted London on 15 March, having taken leave of the King and Queen. The King had knighted him and given him a collar worth 500 ducats, and a horse, very handsome and small, belonging to the King himself. Also how he had quitted the island, and had crossed from Dover to Calais for Flanders, where he intended to remain for some days at Antwerp, and then set out on his way home.'

He arrived on 18 May, 'with beard and in mourning for the death of his father and mother' and duly reported to the Senate on his embassy. 'Much honour had been paid the Ambassador; his legation had technically lasted 11 months and 15 days, and he had expended in all 4,300 ducats. He then mentioned many details, which pleased everybody.'

Marin Sanuto did not record 'the details which pleased everybody' and Trevisano's 'Relation', which it was customary for

Venetian ambassadors to present at the end of their term of office, has not survived. However, it must certainly have been based on a 'relation' which was prepared for the purpose by a secretary or assistant and which later found its way into a Venetian library. This provides the first impressions of England by a traveller from Italy since those of Julius Caesar.

Like Caesar, the writer begins with a geographical description: 'The Kingdom of England is situated in the island named Britain which is in the Ocean, between the north and the west. Her form is triangular, like that of Sicily, and she lies, though at a considerable distance, over against Germany, which is opposite her to the north, France, to the east and south, and Spain to the south, a little to the west.

'I cannot say what the circumference of this island is, because the islanders of our day do not care to understand such matters, and I find that writers differ on the subject. Julius Caesar, counting the three sides of the island, sets it at 2,000 miles; Bede, an English priest who had read the Commentaries, at 3,600 miles.

'The climate is very healthy and free from many complaints with which Italy is afflicted; though so far to the northwest the cold in winter is much less severe than in Italy and the heat proportionately less in summer. This is owing to the rain, which falls almost every day during the months of June, July and August; they never have any spring here, according to the islanders.'

It is to be hoped that Trevisano did not mislead the Senate with his secretary's second-hand report on the weather during months they had not been in England. Apart from the idea that there is no spring, England, by the time the Ambassador and his secretary had returned home, happened to be at the onset of one of the worst droughts recorded, rather than a three-month period of almost daily rain. In other matters the writer seems to have been better informed.

'Agriculture is not practised in this island beyond what is required for the consumption of the people; because were they to plough and sow all the land that was capable of cultivation, they might sell a quantity of grain to the surrounding countries. This negligence is, however, atoned for by an immense profusion of every comestible animal, such as stags, goats, fallow-deer, hares, rabbits, pigs, and an infinity of oxen, which have much larger horns than ours, which proves the mildness of the climate, as horns cannot bear excessive cold. But above all they have an enormous number of sheep which yield them quantities of wool of the best quality. They have no wolves although it is said that they still exist in Scotland. Common fowls, pea-fowls, partridges, pheasants and other small birds abound here above measure, and it is a truly beautiful thing to behold one or two thousand tame swans upon the River Thames, as you and I have seen, which are eaten by the English, like ducks and geese. Nor do they dislike what we so much abominate, i.e. crows, rooks, and jackdaws; and the raven may croak at his pleasure, for no one cares for the omen; there is even a penalty attached to destroying them, as they say that they keep the streets of the towns free from all filth.'

All this was true. The demand for English wool made it far more profitable to keep sheep than to cultivate the land, and arable farming had fallen into decline. Wolves had only recently been exterminated; swans, as royal birds, were preserved but available for eating in small quantities. The English landscape had impressed the Venetians. 'It is all diversified by pleasant undulating hills and beautiful valleys, nothing to be seen but agreeable woods or extensive meadows or lands in cultivation; and the greatest plenty of water springing everywhere.'

The English people impressed them rather less. 'The English are for the most part handsome and well-proportioned [see illustration, page 127], though not quite so much so, in my opinion, as it had been asserted to me before you went to that kingdom. They are great lovers of themselves and of everything belonging to them; they think that there are no other men than themselves, and no world but England. Whenever they see a handsome foreigner they say that "he looks like an Englishman" and that "it is a great pity that he should not be an Englishman"; and when they partake of any delicacy with a foreigner they ask him "whether such a thing is made in *their* country?" They take great pleasure in having a quantity of excellent victuals, and also in remaining a long time at table, being very sparing of wine when they drink it at their own expense and not considering it any inconvenience for three or four persons to drink out of the same cup. Few people keep wine in their own houses, but buy it, for the most part, at a tavern; and when they mean to drink a great deal they go to the tavern, not only the men but ladies of distinction. The deficiency of wine however is amply supplied by the abundance of ale and beer, to the use of which these people are become so habituated that, where there is plenty of wine, they will drink them in preference to it, and in great quantities. Like discreet people, however, they do not offer them to Italians, unless they should ask for them.

'They all wear very fine clothes and are extremely polite in their language; which, although it is derived from the German, has lost its natural harshness and is pleasing enough as they pronounce it. They are very quick at everything they apply their minds to; few however, excepting the clergy, are addicted to the study of letters; and this is the reason why anyone who has learning, though he be a layman, is called by them *a Clerk*. And yet they have great advantages for study, there being two general universities in the kingdom, Oxford and Cambridge in which are many colleges founded for the maintenance of poor scholars.

'They have an antipathy to foreigners, and imagine that they never come into their island but to make themselves masters of it and to usurp their goods; neither have they any sincere and solid friendships amongst themselves, insomuch that they do not trust each other to discuss either public or private affairs together, in the confidential manner we do in Italy. And although their dispositions are somewhat licentious, I have never noticed anyone, either at court or amongst the lower orders, to be in love; whence one must conclude, either that the English are the most discreet lovers in the world, or that they are incapable of love. I say this of the men, for I understand it is quite the contrary with the women who are very violent in their passions. Howbeit the English keep a very jealous guard over their wives, although anything may be compensated in the end by the power of money.'

Like most foreign visitors the Venetians were astonished by the habit of the English gentry of turning their younger sons out of the manor-houses to seek their fortunes elsewhere, usually as apprentices to merchants or craftsmen in the towns. The English preserved their great estates by leaving all the land and most of the money to the eldest son and did not want their younger sons leading idle lives like the impoverished nobles of France and Italy, who were too proud to work. The Venetians saw it quite differently. 'The want of affection in the English is strongly manifested towards their children, for after having kept them at home till they are seven or nine years old at the most, they put them out to hard service in the houses of other people, binding them generally for another seven or nine years. These are called apprentices and few are born who are exempted from this fate. On enquiring the reason for this severity they answered that they did it that their children might learn better manners. But I believe that they do it because they like to enjoy all their comforts themselves.

Besides which, the English being great epicures, and very avaricious by nature, indulge in the most delicate fare themselves and give their household the coarsest bread and beer and cold meat baked on Sunday for the week, which however they allow them in great abundance. If they had their own children at home they would be obliged to give them the same food they had themselves.'

The English respect for primogeniture, and lack of respect for the rights of a wife to her own property, enabled the landowners to increase their estates; their belief in the benefits of hard work, and the demand in Europe for their tin and wool, made it possible for those who left the land to do well in commerce. England was in an enviable position.

'The riches of England are greater than those of any country in Europe, as I have been told by the oldest, most experienced merchants and as I can vouch from what I have seen. Everyone who makes a tour in the island will soon become aware of this great wealth for there is no small innkeeper, however poor and humble he may be, who does not serve his table with silver dishes and drinking cups.'

Finally there was the legal system. Here the Italians had the advantage. 'If anyone should claim a sum and the debtor denies it, the judge would order that each of them make a choice of six arbitrators. After these have heard both parties, they are shut up in a room, without food or fire, or means of sitting down, and there they remain until the majority have agreed upon their verdict. Each of them endeavours to defend the cause of him who named him, whether just or unjust; but those who cannot bear the discomfort yield to the more determined for the sake of getting out sooner. Therefore the Italian merchants are gainers by this bad custom every time they have a dispute with the English; for although the native arbitrators chosen by the English are anxious to support the cause of their principal before they are shut up, yet they cannot stand out as the Italians can, who are accustomed to fasting and privations, so that the final judgment is generally given in favour of the latter.'

PART THREE

Sixteenth-century Travellers

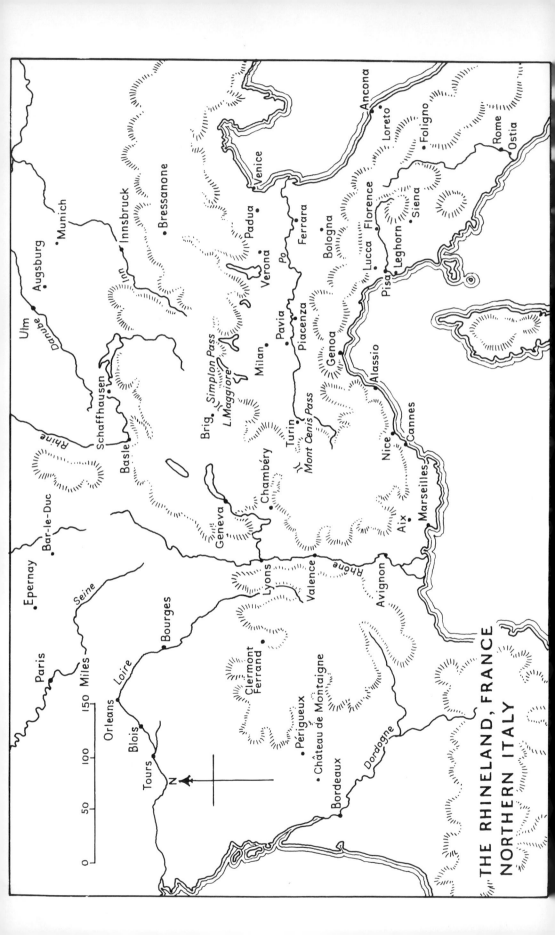

THE RHINELAND, FRANCE
NORTHERN ITALY

Andrea Badoer

'When the King saw me he wept'

Venice to London, 1509–15

Ten years and a few months after Trevisano's return to Venice, that is on 30 January 1509, the Senate decided to send another ambassador to the Court of Henry VII, now in the last year of his life. Europe was combining to form the League of Cambrai in the hope of destroying Venice and it was essential that the King of England, or his son who was expected soon to inherit the throne, should be dissuaded from joining the conspirators. Hieronimo, one of the Giustinian family, refused the appointment. If he was threatened with a penalty, as Trevisano had been, for refusing, he presumably preferred to pay it. The noble families of Venice were still men of individual wealth but the Senate was always in financial difficulties and seems never to have had enough money to pay its representatives properly. An embassy had other disadvantages. The envoy, who had to be a patrician, was not allowed to take his wife with him, although he was positively ordered to take a cook, and he was compelled to hand over to the Senate even the smallest presents which he might be given.

Andrea Badoer was finally chosen to go to England on a basis of one hundred ducats a month for expenses, 'for which he was not bound to show any account to the Signoria' (the Signoria was the inner council of the Republic, consisting of the Doge and his six councillors). Out of this he was 'to keep five servants and as many horses.' In view of the conditions in Europe he was to travel incognito, revealing his identity only on arrival, and his commission was sent to the Venetian Consul in London lest it should be found on Badoer's person during his journey. According to the commission, Badoer was to 'discover to the King the deeply rooted and detestable greediness of the King of France [Louis XII] and others' in spite of the great service of the Signoria 'in securing to them the Milanese in observance of her promise'. The King was to be warned of the consequences of supporting these people and advised precisely how it would be advantageous, to his own country as well as to the Venetians, for him to act. As a final piece of diplomatic nicety, the Senate were to send the commission by way of Germany, 'but not the credentials, lest the leaden seal cause their miscarriage'. These were to be forwarded by another channel and, the Senate minute added ominously, *if* the Ambassador were to arrive, the Consul in England should certify his credentials to the King.

Andrea Badoer was deeply to regret at times that he had been chosen as Ambassador and three years later he wrote his brother a letter describing his journey to London and its consequences. It began, he wrote, in January 1509, when the hostility of France towards Venice first manifested itself.

'Those appointed to govern us determined to send privily an ambassador to induce the English King to attack France (on whose crown he has claims: it is justice appertaining to him), and to arouse him to make a diversion over there in our favour; the need being extremely urgent though, as the roads were intercepted everywhere, it was impossible to effect the journey save at the most manifest peril of one's life.

'I was elected to this mission, without my knowledge, and when the Doge sent for me I stared at him in surprise. But, pardon my presumption, brother, no one save myself was capable of executing this mission, being well acquainted with the French and German tongues as well as English, which is as little known in Venice as modern Greek or Slavonic in London.

'I therefore left my affairs in confusion, starting with a trifle of money, induced by the hope of obtaining great credit with the Government, besides the certain promise of one hundred ducats per month. After riding twenty-six days I reached London, where I am now, nor do I know what more could have been expected of a man at my age, which was then sixty-two years, and encountering on the road such disasters as the following: first, I rode incessantly day and night in disguise, crippling and laming myself, so that I shall never again be as sound as I was; for when on the Mount St. Gothard my horse fell under me whilst riding over ice and in the dark. My right leg was bared to the bone by a wound two inches deep but by good fortune he fell to the right. Had he slipped on the other side I should have gone down a precipice. At length I got to an inn but being late I could get nothing but bread and wine for my supper and dressed my leg myself.

'On the following morning I got to Basle and there embarked, to proceed by water, the Rhine being very much swollen. Having gone some way down stream, we went into a large vessel loaded with merchandise, and also with my horses, and the bottom of this boat struck some sedges under water and went over on its side. The planks of the boat separated and she was carried to the shoal, on which we all jumped, landing the horses also, and the boat filled with water. We passed the night counting the hours and I, with my wounded leg, and all the rest of us well drenched. Finally, the boat was repaired and took us safe to Strasbourg.

'For the rest it will suffice to say that, as suspicion was everywhere alive, it behove me to give account to everybody of what I was doing, and not change colour whilst I was telling my tale. Sometimes I passed for an Englishman, sometimes for a Scotchman, whilst at others I thought it safer to make myself out a Croat on my way to the court of the Emperor [Maximilian I] who was then on the borders of Flanders. With this pretence I went on for some days, having made my face very black according to a device of my own.

'When I had passed the territory where the Emperor was, I replied to enquiries that I was a messenger of the King of England's, returning from court, and I went on thus until I got near Calais, which is a fortified town in Picardy belonging to the King of England. I experienced greater difficulty in getting into this place than had befallen me throughout the rest of my journey, there being numerous fortified towns belonging to the French on the borders which are very strictly guarded from fear of the English. I was thrice stopped by French companies but when I answered haughtily that I was an Englishman coming from Flanders, and on my way home, they let me pass. They rode after me to within a bow-shot's distance from the walls of Calais, where I found an English armed bark bound to London on which I took passage with my horses and in one day and night reached London in safety.

'Having reached London, picture to yourself, noble brother, what a stately mission mine was, for, on leaving Venice, to avoid suspicion, I took nothing but what was on my back—namely, two shirts, one over the other, and a doublet in the English fashion, all patched and motheaten, without purse or pocket. In short, on arriving here I had to clothe myself anew from head to foot, as a Venetian ambassador, just as if I had only then come into the world.

'Here they manufacture no cloths of silk, receiving all such from Genoa, Florence and Lucca, so it behoved me to take what I could get, and shut my eyes. Think what a figure I shall make in Venice. I shall be unable to use my apparel in Venice anyway as it is all made according to the English fashion, not that of Italy.

'I found that the King, his present Majesty's father, was sick and could not give me an audience, and a few days afterwards he died and was succeeded by his son [Henry VII died on 21 April].'

Badoer's letter of credence was no longer valid since it was made out to Henry VII and the new letter he requested from Venice did not arrive until six months later. An English nobleman whom Badoer had known in Venice intervened and the new King accepted the old letter. He took a liking to Badoer immediately and was persuaded by him to write to the Pope in favour of the Venetians. He was also prevailed upon to write suitable letters to King Ferdinand of Spain and the King of France and 'endless letters to the Emperor', Maximilian I.

According to Badoer, the King wrote strongly to Louis XII. 'He was to desist from the league against the Venetians, having obtained what belonged to him in the Duchy of Milan. If he chose to continue in amity with his Majesty here, he was to cease molesting the Venetians, his good friends who had proved themselves the bulwark of Christendom by a most immense outlay, both of blood and treasure. Upon this the King of France took offence and answered sharply, I fanning the flame from time to time.

'After so much exertion and toil I was seized with a malignant fever which never left me for thirty-seven days. I had two physicians, each of whom chose to receive a noble [6s 8d] per diem, and their coming was as beneficial to me as if they had stayed away. When I had completed my fever the King received a reply from the Emperor and, not knowing I was so very ill, sent to tell me to come and speak with him; so, regardless of the fever, I rose from my bed on 24 November and went to the Court at Greenwich, six miles hence, by water, though all dissuaded me from doing so, thinking it would be my death. When the King saw me he wept for very pity at my having come, it seeming to him that I had been taken out of my grave.'

But at home in Venice Badoer's troubles were either unknown or unappreciated. One senator proposed that he be brought back and another, Lorenzo Orio, who later became Ambassador himself, proposed that his hundred ducats a month be reduced to seventy. With this economy agreed, the Senate decided the embassy could remain in London, but Badoer was not told about it until three months later. He was, he told his brother, naturally furious but there was even worse to report: he had been in London for nineteen months without receiving a single ducat and ten months without so much as a letter.

'Seeing that no money was sent me, I lived plainly and on credit, just as if I had been at an hostel, paying three for what was worth one, and taking up money at usury on bills, so that I am in debt for life.'

No one believed him. No one remembered the risk to his life when he had risen from his sick bed and gone to Greenwich in depth of winter. From Ambassador they had degraded him to secretary in spite of all he had persuaded the King to do on behalf of Venice. As the letter ends, the complaints become almost hysterical and Badoer has nothing to hope for but death. At least, 'he who dies a noble death is respected by the whole country.'

Much of what Badoer wrote to his brother was true. The Venetian State archives record again and again that 'Badoer has arrayed himself like an ambassador but has no money and so demands a remittance'; 'letter from Badoer narrating how he is there without plate; cannot do honour to the Signoria; would require money etc.'; 'his means are exhausted, he has neither plate nor anything else to pawn'; 'he is residing there in shame, nor will anyone accommodate him, and it is a reproach to the Signoria.' In 1510, two years before Badoer's letter to his brother, the Senate, 'considering the excessive cost of the embassy and the necessity of retrenchment owing to the great need of money' decided to recall Badoer and entrust the State's affairs to the Consul in London. Meanwhile his monthly salary was to be reduced to fifty ducats. But there were second thoughts. The King might take umbrage. Badoer was to remain with only seventy ducats a month for expenses until the Senate determined otherwise. Badoer replied graciously: he did not go to England to benefit himself, but for his country's sake, and he is content with what the Signoria pleases to give. The Senate, at the end of 1511, 'lately remitted him two hundred ducats and will forthwith send as many more; so recommend him to be of good cheer and to serve the State diligently, as hitherto.'

Privately, the Senate felt that Badoer had been in England long enough. His complaining letters to various members of his family and friends elsewhere were not of benefit to the State's repute. In July 1512 Francesco Capello was elected Ambassador and instructed to proceed to England and announce himself as Badoer's successor. Capello, though, was even less fortunate than Badoer. He was detained on the way to England by the Emperor Maximilian on several grounds, among them being the charge that he had been sent by the Venetians to poison the Emperor. (There is no evidence that this was true, although it may well have been.) Eventually Capello was released but compelled to return to Venice, 'by such impassable and rugged roads', according to a letter from the Senate to Badoer, 'that he was seized with an illness of which he at length died.' Thus the wretched Badoer was condemned to more months in England without money until a successor could be found; he was borrowing wherever he could and, as a result, was held in such small account that he was the only ambassador to be neglected when the King and Queen attended the launching of a new ship.

Eventually, at the end of 1514, it was decided that two ambassadors should be appointed to serve France and England jointly. Francesco Donato and Pietro Pasqualigo were named and, to avoid a fate such as had befallen Francesco Capello, they were to go by way of Ferrara, Florence and Genoa and thence by sea. Fate was still against Badoer: on the eve of their departure Donato had an apoplectic fit and Pasqualigo was sent on alone, to await further instructions. At last, Sebastian Giustinian was elected in his place. 'He took time to reply until the following morning' but then accepted the post. He may have been encouraged by the fact that the Senate had decided to send him a bill of exchange for one thousand ducats to pay Badoer's debts; he may or may not have known that implementation by no means necessarily followed decision in the case of the Venetian Senate.

13

Sebastian Giustinian

'I answered that I had no present'

Venice, Paris and London, 1515

Sebastian Giustinian left Venice on the morning of 10 January and before he had reached Ferrara he received news of the death of Louis XII of France. He passed this on to the Signoria and was told to make for Lyons where he would meet his colleague, Pietro Pasqualigo, and then proceed to Paris. It was to be another ten days before he had crossed the Apennines and he then went by sea to Genoa and Nice, where he arrived on 9 February. Another sixteen days took him to Lyons where he found Pasqualigo, but not his baggage which had been sent by road. Pasqualigo was in the same position and, after waiting until 3 March, they bought new clothes and set out for Paris with the intention of trying 'to make shift in court until our effects arrive and pray God to send them quickly'. Fresh instructions had been sent to them as to how they were to ingratiate themselves, not only with the new King Francis (Louis's nephew) and his Queen, but also with his mother, 'she being, as we understand, a person of great authority and power at Court'. A delicate matter was then broached:

'The presents now in your hands, you will keep thus until further orders from us and on your departure from France you will leave them with your predecessor, not giving it to be understood to anyone that you have any presents with you.'

It was not easy to accomplish their first task, 'to make loving speeches to the King', when they eventually arrived in Paris three months after leaving Venice. An Italian nobleman soon warned them what to expect, and Marin Sanuto summarized their report to Venice in his official diary:

'The King's mode of life is in this wise: he gets out of bed a little before noon, then, after dressing and hearing mass, he forthwith

19. 'He remains for two or three hours with his mother'. Louise of Savoy, mother of King Francis I. From a miniature in Catherine de' Medici's Book of Hours.

dines and remains for two or three hours with his mother and afterwards visits his mistresses [*va a morose*] or goes out hunting, then during the whole night visits here and there so that only with difficulty can one find an opportune moment for transacting business.'

Paris, the Ambassadors reported, stank of mud and abounded in horses—ten thousand of them were seen daily. The whole Court dressed in silk and even pages trailed silk on the ground. When

they were eventually sent for by the King he behaved graciously:
'He rose from his seat, as did all the others, cap in hand; we made
due obeisance, and notwithstanding all our efforts, he would not
allow us to kiss his hand, but embraced us, evincing the greatest
goodwill and esteem for your Serenity, positively commanding,
after we had presented our credentials, that we should sit beside
him.'

As Henry VIII had remarked to Andrea Badoer a few weeks
earlier, and as Badoer had immediately reported to the Signoria,
'this King of France was indeed a worthy and honest sovereign,
but nevertheless a Frenchman, and not to be trusted.'

20. 'A Frenchman, and not to be trusted'. Francis I, by Jean Clouet.

After the interview with the King and the new Queen, the Ambassadors had to call on the widowed Queen, the sixteen-year-old sister of Henry VIII who had been married to Louis XII, then fifty-three, the previous August. The Signoria had no intention of wasting the valuable present they had given Pasqualigo on a dowager of that age who, with her husband's death, had lost all influence. As they had been given to understand, the new King's mother, Louise of Savoy, was likely to play a far more considerable role in the history of France and events proved them right. Pasqualigo, though, had been warned by a friend of a complication likely to arise, as he reported home after the interview: 'My friend told me the Queen knew that I was bringing her a handsome present from you and that on this account she would give us a very good reception and he said that this had been heard through letters from his brother [who was French Ambassador in Venice]. I answered that I had no present with me, and knew not this, turning the conversation immediately.'

The Ambassadors must have been pleased to complete their mission in Paris, with its various embarrassments, and by 4 April they were in Boulogne. They were still there on the seventh 'meaning to make the passage either from hence or Calais as soon as possible'. At last, on the tenth, they left Boulogne. A week's delay before being able to cross the Channel was longer than average, but not exceptional. The normal time for news and letters to reach Venice from Calais was fourteen days and from London twenty-four days; ten days between London and Calais was therefore to be expected. On the other hand, if the weather was in the traveller's favour the journey between London and Venice could be done in as little as nine days.

Two days after leaving Boulogne the Ambassadors wrote from Canterbury that they had landed at Dover. 'We had been at sea during twenty-four hours, owing to the foul weather which buffeted us mercilessly. Today, early, we arrived here and shortly after the French Ambassadors also arrived on their return to the King. We visited them immediately, using such friendly expressions as we deemed becoming.'

In return they picked up some useful political gossip. On 21 April their three-month journey from Venice ended and they were able to write from London: 'In order to await his Majesty's instructions respecting our entry into this city we came as far as Rochester, twenty-four miles hence, where we found the Consul with some of our countrymen who, to honour you, had come thus far and with them we betook ourselves to Deptford, some twelve Venetian miles from here. From thence, on the 18th, there came to escort us, in the name of the King's majesty, a doctor of the Parliament and another cavalier with an honourable company of about fifty horsemen, all in one livery, who, after addressing us in friendly terms, accompanied us as far as our dwelling in this town. On the road we were met, first by the rest of our countrymen, and then by the Ambassador Badoer and others, so that on entering London we numbered upwards of two hundred horses. His Majesty is at Richmond, seven miles off, where he means to celebrate the approaching festival of St. George, the patron of his Order of the Garter, and he has given us to understand that he will there, and on that day, give us our first audience, for the sake of doing greater honour to you.'

As soon as the retiring Ambassador, Badoer, had his reliefs to himself he turned to the subject with which his mind was preoccupied. 'We have presented his letters of recall to Ambassador Badoer who answered us that he is unable to depart hence without a good sum of money; and he enquired of me, Sebastian, whether I had brought him any supply, but I answered him in the negative; for although in the commission given me on leaving Venice it was stated, among other things, that a bill for one thousand ducats had been consigned to me for this purpose by Almoro Pisani of the bank, I never received either the bill or anything else. We have chosen to notify this that you may be acquainted with the whole, and take such steps as you shall think fit.'

The King kept his promise to receive the three Ambassadors on St. George's Day and they were conducted by the Thames to Richmond Palace. The King was in the robes of the Garter and eight other knights of the Order were present at the ceremony. He listened attentively to Giustinian's praises and the new Ambassador began his service at the Court of Henry VIII which was to last for four years.

There was no release yet for the unhappy Badoer; no money came from Venice and without it he had no alternative but to remain in England. On 5 August there was some compensation and he was able to send the good news to Venice that the King had honoured him with a knighthood. It was not until 19 November, more than six months after his reliefs had arrived, that his debts were at last paid and he was able to leave. Giustinian echoed the words of his predecessor Trevisano in writing to Venice that 'all the great personages of the kingdom consider him quite in the light of a native Englishman by reason of his excellent qualities'. They knew no higher praise.

Badoer made his journey home in leisurely fashion, arriving on 25 April 1516. Marin Sanuto was among those who greeted him after his seven-year absence and found him looking very well indeed. Badoer 'presented a letter to the Signoria from the King of England much to his praise' and he was commended by the Doge. But he was not allowed to keep the gold chain which the King had given him; forty-seven senators voted against the proposal, a hundred and fifteen in its favour, and the majority was not enough to carry the motion.

Three years later, in 1519, Giustinian returned. He had not been knighted, as had both Trevisano and Badoer, but Cardinal Wolsey had given him a chain worth 450 ducats 'in the name of the King of England'. The record of his report to the Senate ended with the words: 'The Ambassador mentioned the chain received from the King of England which he requested as a gift from the Signoria, beseeching that it might be conceded him. *Bene dixit sed non bene persuasit.*'

Well spoken, the request had been, but not persuasively enough for the Venetian Senate.

14

Erasmus

'Go I would, in an open carriage'

Basle to Louvain, 1518

(Map on p. 154)

In the autumn of 1518 Desiderius Erasmus was asked as a matter of
urgency to leave Basle, where he was living, and join the monks of
Louvain for a theological discussion. It may be presumed that the
activities of Martin Luther were also on the agenda. Erasmus was
ill, and determined not to become involved with Luther, but he
accepted the summons and set off on a journey which was to prove
extremely unpleasant. He was in his early fifties at the time,
probably the most famous man in Europe, and, although he had
always avoided the temptation to become rich, he was normally
used to travelling and living in some comfort. He described his
journey in a Latin letter to Beatus Rhenanus, a scholarly friend
some twenty years younger than Erasmus himself. The letter is
very freely translated here by J. A. Froude, the Victorian historian.

'Listen to the tragedy of my adventures. I left Basle relaxed and
worn out. The river part of my journey was well enough, save for
the heat of the sun. We dined at Breisach [30 miles north of Basle,
then under Habsburg rule]. Dinner abominable. Foul smells and
flies in swarms. We were kept waiting half an hour while the
precious banquet was preparing. There was nothing that I could
eat, every dish filthy and stinking. At night we were turned out of
the boat into a village—the name I forget, and I would not write if I
remembered. It nearly made an end of me. There were sixty of us
to sup together in the tavern, a medley of human animals in one
small heated room. It was ten o'clock, and oh! the dirt and the
noise, especially after the wine had begun to circulate. The cries of
the boatmen woke us in the morning. I hurry on board unsupped
and unslept. At nine we reached Strasbourg [50 miles] when things

mended a little. Schurer [his publisher at Strasbourg] supplied us with wine, and other acquaintances called to see me. From Strasbourg we went on to Speyer [on horseback; a two-day journey of 68 miles]. My English horse had broken down, a wretch of a blacksmith having burnt his foot with a hot shoe.

'I escaped the inn at Speyer and was entertained by a friend, the Dean. Two pleasant days with him, thence in a carriage to Worms [20 miles] and so on to Mainz [25 miles] where I was again lodged by a Cathedral canon. So far things had gone tolerably with me. The smell of the horses was disagreeable and the pace was slow, but that was the worst. [He returns to the Rhine boat and goes on to Boppart, the Customs frontier between the Emperor and the Archbishop of Treves.] I called on my friend Christopher, the toll-collector [telones] to his great delight. On his table I saw the works of Erasmus. He invited a party to meet me, sent the boatman a pitcher of wine and promised to let them off the Customs duty as a reward for having brought him so great a man. Thence to Bonn, thence to Cologne [115 miles from Mainz] which we reached early on Sunday morning.

'Imagine a toll-collector reading my books. Christ said the publicans and harlots would go into the kingdom of Heaven before the Pharisees. Priests and monks live for their bellies and toll-collectors take to literature.

But, alas, the red wine which he sent to the boatmen took the taste of the bargeman's wife, a red-faced sot of a woman. She drank it to the last drop, and then flew to arms and almost murdered a servant wench with oyster-shells. Then she rushed on deck, tackled her husband, and tried to pitch him overboard. There is vinal energy for you.

'At the hotel in Cologne I ordered breakfast at ten o'clock, with a carriage and pair to be ready immediately after. I went to church, came back to find no breakfast and a carriage not to be had. My horse being disabled I tried to hire another. I was told this could not be done either. I saw what this meant. I was to be kept at Cologne, and I did not choose to be kept; so I ordered my poor nag to be saddled, lame as he was, with another for my servant, and I started on a five hours journey for Bedburg [16 miles west of Cologne. There he stays with 'the Count Nova Aquila'.]

'I had five pleasant days with the Count whom I found a young man of good sense. I had meant, if the autumn was fine, to go on to England and close with the King's repeated offers to me [from his accession in 1509 Henry VIII had been pressing Erasmus to join

21. 'I was to be kept in Cologne'. Cologne in the time of Erasmus.

his Court]. From this dream I was precipitated into a gulf of perdition [*in extremum exitium*]. A carriage had been ordered for me for the next morning. The Count would not take leave of me overnight, meaning to see me before I started. The night was wild. I rose before dawn to finish some work. At seven, the Count not appearing, I sent to call him. He came and protested that I must not leave the house in such weather. I must have lost half my mind when I went to Cologne. My evil genius now carried off the other half. Go I would, in an open carriage, with wind enough to tear up oak-trees. It came from the south and charged with pestilence. Towards evening wind changed to rain. I reached Aix [Aachen] shaken to pieces by the bad roads. I should have done better on my lame horse.'

The stay at Aix was disastrous. Erasmus supped at the house of the Precentor but, hungry as he was, there was nothing to eat but cold carp. Next day he was taken to the Vice-Provost who, owing to the weather, had nothing to offer but eels. These Erasmus could not touch and he had to fall back on salt cod, called 'bacalao' from the sticks they beat it with.

'It was almost raw. Breakfast over, I returned to the inn and ordered a fire. The canon stayed an hour and a half talking. My stomach then went into a crisis. A finger in my mouth brought on vomiting. Up came the raw cod and I lay down exhausted. The

22. 'I reached Aix shaken to pieces'. The Minster at Aix, by Dürer, 1520.

pain passed off. I settled with the driver about my luggage, and was then called into the *table d'hôte* supper [*ad nocturnam compotationem*]. I tried to excuse myself. I knew from experience that I ought to touch nothing but warm sops. However, they had made their preparations for me, so attend I must. After the soup I retreated to the Precentor's to sleep. Another wild night. Breakfast in the morning, a mouthful of bread and a cup of warm beer, and then to my lame beast. I ought to have been in my bed, but I disliked Aix and its ways, and longed to be off. I had been suffering from piles, and the riding increased the inflammation. After a few miles we came to the bridge over the Meuse [the frontier town of Maastricht] where I had some broth, and thence on to Tongres [25 miles from Aix]. The pain then grew horrible. I would have walked, but I was afraid of perspiring or being out after nightfall. I reached Tongres very ill all over. I slept, however, a little, and ordered a closed carriage [*bigam tectam*].

'The road turned out to be paved with flint [*ob silices*, probably cobbles]. I could not bear the jolting and mounted one of the horses. A sudden chill, and I fainted, and was put back into the carriage. After a while I recovered a little and again tried to ride. In the evening I was sick and told the driver I would pay him double if he would bring me early to my next stage. A miserable night— suffering dreadful. In the morning I found there was a carriage with four horses going straight to Louvain. [This was a *quadriga* as opposed to the *biga*, with two horses, used before—the first references to wheeled transport in these pages since the letter of Pliny the Younger on page 21.]

'I engaged it and arrived the next night in an agony of pain. Fearing that my own rooms would be cold, I drove to the house of my kind friend Theodoric, the printer. An ulcer broke out in the night and I was easier. I send for a surgeon. He finds another on my back; glands swollen and boils forming all over me. He tells Theodoric's servant that I have the plague and that he will not come near me again. Theodoric brings the message. I don't believe it. I send for a Jew doctor, who wishes his body was as sound as mine. The surgeon persists that it is the plague, and so does his father. I call in the best physician in the town, who says that he would have no objection to sleep with me. The Hebrew holds to his opinion. Another fellow makes a long face at the ulcers. I give him a gold crown and tell him to come again the next day, which he refused to do. I send doctors to the devil, commend myself to Christ, and am well in three days. Who could believe that this frail body of mine could have borne such a shaking? When I was young I was greatly afraid of dying. I fear it less as I grow older. Happiness does not depend on age. I am now fifty, a term of life which many do not reach, and I cannot complain that I have not lived long enough.'

15

Albrecht Dürer

'I have suffered loss in the Netherlands'

Nuremberg to the Netherlands, 1520–1

(Map on p. 154)

Erasmus arrived in Louvain in October 1518 and remained in the Netherlands long enough to meet Albrecht Dürer there on 5 August 1520. Dürer had himself been in the Netherlands for only a month, having left his home in Nuremberg with his wife and her maid in July to attend the coronation of the young Emperor Charles V; it was, he felt, desirable to make his mark at Court as soon as possible. For the whole year that he was away Dürer kept a diary in which he entered the minutest details of travel, although few personal impressions.

Dürer was in his fiftieth year at the time and best known for his engravings, his immense talent coinciding with the new developments in printing. It was his first visit to the Netherlands but he had been twice to Italy, the first time in 1494. On his way there then he had drawn a series of water colour sketches of places he passed through which were the earliest purely topographical landscapes known (see illustration on page 66). By the time of his second visit, twelve years later, his engravings had made him famous and while he was living in Venice he met all the artists working there at this momentous period. It would be too much to say that he became friends with them: his letters from Venice do not show him as a friendly man. His Netherlands diary must have been written simply as a record of expenses and places visited, yet, from within its apparently lifeless pages, a narrative emerges.

'On Thursday 12 July I, Albrecht Dürer, at my own charges and costs, took myself and my wife and maid Susan away to the Netherlands. And the same day, after passing through Erlangen, we put up for the night at Baiersdorf.'

They were travelling down the River Main and Dürer notes that he paid six florins in gold to the boatman who took him from Bamberg to Frankfurt (a florin was worth a tenth of a pound sterling). They spent the next ten nights at towns on the river and at Frankfurt Dürer made a new bargain to be taken to Mainz, where the Main flows into the Rhine, and Cologne in two days. At each stopping-place, not only night stops, Dürer had to show a pass which freed him from Customs dues and at some later stages he had to leave a deposit which would be refundable on his return.

'And so we came to Köln [Cologne] where I paid 7 pf. [pfennigs = pence] for landing my things and I gave the boatmen 14 hellers [farthings]. And I gave my cousin Niklas my black fur-lined coat, edged with velvet, and to his wife I gave a florin. At Köln Hieronymus Fugger gave me wine; Johann Grosserpecker also gave me wine; and my cousin Niklas, he also gave me wine.

'After three days we travelled from Köln to a village called Büsdorf where we stayed overnight and [after five nights on the road] we came next to Antwerp.

'At Antwerp I went to Jobst Plankfelt's inn and the same evening the Fuggers' [the bankers] factor invited me and gave us a costly meal. My wife however dined at the inn.

'On Sunday the painters invited me to the hall of their guild, with my wife and maid. All their service was of silver and they had

23. 'We came next to Antwerp'. The port of Antwerp, by Dürer.

24. 'Herr Erasmus has given me a small Spanish mantilla'. Erasmus, by
Dürer, 1520.

other splendid ornaments and very costly meats. All their wives
were also there. And as I was being led to the table the company
stood on both sides as if they were leading some great lord. Six cans
of wine were presented and speeches made and when we had spent
a long and merry time together till late in the night they
accompanied me home with lanterns in great honour.

'I have also been in Master Quentin Massys's house [but the
Antwerp painter was away].

'Paid 1 st. [stiver, a penny] for pears and bread, 2 st. to the
barber. Master Joachim de Patinir has once dined with me, and his

apprentice once. I gave Master Joachim 1 fl. worth of prints for lending me his apprentice and his colours, and I gave his apprentice some prints.

'Herr Erasmus has given me a small Spanish mantilla and three men's portraits.

'After two weeks in Antwerp I owe my host 7 fl. 20 st. For sitting-room and bedroom and bedding I am to pay him 11 fl. a month. I came to a new agreement with my host on 20 August. I am to eat with him and to pay 2 st. for the meal and extra for what is drunk. My wife however and the maid can cook and eat up here.'

On 26 August Dürer travelled to Brussels where he saw four paintings by Roger van der Weyden, burnt in 1695, and 'the things which have been brought to the King from the new land of gold'. This was Mexico, where the overthrow of the Aztec empire by Hernan Cortez had begun the previous year but was not yet completed. Nevertheless, 'all kinds of wonderful objects of human use' had arrived, 'so precious that they are valued at 100,000 florins. All the days of my life I have seen nothing that rejoiced my heart so much as these things.' He also saw a fish bone in Brussels, 'a fathom long and very thick, weighing up to 15 cwt' but, more important, Lady Margaret, the all-powerful regent of the Netherlands and guardian of her nephew Charles V, 'sent after me to Brussels and promised to speak for me to King Charles, and she has shown herself quite exceptionally kind to me.' But 'six people whose portraits I drew at Brussels have given me nothing'. Dürer was in fact selling a few engravings but giving away many more and he complains constantly of the small amounts he was receiving and the continuing expenses. 'I have presented a whole set of all my works to Lady Margaret the Emperor's [Maximilian I] daughter, and have drawn her two pictures on parchment with the greatest pains. All this I set at as much as 30 fl. And I have had to draw the design of a house for her physician, according to which he intends to build one; and for drawing that I would not care to take less than 10 fl.'

'Dined out', 'dined out' recurs but on 1 October 'I dined once with my wife.' Then, on 4 October, Dürer set off for Aix where he stayed until the 23rd for Charles's coronation. 'There I saw all manner of lordly splendour, more magnificent than anything that those who live in our parts have seen.' While in Aix he bought a sketchbook which he refers to frequently in his diary as 'my little book'. 'I made the portraits of Paulus Topler and Martin Pfintzing

25. 'I made the portraits of Paulus Topler and Martin Pfintzing in my little book'. Page 1 of Dürer's sketchbook.

in my little book,' he writes, and the drawing (above) shows an elderly, bearded man, aged 'LXI' according to Dürer's inscription, with a young, clean-shaven man beside him. The drawings were made in silverpoint, the lines of which cannot be erased, and it is characteristic of Dürer's mastery of his art that he should use such a technique for a 'sketchbook'. The book has long been broken up and the leaves dispersed but it has proved possible from Dürer's diary to reconstruct the order in which the drawings were made.

After the coronation was over Dürer went on to Cologne for a second visit instead of returning to Antwerp immediately. He stayed for fourteen days and was guest of friends from Nuremberg, Leonhard Groland and Hans Ebner, who had taken the regalia for the coronation from Nuremberg to Aix. They would take no payment from him but he 'had to give' a great ox-horn to Groland and a cedarwood rosary to Ebner. For himself he bought a tract of Luther's, candles, shoes, a little ivory skull and a small turned box. He also gave 2 pfennigs for Stefan Lochner's altarpiece, then in the Town Hall chapel, to be opened; it is now in the Cathedral, the only firmly attributed painting of its school, and that thanks to Dürer's diary entry.

At last, on 12 November, Groland and Ebner were able to

inform Dürer that they had received from the Emperor Charles confirmation of the grant of a pension of 100 florins for life. This pension had already been granted by Maximilian but on his death the previous year it had lapsed and Dürer had written earlier in the year begging for it to be renewed 'as I am losing my sight and freedom of hand and my affairs do not look well.' He truly noted in his diary that the long-awaited confirmation had come only 'after great trouble and labour.'

The main object of his visit to Cologne achieved, Dürer set off on 15 November for a three-day trip down the Rhine to Nijmegen; but for a 'great storm of wind' at Emmerich it would have taken only two days. He then left the Rhine and continued on the Meuse to Bommel where there was another storm 'so we hired cart-horses and rode without saddles to Herzogenbosch' (Bois-le-duc). There the goldsmiths came to see him and did him much honour but at the next town, Baarle, 'my companions quarrelled with the host so we went on in the night to Hoogstraten.' From there they went to Antwerp, evidently by coach since Dürer 'paid the driver 15 st.' He had been away seven weeks and in his absence his wife and maid had spent too much money, and his wife's purse, worth another florin, with some keys in it had been stolen while they were in church.

On 24 November there was news: 'At Zierikzee in Zeeland a whale has been stranded by a high tide and a gale of wind. It is much more than 100 fathoms long and no man living in Zeeland has seen one even a third as long as this. The fish cannot get off the land; the people would gladly see it gone as they fear the great stink, for it is so large that they say it could not be cut in pieces and the blubber boiled down in half a year.'

This could not be missed. On 3 December, he wrote: 'I rode out of Antwerp to Bergen op Zoom where I bought my wife a fine Netherlandish cloth for the head and paid 6 st. for three pairs of shoes and 1 st. for a pair of spectacles. I made portraits in charcoal of Jan de Has [his host] and of the girl and old woman in metalpoint in my little book.'

Again, as with the drawing of the old Topler and the young Pfintzing on the same page (opposite), Dürer seems to take pleasure in juxtaposing a young girl and an old woman (overleaf); in this case he goes out of his way to emphasize that the drawings were made 'in metalpoint'. He continues:

'On 7 December I started with my companions for Zeeland and Sebastian Imhof lent me 5 fl. [the Imhofs had long been Dürer's

26. 'I made portraits . . . of the girl and old woman in metalpoint in my
little book'. Page 5 recto of Dürer's sketchbook.

bankers]. The first night we lay at anchor in the sea; it was very
cold and we had neither food nor drink. We passed by a sunken
place and saw the tops of the roofs standing up out of the water.
Then we went to Arnemuiden.

'At Arnemuiden, where I landed, a great misfortune befell me.
As we were pushing ashore, and getting out our rope, a great ship
bumped hard against us as we were in the act of landing and in the
crush I had let every one get out before me so that only Georg
Kötzler [from Nuremberg], two old wives and the skipper with a
small boy were left in the ship. The rope then broke and in the same
moment a storm of wind arose which drove our ship back with
force. We all cried for help but no one would risk himself for us.
The wind carried us away out to sea, thereupon the skipper tore his
hair and cried aloud, for all his men had landed and the ship was
unmanned. We were in fear and danger for the wind was strong
and only six persons in the ship. I spoke to the skipper that he
should take courage and consider what was to be done. He said that
if he could haul up the small sail he would try if we could come
again to land. So we toiled all together and got it feebly about half-
way up and we went on again towards the land. And when the
people on shore, who had already given us up, saw how we helped
ourselves they came to our aid and we got to land.

'From thence I went to Middelburg, a good town with a very beautiful Town Hall. Early on Monday [9 December] we started again by ship and went by the Veere and Zierikzee and tried to get sight of the great fish, but the tide had carried him off again. I paid 2 fl. for fare and expenses and 2 fl. for a rug [or basket, *Kotzen*], 4 st. for a fig-cheese and 3st. for carriage and I lost 6 st. at play, and we have come back to Bergen.'

Once back at Antwerp, the losses 'at play' increase in frequency although not very much in amount. Social life continued, portraits were drawn, and sometimes sold, engravings were sold or given as presents. Everything bought is carefully noted, with its price, not always paid in cash—'I gave Jan Türck 12 ducats worth of prints for an ounce of good ultramarine'. But the Zeeland adventure had brought more than disappointment over the whale's escape: Dürer had contracted a fever of some kind which was never to leave him. 'I bought 14 pieces of French wood for 1 fl.' is an ominous entry, for *lignum guajacum* or *lignum vitae* is a drug.

There was a visit down the Scheldt to Bruges where he saw, among other things, the 'Madonna, sculptured by Michelangelo of Rome'; Dürer had none of the doubts since cast on the sculpture, then only a few years old, and his opinion must carry weight. At Ghent he saw the van Eyck altar-piece, 'a most precious painting, full of thought', and there 'the painters did not leave me alone, but they ate with me morning and evening and paid for everything.' Back at Antwerp his health did not improve.

'Three weeks after Easter a violent fever seized me, with great weakness, nausea and headache. And before, when I was in Zeeland, a wondrous sickness overcame me, such as I have never heard of from any man, and this sickness remains with me.'

'Paid the Doctor . . . the surgeon . . . the apothecary' now becomes the theme, but portraits, often in charcoal, are drawn, if anything more frequently. Dürer goes to Joachim Patenir's second wedding, and draws him 'with the metal-point'; pays for cleaning an old cap, but finds it clumsy and exchanges it for a new one; designs three sword-hilts in return for a small alabaster bowl; receives 1 fl. from an Englishman for painting his coat of arms— but 'for the more part of my work I have received nothing.'

At last, on 5 June 1521, 'I gave over my great bale at Antwerp to a carrier to take it to Nuremberg; and I am to pay him for the carrying of it $1\frac{1}{2}$ fl. for every hundredweight. And he is to answer for it to Hans Imhof the elder.'

Two days later there was another disappointment. 'On 7 June I went with my people to Lady Margaret at Mechlin [Malines]. The painters and sculptors bade me as guest at my inn and did me great honour in their gathering. I went to Lady Margaret's and showed her my *Emperor*, and would have presented it to her, but she so disliked it that I took it away with me.'

This is probably the portrait now in Vienna. Dürer must have taken the rebuff with good grace since he returned to Lady Margaret the following day and 'she showed me all her beautiful things'. On his return to Antwerp he exchanged prints and books for three rings, said to be worth 54 florins, but he quickly found he had made a mistake. 'The man with the three rings has overreached me by half. I did not understand the matter.'

The trunk had now left for Nuremberg but a packing-case had to be bought. Prints were being exchanged for books, glasses, brushes and other things to be taken home. The bill had to be paid.

'I reckoned up with Jobst and found myself 31 fl. in his debt, which I paid him; therein were charged and deducted the two portrait heads which I painted in oils, for which he gave 5 pounds of borax. In all my doings, spendings, sales and other dealings, in all my connections with high and low, I have suffered loss in the Netherlands; and Lady Margaret in particular gave me nothing for what I made and presented to her.

'I have engaged with a carrier to take me from Antwerp to Köln. I am to pay him 13 florins and am to pay the expenses of another person and a lad besides.

'I exchanged my portrait of the Emperor for a white English cloth which Tomasin's son-in-law gave me.

'Alexander Imhof has lent me 100 gold florins for which I gave him my bond to repay the money with thanks at Nuremberg. I paid the apothecary . . . paid for cord . . . gave away leaving gifts. . .'

Suddenly, the preparations for departure were interrupted. 'As I was just about to leave Antwerp, the King of Denmark [Christian I] sent for me to come to him at once and take his portrait, which I did in charcoal. I also did that of his servant Anton, and I was made to dine with the King and he behaved graciously towards me. I have entrusted my bale to Leonard Tucher and given over my white cloth [exchanged for the *Emperor* portrait] to him. The carrier with whom I bargained did not take me, I fell out with him. I gave the new carrier the great turtle shell, the fish-shield, the long pipe, the fish-fins and the two little casks of lemons and capers to take home for me.

'Next day [3 July] we travelled to Brussels at the command of the King of Denmark and I engaged a driver. I gave the King of Denmark the best of all my prints [they are still in Copenhagen, in the Museum]. I noticed how the people of Antwerp marvelled greatly when they saw the King of Denmark, to find him such a manly, handsome man and come hither through his enemy's lands with only two attendants. I saw too how the Emperor rode forth from Brussels to meet him and received him honourably with great pomp.

'On 7 July the King of Denmark gave a great banquet to the Emperor, Lady Margaret and the Queen of Spain [in fact, Portugal] and he bade me in and I dined there also.'

Five days after this climax, on 12 July 1521, exactly a year after their departure from Nuremberg, he wrote: 'We set off from Brussels and I am to pay the driver 10 fl. I paid my hostess 5 st. further for the single night. We passed through three villages and stopped for the night and I spent 9 st. . . . We came to Maastricht . . . We went early thence to Aix . . . Then we travelled to Köln. . .'

And so Dürer's travels ended. Seven years later, in 1528, the illness, which was all his curiosity to see the stranded whale had brought him, finally overcame him and the process began of scattering the drawings of his Netherlands year among the museums and collections of the world.

16

Benvenuto Cellini

'I'll show you with this'

Ferrara to Venice, 1535

The Po has been encountered bearing a number of travellers up and down its course and into its tributaries. It can have carried few as quarrelsome or as talented as Benvenuto Cellini who tells of the troubles he made for himself on the river in 1535.

Having killed a man in Rome in a street fight, he decided it would be wise to retire for a time. He travelled 'with the post bound for Florence' where he had a sculptor friend called Niccolo di Raffaello, known by the nickname of 'Tribolo'. Tribolo told Cellini he was going to Venice, where Jacopo Sansovino had promised to employ him, and the pair decided to travel together. They went on horseback all the way to Ferrara, preferring this to the water route from Bologna which most other travellers, including Tafur and many later ones, seem to have taken.

Cellini was thirty-five years old at the time, and behaving as an odious bully who caused trouble wherever he went. His friendship with Michelangelo and his skill as a craftsman had brought him the patronage of those who counted most in Florence and Rome and they were prepared to tolerate all but his worst excesses. It has been the good fortune of later generations (although not until nearly two centuries after his death) to be able to enjoy one of the most readable autobiographies ever written without having to endure the man. Here he is with Tribolo at Ferrara; inevitably the evening had ended in a brawl, with Cellini brandishing his sword and threatening to kill everyone in sight.

'After we had supped, a boatman appeared and offered to take us to Venice. I asked if he would let us have the boat to ourselves; he was willing, and so we made our bargain. In the morning we rose early and took our horses to go to the landing-stage which is a few miles from Ferrara. On arriving there, we found the brother of Niccolo Benintendi [one of those involved in the evening's brawl] with three comrades, waiting for me. They had among them two pikes and I had bought a fine big spear [*giannettone*] in Ferrara. Being also very well armed I was not at all frightened, as Tribolo was, who cried: "God help us! these people are here to murder us." Lamentone [the courier] turned to me and said: "The best thing you can do is to go back to Ferrara, for I see the affair is likely to be ugly; for mercy's sake, Benvenuto, do not risk the fury of these mad beasts." To which I replied, "Let us go on, for God helps those who are in the right; you shall see how I will help myself. Is not this boat engaged for us?" "Yes," said Lamentone. "Then we will stay in it without them, unless my manhood has deserted me." I put spurs to my horse, and when I was within fifty paces, I dismounted and marched boldly forward with my spear. Tribolo stopped behind, all huddled up on his horse, looking the very picture of frost. Lamentone, meanwhile, was puffing and snorting like the wind. That was his usual habit, but he did it more than usual, being in doubt how this devil's affair would end.

'When I reached the boat the boatman set himself in front of me and said that those Florentine gentlemen wanted to join our party in the boat if I had no objection. I replied: "The boat is engaged for us and no one else, and it grieves me to the heart that I am not able to have their company." At these words a brave young man of the Magalotti family spoke out: "Benvenuto, we will make you able to have it." I answered: "If God and the right that I have, together with my own strength, have any will or power, you will not make it possible for me to do what you say." So saying I leapt into the boat and, turning my spear's point against them, added: "I'll show you with this that I am not able." Wishing to prove he was in earnest, Magalotti then drew his weapon and came forward. I jumped up on the edge of the boat and hit him such a blow that, if he had not tumbled backwards, I must have pierced his body. His comrades, instead of helping him, turned to flee and when I saw that I could kill him, instead of striking, I said: "Get up, brother; pick up your arms and begone. I have shown you that I cannot do what I do not want to do, and what I could do I have not chosen to do." Then I called for Tribolo, the boatman and Lamentone to embark, and so we proceeded for Venice. When we had gone ten miles on the Po we sighted those young men who had got into a skiff [*fusoliera*) and caught us up and, when they were level with us, that idiot Piero

Benintendi sang out to me: "Come along now, Benvenuto, for we shall see each other again in Venice." "Go along, for I am coming," I shouted, "and any man can meet me where he chooses." In due course we arrived at Venice, where I applied to a brother of Cardinal Cornaro asking him to procure for me the favour of being allowed to carry my arms. He told me I could do so freely, saying that the worst risk I ran was that I might lose my sword.'

They then visited Jacopo Sansovino who, having completed the church of San Francesco della Vigna the previous year, was about to start work on the Library of St. Mark's, the Mint and the Loggetta below the Campanile, which were to occupy him for more than twenty years, including a short spell in prison when part of the Library collapsed. According to Cellini, Sansovino had sent for Tribolo but, although he invited the couple to stay for dinner, he said he had no work for Tribolo at the moment. This, and what he called Sansovino's boastfulness and abuse of Michelangelo, gave Cellini an excuse for another quarrel and he left the house without finishing his dinner but after lecturing Sansovino on the evils of conceit. Later the same day he ran into the Benintendi brothers and their friends near the Rialto but, seeing that he was outnumbered, avoided another quarrel by turning into an apothecary's shop. A few days later Cellini and Tribolo left Venice to return to Florence.

'We lay one night at a place on this side of Chioggia, on the left-hand side as you go towards Ferrara. Here the host insisted upon being paid before we went to bed, according to his mode of reckoning, and when I observed that it was the custom everywhere else to pay in the morning, he answered: "I want to be paid in the evening, and according to my own reckoning." I retorted that men who wanted everything their own way ought to make a world after their own fashion, since things were managed differently in this world. Our host told me not to go on bothering his brains because he was determined to do as he had said. Tribolo stood trembling with fright and nudged me to keep quiet, lest things should be worse for us, so we paid him according to his way and went to bed.

'We had, I must admit, the most capital beds, entirely new and very clean. For all this I could not sleep at all because I kept thinking how I could revenge myself. At one time it came into my head to set fire to his house; at another to cut the throats of four fine horses which he had in the stable. I saw clearly that it would be easy enough for me to do this but I could not see how it was easy to secure myself and my companion. At last I resolved to put my things and my comrade's on board the boat and so I did. When the horses had been harnessed to the tow-rope [*alzana*: Cellini uses the Venetian word] I told them not to start the boat until I returned for I had left a pair of slippers in my bedroom. Accordingly I went back to the inn and called the innkeeper who replied that he had nothing to do with us and we could go to blazes [*al bordello*]. There was a ragged stable-boy about, half asleep, who cried out to me, "The master would not move to please the Pope because he has got a wench in bed with him whom he has much coveted." Then he asked me for a tip and I gave him a few Venetian coppers and told him to make the boatman wait until I had found my slippers and returned. I went upstairs, took out a small knife that cut like a razor, and cut the four beds that I found there into ribbons. I had the satisfaction of knowing that I had done a damage of more than fifty crowns. Then I ran down to the boat with some pieces of the bed-covers [*sarge*] in my pouch and told the boatman to start at once. We had not gone far before my crony Tribolo said that he had left behind some small straps belonging to his travelling-bag and that he must be allowed to go back for them. I answered that he need not worry about two small straps since I could make him as many big ones as he liked [*coreggine* means fart as well as strap]. He told me I was always joking but that he must really go back for his straps. Then he began ordering the man with the tow-rope to stop while I kept ordering him to go on. Meanwhile I informed my friend what kind of trick I had played on the innkeeper and showed him pieces of the bed-covers and other things. This threw him into such a trembling fright that he roared out to the tow-rope man: "On with you, on with you, as quick as you can!" and never thought himself quite safe until we were within the gates of Florence.

'When we arrived there, Tribolo said: "Let us pack up our swords, for the love of God, and play me no more of your games, I beg; for all this while I've felt as though my guts were in a saucepan." I answered him: "Dear old Tribolo, you need not pack up your sword for you have never loosened it," and I said this at random, because I never once had seen him show a sign of manhood during that journey. When he heard the remark, he looked at his sword and cried out: "In God's name you speak true. Here it is packed up just as I arranged it before I left home." To this comrade of mine it seemed that I had been a bad travelling companion to him because I resented affronts and defended myself against those who would have done us injury; to me it seemed that he had done much worse by never coming to my assistance in such needs. Let him judge between us who stands by and has no personal interest in our adventures.'

17

Nicander Nucius

'They possess a curious language, as I conjecture'

France to England, 1546

Nicander Nucius was a Greek who found himself in Venice in 1545. He there fell in with an old acquaintance from Flanders, called Gerardus, who was on his way to Constantinople as the Emperor Charles V's ambassador to Suleiman I. Gerardus made Nicander a member of his suite and so Nicander remained, not only during the short, and unsuccessful, mission to Constantinople, but on the journey back to report to the Emperor in Brussels and a later mission to Henry VIII in England.

Nicander was a curious and observant traveller who recorded all his adventures in the form of a letter to a friend. He had none of the sophistication of a Venetian ambassador, nor did he move in high places with his friend Gerardus, but his letter provides an early account of England as seen through the eyes of a foreigner—a type of essay that was to proliferate over the next three centuries. Like others, he begins with the crossing from Calais:

'At first we moved out of the harbour by rowing. It being now night, we were being borne along by the tide and were accomplishing our voyage in smooth water. The master however gave orders to take in sail, in spite of the favourable wind, because he said it was best for us to pass the night at sea rather than approach the island about the first watch when there would be fear of our grounding on shallows.

'Thus indeed spoke the master: but it fell not out as he conjectured. It being now midnight, a certain wind called the north wind having sprung up, the sea was suddenly ruffled. The sound of the approaching storm was now heard and instantly, an impetuous and violent blast having fallen on us, it filled the sailors with unlooked-for consternation.'

It may have been no more than a Channel storm but Nicander and his fellow passengers, perhaps the crew too, 'entertained slender hopes of being saved'. The ship was driven back to the Flemish coast where it took shelter for three days, eventually setting out on another attempt to reach Dover, this time successfully.

'Dover is a small town, full of inns, and having disembarked and tarried one day in the inns, on the morrow we mounted and proceeded on our journey to the King [Henry VIII] and arrived in Greenwich, a village in the neighbourhood of London, the capital of England. Whereupon, having been presented to the King, who was at this time residing in his palace, Gerardus laid before him the instructions he had received from the Emperor; to which the King having both graciously acceded and appointed for us suitable lodgings, he himself returned to London. And we, continuing still in Greenwich, on the fifth day removed to London. Having apartments near the royal palace [Whitehall] we awaited the King's final despatch of the affairs laid before him and it appeared good to me to investigate the peculiarities of the island as far as lay in my power.'

London had for long surpassed all other cities of England and Nicander was particularly struck by its single bridge, 'with the houses and turrets upon it, with the ferry boats and barges, plying in great numbers on the river'. There was also 'a castle, built very near the river, and very beautiful and strong'. But it was the multiplicity of nations among the people, and their industry that impressed him most.

'Almost all, indeed, except the nobles and those in attendance on the royal person, pursue mercantile concerns. Not only men, but to a great extent women also. One may see in the markets married women and damsels employed in arts and affairs of trade undisguisedly. But they display great simplicity and absence of jealousy in their usage towards females; even those who have never seen them kiss them on the mouth with salutations and embraces and to themselves this appears by no means indecent. [Erasmus in 1500 had remarked on this English practice.]

'They possess a curious language, having received contributions from almost all the rest, as I conjecture. For although they speak somewhat barbarously, yet their language has a certain charm and allurement, being sweeter indeed than that of the Germans and Flemish.

'Their nobles and rulers are replete with benevolence and good

order, and are courteous to strangers, But the rabble and the mob
are turbulent and barbarous in their manner. Towards the
Germans and Flemish and Italians, and the Spanish also, they are
friendly disposed. But toward the French they entertain not one
kindly sentiment of goodwill.

'In their persons the men are tall and erect; the hair of their
beard and head is of a golden hue, their eyes blue and their cheeks

27. 'The men are tall and erect'. The English in the eyes of a foreigner: a
visiting German artist's impression of Queen Elizabeth receiving Dutch
ambassadors.

28. 'Flesh-eaters and insatiable of animal food'. Detail from Sir Henry
Unton's portrait, sixteenth century.

ruddy. They are martial and valorous; flesh-eaters and insatiable
of animal food; sottish and unrestrained in their appetites; full of
suspicion. But towards their King they are wonderfully well
affected, nor would any one of them endure hearing anything
disrespectful of the King.

'The western portion of the island is called Scotland and there is
a considerable river called the Tweed and it separates England
from Scotland. England possesses its own King and Scotland
likewise appoints a King from among its own people. And ever as it
were these Kings, being inimical, perpetually fighting about the
limits of their country, cruelly destroy each other in a kind of
barbarous and savage warfare. The Scotch are a more barbarous
people in their manner of living than the English but they possess a
soil as favourable to fruit and corn as that of the English.

'The greatest portion of the country of the Britons, laved
continuously by the ebb and flow of the ocean, is marshy; from the
exhalation and denseness of which, the atmosphere throughout
that portion appears for the most part misty. Whence, as the waters
flow and ebb it accumulates a certain slimy deposit from which the
exhalations are drawn.

'Marble and smooth rocks, such as those very solid ones with us,
they have not, but certain porous and terceous stones; they are
easily obtained and easily polished. But the stone used for fire and
black is found in most places. They have not much gold but very
much silver and tin.'

After the mission of Gerardus was completed he was recalled by the Emperor but Nicander preferred to stay. Undeterred by the 'barbarous' Scots he joined the King's troops against those of Scotland and helped to 'lay waste the country and sack some of the small towns of that kingdom.' He found himself among Italians and Spaniards and even a Greek, Thomas from Argos in the Peloponnese, who was his commander. He may well have stayed when Henry 'sent forces to Boulogne' but his narrative breaks off in mid-sentence, so we shall never know.

18

Michel de Montaigne

'I gave a ball'

France and Italy, 1580–1

(Map on p. 92)

The writer of the notes that follow is seemingly an uncomplicated man, travelling in search of a cure for kidney stone. As his tale proceeds his faith in the chances of finding a cure diminishes but he remains determined to enjoy the journey whatever the outcome.

Michel de Montaigne, who wrote or dictated the notes, was in fact a man of extreme subtlety of mind who can be known only to a reader of his one original literary work, the *Essays*. He was born in 1533, great-grandson of a successful merchant who had bought the Château de Montaigne, son of a mayor of Bordeaux who had accordingly changed his name from Eyquem to Montaigne. Michel was put out to nurse with a peasant woman and provided with a German tutor who taught him Latin before French. He became a lawyer, married and had five children, four of whom died without causing him too much grief, and in 1568 he inherited the estate of Montaigne on his father's death. By this time he had become a member of the Bordeaux *parlement*, had been sent to the Court of Henry III for some eighteen months and was inevitably involved to some extent in the disorderly times in which he lived.

If Montaigne ever had political ambitions they were short-lived and three years after his father's death he entered upon a life of reflection, resigning from *parlement* and abandoning the law. From 1571 to 1580, with one three-year interruption caused by the civil war with the Huguenots, he was engaged on the first two books of his *Essays*. During the last two years of this period he was troubled by his kidneys and immediately after publication in 1580 he set out on the journey on which we are to follow him.

Many of Montaigne's tastes and inclinations become abundantly clear as his journal progresses, but there can be no better introduction than a few extracts from the last *Essay* he wrote in which he reports on his bodily requirements with the same curiosity that he has long applied to the exploration of his mind.

'I would feel as uncomfortable without my gloves as without my shirt, or without washing when I rise from table or get up in the morning, or without canopy and curtains for my bed which are to me really necessary things. I could dine without a tablecloth but very uncomfortably without a napkin, German fashion; I soil napkins more than they or the Italians do, as I make little use of spoon or fork. I am sorry that they do not keep up with the fashion which was begun in my day, after the example of kings, of changing napkins with the plates, with each course. [Napkins are repeatedly referred to throughout the diary, the reason made clear by this passage.]

'I have seen many soldiers inconvenienced by the irregularity of their bowels; mine and I never fail the moment of our assignation, which is on leaping out of bed. We should not pamper ourselves, as I have done as I grew old, by being tied for this function, and make it a burden by prolongation and fastidiousness. I have trouble getting under way and am late in everything; getting up, going to bed, at meals. Seven o'clock is early for me, and where I am in charge I do not dine before eleven or sup till after six. I like to sleep hard and alone, even without a woman [*voire sans femme*: without my wife?], in the royal style, rather well covered up. Sleeping has occupied a large part of my life and even at this age [55] I continue to sleep eight or nine hours at a stretch.

'I am not excessively fond of salads or fruits, except melons. My father hated all kinds of sauces: I like them all. I am not yet really certain that any kind of food disagrees with me, nor have I noticed that I am affected by full or new moons, by autumn or spring. There are changes that take place in us, irregular and unknown. I have changed more than once from white wine to red [*clairet*] and then back from red to white. I am very fond of fish; for me lean days are fat, and fast days are feasts. Besides I believe what some say, that it is easier to digest than meat. I drink pretty well for a man of ordinary build; in summer or at an appetizing meal up to five glasses, about three *demyseties* [i.e., $\frac{3}{4}$ litre] for the little glasses are my favourites and I enjoy emptying them. I dilute my wine generally with a half but sometimes with a third part of water. And when I am at home they mix what I need in the buttery two or three hours before serving it. It is bad manners, besides being harmful to

29. 'No good our mounting on stilts'. Montaigne, in an engraving after
Thomas de Leu.

health and even to pleasure, to eat greedily as I do. I often bite my tongue and sometimes my fingers in my haste.

'My eyes are hurt by any brilliant light. I could not now sit at dinner facing a bright, blazing fire. When it was my habit to read more than I do now, I used to place a sheet of glass on my book to deaden the whiteness of the paper, and this gave me great relief. Even to this day I have never had to use spectacles, and can see as far as ever I did, or as any other man.'

Almost at the end of this essay Montaigne wrote: 'A man who knows how to enjoy his existence as he ought has attained to an absolute perfection, like that of the gods.' And, years later, he added to his own copy: 'Yet it is no good our mounting on stilts, for even on stilts we have to walk on our own legs; and upon the most exalted throne in the world it is still our own bottom that we sit on.'

The first half of the travel journal was written by a secretary, or servant, largely at his master's dictation but with occasional interpolations from Montaigne. Later, as will be seen, it was written by Montaigne himself.

The diary first came to light almost two hundred years after it had been written and was first published in 1774. Some time after that the manuscript disappeared but the first few pages had always been missing so it is not possible to be certain who the members of Montaigne's party were. They certainly included his younger brother and brother-in-law and a young friend entrusted to his care by his mother. A fourth member, Comte du Hautoy, is occasionally mentioned. As for servants, Montaigne admitted that he could not travel without a goodly number and the party must have consisted at the outset of at least a dozen members.

They set out on 4 September 1580 and went across France, through Epernay and Epinal, to Plombières which they reached after twelve single-night stops. Here they stayed for eleven days and Montaigne took the cure, consisting of drinking and bathing in water from the hot springs. Their lodgings at the Angel inn were comfortable and very cheap, costing only fifteen sous a day, a quarter the price they would have cost in the crowded season. The cure was quite ineffective and they passed on, through Germany, to Baden in Switzerland. This was far more expensive, costing a crown a day (sixty sous) for each of the masters, nine sous for each servant and fourteen for each horse—'but besides that they added several thievish charges.' The results were no better and, after five days, they set out for Austria and the Alps. They reached Brixe (Bressanone), on the south side of the Brenner Pass, after eighteen more one-night stops, pausing only in Innsbruck for two days. By this time Montaigne's secretary had committed some 25,000 words to paper at his dictation, recording every detail of the journey, every story of interest which they had heard from chance acquaintances, and much of the behaviour of Montaigne's stones and gravel. The time had now come for some reflections.

'Monsieur de Montaigne said that all his life he had distrusted other people's judgments on the matter of the amenities of foreign countries, since every man's taste is governed by the ordering of his habit or the usages of his village; and he had taken very little account of the information that travellers gave him; but on this spot he wondered even more at their stupidity, for he had heard, and especially on this journey, that the passes of the Alps in this region were full of difficulties, the manners of the people uncouth, roads inaccessible, lodgings primitive, the air insufferable. As for the air, he thanked God that he had found it so mild, for it inclined rather toward too much heat than too much cold. But for the rest, if he had to take his daughter, who is only eight, for a walk, he would as soon do so on this road as on any path in his garden. And as for the inns, he had never seen a country in which they were so plentifully distributed and so handsome, and more reasonable than elsewhere.'

The machine used for turning the spit at Bressanone was then described; indeed, almost every machine on the journey was described, whatever its purpose. There was no question of turning back. Three more days took them to Bolzano, 'very disagreeable compared with other towns in Germany', and so into Italy. Hitherto, distances had been referred to in leagues (*lieues*), equivalent to $2\frac{1}{2}$ English miles; now they were going by Italian miles (*milles*), rather longer than English miles in most states but a little shorter in some. German miles, the secretary noted, were much longer, almost five English miles. At Rovereto he recorded his own reflections: 'I believe, in truth, that had he [Montaigne] been alone with his attendants, he would rather have gone to Cracow or towards Greece by land, than have taken the trip to Italy, but the pleasure he took in visiting strange countries, which he found so great as to make him forget the weakness of his health and his age, he could not infuse into any of his party, all of whom wanted to return home.

'I never saw him less tired, and never heard him complain less of his pains; his mind so on the alert for what he might encounter, and seeking every occasion for conversing with strangers, that I believe it made him forget his malady. When they complained to him that he often led the company by divers roads and districts, often returning to very near the spot whence he had set out, he would reply "that for his part he went to no place except where he happened to be, and that he could not miss his route seeing that he had no plan but to go to unknown places; and provided that he did not travel twice by the same road he did not fail in carrying out his design." And as to Rome, which the others regarded as their goal, he was less desirous of seeing that than other places, because everybody knew it; and there was not a lackey who could not give an account of Florence and Ferrara. He also said that "he appeared to himself like a person who is reading a fine book and begins to be afraid that he is getting towards the end of it; he took such great pleasure in travelling that he hated the very approach to the place where he was to rest."'

So, with these words of a true traveller, they proceeded down the Adige valley, leaving the secretary in charge of the baggage which was to be taken down the river itself on a barge as far as Verona. There Montaigne found the Arena 'the finest building he had seen in his life' and in Vicenza there were 'plenty of noblemen's palaces'; Palladio had died only a few months earlier and the palaces with which he had bejewelled the city must still have been pristine. In Padua the hostelries were in no respect comparable to those in Germany, although it was true that they were cheaper by a third, about the same as those of France. They left very early in the morning 'by a very fine causeway along the river [Brenta], the road plentifully furnished with handsome pleasure-houses', most of them recently built by Palladio or his followers. They arrived in time to dine at Fusina which is called 'La Chaffousine' in the diary (from Ca Fusina?). It was 'only a hostelry where one takes to the water to get to Venice'. Here 'all the boats along the river land, by means of machines and pulleys turned by two horses in the manner of those that turn the oil-mills. They transport these boats, with wheels that they put underneath, over a wooden flooring, and launch them into the canal which goes into the sea [lagoon] in which Venice is situated.'

The dam which closed the Brenta Canal at Fusina was a necessary part of the water system at the time, and will be encountered on more than one occasion later. Once the barge was in a position to continue its passage across the lagoon, the traveller had the choice of rejoining it or taking a gondola (as Comines had done, page 80). Montaigne and his party also preferred to dine at Fusina and crossed the lagoon by gondola at their leisure in time to sup at Venice.

He had little to say about Venice—'the curiosities of this city are sufficiently well known'—and after a week there, moved on to Abano, famous then, as now, for its hot springs. Montaigne found the water tasted more of salt than anything else and soon passed on, travelling by water wherever possible, to Ferrara and Bologna. He was making for Rome but preferred to go via Florence because he had been warned of bandits on the road through the Marches from Ancona. Montaigne enjoyed himself, according to his secretary.

'He took all possible delight in the rivalry between the landlords. They have a custom of sending seven or eight leagues to meet strangers to implore them to choose their inn. You will often meet the landlord himself on horseback and in various places several well-dressed men are on the watch for you. All along the road he amused himself by humouring them and listening to the various offers made by each. There is nothing they will not promise [someone, probably Montaigne himself, has added in the margin "*anche ragazze e ragazzi*", "even girls and boys"]. There was one who offered him a hare purely as a gift if he would only inspect his house. Their disputes and rivalry stop at the gates of the town and they do not venture to say a word more. They have it in common that they offer you a guide on horseback, at their own expense, to guide you and carry part of your baggage to the inn you are going to; which they always do and pay the expense. I do not know whether they are obliged to do this by some regulation, because of the danger of the roads.

'We had made our bargain before we left Bologna for what we had to pay and get in return at Lojano, being strongly advised to do so by the people of the inn where we stayed. So he had sent one of us to inspect all the inns, the provisions and wines, and learn the conditions before dismounting, and he chose the best. But it is impossible to make such careful terms that you escape their trickery; for they will keep you short of wood, candles, linen, or they will fail to supply the hay which you have omitted to specify.

'This route is full of travellers for it is the ordinary high road to Rome.'

Two days were enough for Florence on this occasion. In the church of S. Lorenzo they saw examples of 'flat painting' (*plate*

30. 'This route is full of travellers'. Travellers, with packs on their heads, at the junction of Via della Spada and Via delle Belle Donne in Florence, about 1540.

peinture) which must have been the frescoes completed by Bronzino some ten years previously. The wall-tombs of Giuliano and Lorenzo de' Medici in the same church drew a reference to their sculptor, Michelangelo; on no other occasion throughout the journey is an artist mentioned by name except for an obscure designer of fountains. Montaigne found the inn poor, as throughout Italy. There was no hall. The windows were large and wide open and if you used the large wooden shutter to keep out the sun and the wind you kept out the light as well; this was more intolerable and irremediable than the want of curtains in Germany. Anyone who hated to lie hard would be very uncomfortable in the little cots with wretched canopies and there was a great lack of linen. Indeed, Montaigne could not understand why Florence should have been described in Münster's guidebook as '*la belle*'— although the following year, on returning, he admitted the epithet was justified.

'The next day M. de Montaigne was the first of us to ascend to the top of the cathedral, where there is a globe of gilt brass which from below seems about the size of a ball and when you get up to it you find it capable of holding four people. He observed there that the marble with which this church is encrusted is in many places already beginning to give way, and crackling in the frost and sun, even the black, for it is all variegated and carved; which made him suspicious that the marble was not very natural.' (Brunelleschi's cupola was finished in 1434 and the lantern above it in 1461, 120 years earlier.)

Later the same day, Montaigne and one of his companions dined with Francesco de' Medici, Grand Duke of Tuscany, and Bianca Cappello, Grand Duchess since 1578 after many years as Francesco's mistress. She was 'handsome, according to Italian ideas, an imperious and agreeable face, big bust and breasts, as they like them.' (The Italian's idea of beauty is *'grosse et massive'*, Montaigne had written in one of his *Essays*.)

'They bring drink to the Duke and his wife in a basin in which there is an uncovered glass full of wine and a glass bottle full of water; they take the glass of wine and pour as much as they do not want into the basin, then fill it up with water themselves and replace the glass in the basin which the cup-bearer holds for them. He put in a good deal of water; she hardly any. The fault of the Germans is to make use of glasses large and out of proportion; here on the other hand they are extraordinarily small.'

On 24 November the party left Florence and covered the 32 miles to Siena in one day in four stages 'for they make them of eight miles, usually longer than ours.' They lodged at the Crown, 'tolerably well, but still without window-panes or frames' and on the 26th continued the journey to Rome.

'The inns on this road are among the best, since it is the ordinary post highway. You are put to no trouble about the care of the horses for from place to place the landlords take charge of the horses of their fellow-landlords; indeed if the one you have hired fails, they stipulate that you may replace it by another at some other place on the road. We saw for ourselves that at Siena a Fleming who was in our company, a foreigner, unknown and quite alone, was trusted with a hired horse to take him to Rome; you only have to pay the hire before leaving, but in other respects the horse is at your mercy and they trust to your good faith to leave it at the place you have promised.

'M. de Montaigne was pleased with their custom of dining and supping late, in accordance with his inclinations, for in the good houses they do not dine until two o'clock in the afternoon, nor sup till nine; so that in places where we found actors they did not begin the play till six o'clock, by torchlight, and are at it for two or three hours, and then you go to supper. He said it was a good country for lazy people for you get up very late.

'We started next morning three hours before daylight, so anxious was he to see the *pavé* of Rome. We descried the city of Rome at a distance of fifteen miles and then lost sight of it for a long time. We came across some districts where the roads were raised and paved with very large paving-stones which, to look at them, seemed something ancient; and nearer the city some ruins that were evidently very ancient.

'Rome did not seem to us to make much of an appearance from this road. Far away on the left we had the Apennines; the prospect was unpleasing, a bare soil without trees, a good part of it barren, a country very open for ten miles round and more, a very few houses; through this sort of country we arrived at about eight in the evening on the last day of November at the Porta del Popolo.

'ROME, thirty miles. Here, as elsewhere, they raised some difficulties on account of the plague at Genoa. We took lodgings at the Bear, where we stayed also the next day and on 2 December rented rooms at the house of a Spaniard. Here we were well accommodated with three handsome bedrooms, a dining-room, a larder, stable, kitchen, for twenty crowns a month, for which the landlord provided a cook and fire for the kitchen. M. de Montaigne was annoyed at finding so many Frenchmen here that he hardly met a person in the street who did not salute him in his own language.'

During the first two and a half months in Rome Montaigne continued to dictate to his secretary. The old city, 'where he went every day and took a thousand walks', had by no means been fully excavated and Montaigne immediately realized that the contours had no relation to those of ancient times; 'he felt certain that in many places we were walking on the tops of houses still intact.' They quite possibly were. The Temple of Vespasian, for example, was covered by a mound of earth and Piranesi's etching of 180 years later still shows little more than the frieze and capitals of the columns (overleaf). The journal continued: 'At the beginning he took a French guide but he soon decided that, with various maps and books, he could serve himself better, and he seems to have spent the best part of every day in sight-seeing.' However, it was not the usual descriptions of churches and relics that he dictated, but

31. 'We were walking on the tops of houses still intact'. The Temple of
Vespasian, still partly buried 100 years after Montaigne's visit to Rome.
View by Piranesi.

rather the incidents of the day and, at one point, a series of
reflections on the absence of outward signs of the ancient city. 'He
thought that an ancient Roman, could he see it, would not be able
to recognize the site of his city.'

There were disagreeable incidents to record: his books were
taken for examination by the Customs and not returned until four
months later, and after two weeks he was taken ill. He was
persuaded to take large quantities of cinnamon followed by
Venetian turpentine 'washed down by some tasty syrup; he
observed no other effects from it than a smell of March violets in
his urine.' An attack of colic came next and then he passed 'a large
stone, hard, long and smooth' which took five or six hours in
passing through the final stage of its journey. But his bowels had
been in good order since his baths as a result of which 'he thought
he was safe against any worse'.

The French Ambassador considered he should kiss the feet of
the Pope (Gregory XIII, an eighty-two year old Bolognese), and
he did so, afterwards describing the grotesque ceremony in some
detail. The approach was made in three stages, none directly
towards the Pope himself, the visitor going down on one knee after
each; on reaching the edge of a carpet he went down on both knees
and dragged himself in this posture to the Pope's red slipper,
marked with a white cross to show the place to be kissed. After

being admonished to continue in the devotion he had ever borne the Church, Montaigne was given the signal of dismissal. He then had to move away backwards, always looking the Pope in the face, going down on one knee at the half-way stage and again on reaching the door. Montaigne thought the Pope's Italian smacked of the Bolognese twitter (*ramage*), the worst idiom in Italy.

Early in 1581 Montaigne, in his own words, 'dismissed the man who carried on this fine business' and, as the diary was so far advanced, decided to continue it himself, 'however much trouble it may give me'. He did so conscientiously and when, a little later, he arrived in Tuscany he was so enchanted by the Tuscan speech that he wrote in Italian. He could say whatever he pleased in that language 'in ordinary talk but for serious discourse' he would not trust himself.

As the stay in Rome drew towards its close Montaigne achieved a small ambition which seems to have involved him in considerable effort. 'I sought, and used all my five natural senses, to obtain the title of Roman citizen, if only for its ancient honour and the religious memory of its authority. The authority of the Pope was called into requisition and letters-patent were despatched to me "on the 3rd day before the Ides of March, 1581". It is a vain title but I nevertheless received much pleasure in having obtained it.'

But he did not feel a Roman, and summed up his visit thus: 'There is nothing so injurious to my health as boredom and idleness; here I always had some occupation, if not as pleasant as I could have wished, at least enough to relieve me from tedium: visiting the antiquities and the vineyards, or going to hear sermons or theological discussions which are going on at all times, or again occasionally visiting some woman of the public sort, where I found this drawback, that they will sell their simple conversation as dear (which was what I wanted, to hear them talk and share their *subtilités*) and are as sparing of it as of the whole business. All these diversions kept me busy enough. So this is a pleasant place to live in, and I may conclude how much more I should have liked it if I could have tasted it more intimately; for in truth, however much ingenuity and trouble I employed, I became acquainted only with its outside face, which it offers to the meanest stranger.'

On Wednesday 19 April Montaigne set out with a small party along the ancient Flaminian Way for Ancona and Loreto, having been diverted from it for fear of bandits on the way out. After five

32. 'A pleasant place to live in'. Map of sixteenth-century Rome.

The Seven Hills

1. Quirinal
2. Viminal
3. Esquiline
4. Caelius
5. Capitoline
6. Palatine
7. Aventine

8. Appian Way
9. S. Angelo
10. St. Peter's
11. Flaminian Way

days travelling he noted: 'We became well aware that we were on the way to Loreto, so crowded were the roads with people going and coming; and many, not merely single travellers, but whole companies of rich people, making the journey on foot, dressed as pilgrims, and some with a banner and then a crucifix going on ahead—and these dressed in livery.'

But Loreto itself was much as it is today—'hardly any other inhabitants but those in the service of this cult, such as a number of landlords—yet the inns are dirty enough—and many tradesmen, to wit, sellers of wax images, beads, medals and images, for which there is a large number of fine shops, richly provided.' Yet even Montaigne 'left nearly 50 good crowns there.' He even, 'with great pains, and as a great favour, was able to find room to place a tablet' in the Santa Casa, the little house from Nazareth, in which Mary had lived during the childhood of Jesus and which had been carried by angels, first to Dalmatia in 1291, then across the Adriatic to Recanati and finally to Loreto. The legend was too well-known for Montaigne to dwell on it but he described his tablet in detail; it had four silver figures, 'that of Our Lady, my own, that of my wife and that of my daughter' but it seems soon to have been removed and melted down to make room for others.

Montaigne 'liked Loreto very much' and stayed three days there. He met a rich young Parisian whose leg had been cured after 'all the surgeons of Paris and Italy had failed it' and he found the church people 'as obliging as possible in all matters.' The traveller in him was now tempted to indulge in every kind of diversion—to Pescara, from which he could make Naples by sea in eight days; to Ancona, whence he could get to Dalmatia in ten hours or so, or to Venice by bark for six crowns. In the end he decided to go direct to his final destination, Bagni della Villa, a watering place sixteen miles from Lucca which had been known since the tenth century for its salt and sulphur hot springs, and by daily stages 'of not more than seven or eight hours riding' he reached it on Sunday 7 May.

There were thirty or forty houses close to the baths at Villa, 'the rooms cheerful, quite private and free to do as you please, with a retret [garde-robe or private closet] to each. I inspected nearly all of them before making a bargain and fixed on the finest, especially for the view which commands (at least the room which I chose) the whole of the little valley and the River Lima and the mountains which shelter the valley, all well cultivated and green to the very top, full of chestnut and olive trees, and in other places with vines which they plant all over the mountains and arrange in circles and terraces. From my room I had all night long the gentle murmur of the river.

'Most of the inhabitants of this place stay here in the winter and have their shops, especially apothecaries' shops, for nearly all are apothecaries. My landlord is called Captain Paulini and he is one.

He gave me a dining-room, three bedrooms, a kitchen and also an *apant* [garret?] for our servants, and in them eight beds, two of them with *pavillon* [screens or canopy]. He supplied salt, a napkin every day, a table-cloth every third day, all the iron utensils for the kitchen, and candlesticks, all for eleven crowns a fortnight. The pots, dishes and plates, which are of earthenware, we bought, and glasses and knives; meat is there, as much as you want, veal and kid, scarcely anything else. The wine is not very good but if you so wish you can have it brought either from Pescia or from Lucca. My landlord is bound down by our bargain only for the month of May; we have to make a new one if I wish to stay longer.'

Montaigne stayed six weeks at Villa, although nothing that he did there benefited his health (which he confessed was '*en bon estat*' when he arrived). Occasionally he was much worse for his experimental dosing and he recorded in fine detail the effects on each part of his body of what he took and his theories as to the constituents of the water. He did not want to be a recluse and on Whit Sunday he 'gave a ball to the peasant girls and even dances so as not to appear too reserved.' On the following Sunday he went further.

'I gave a ball with public prizes, as is the custom at these baths and I wanted to give the first one of this year. Five or six days before, I had the party announced in all the neighbouring places. On the day before I sent special invitations to all the gentlemen and ladies who were staying at the two baths inviting them to the ball and to the supper afterwards.'

He had the prizes sent by a friend from Lucca: a leather belt and a leather biretta for the men, aprons, slippers, crystal nets and little necklaces for the women. There were also four pairs of pumps— 'but I gave one of these to a pretty girl not at the ball.' Montaigne himself and the most important ladies acted as judges and he presented the prizes, with a gracious speech to each winner.

'The gentlemen and ladies do not compete, although they take part in the dancing. It is indeed a charming, and to us French an uncommon thing, to see these peasant girls, so graceful and dressed like ladies, dancing so well. I invited them all to supper, for a banquet in Italy is no more than a very light meal in France—a few cuts of veal and a couple or two of fowls, that is all.'

It was now the season of the silk harvest, the most important of the year, and all the inhabitants were 'hard at work, without any regard for holidays, gathering the mulberry leaves for their caterpillars and silk-worms'; in some places they were also beginning to mow the hay. But Montaigne's preoccupation continued to be with the effects of the various treatments, first on himself but also on the many other sufferers who were seeking relief; few seemed unwilling to discuss their symptoms with him. On 1 June his agreement with his landlord expired, but the Captain, 'seeing how much I was in request with all his neighbours', renewed it for a month with only a trifling increase of rent.

Why Montaigne wanted to prolong his stay is hard to understand. He was passing more, not less, gravel on most days and suffering more pain with each expulsion; his eyes were troubling him and his migraines recurring. True he had time to experiment with his body, examining and measuring all that it discharged. He was also meeting doctors, whose company he enjoyed, and was flattered to be called into consultation by them although he claimed that he laughed to himself at the time. Eventually, on 21 June, he left, recording no more reason for doing so than for staying so long and giving no indication in his diary that he had any intention of returning.

Montaigne (for some time he had made no mention of any other members of his party) reached Florence in two days and saw the *palio* on his second day there; he was more pleased with this spectacle than with any other he had seen in Italy for its resemblance to the ancient chariot-races. After five days sightseeing, in spite of an attack of colic, and heat which astonished even the natives, he confessed that Florence was rightly called *la Bella*. But his two weeks there were dismissed in only a few pages of his diary, in contrast to the voluminous record of his treatments at Villa. On Sunday 2 July the party left Florence (he reverts to the pronoun 'we') and travelled the twenty miles to Scala. Three things struck him on the road: 'To see the people working, some at threshing or stacking the corn, some at sewing or spinning, on Sundays; to see the peasants with lute in hand and even Ariosto's *pastorelle* on their tongues (that you may see throughout Italy); to see how they leave the harvested corn in the fields without fear of their neighbour.'

After a bad night at Scala, troubled by toothache, Montaigne and his party followed the Arno valley for the twenty miles to Pisa, arriving at noon.

'Not being satisfied with the hostelry, I rented a house with four bedrooms and a dining room. The landlord was to do the cooking and supply the furniture. A fine house. The whole for eight crowns a month. As the supply of table-cloths and napkins he had promised was too little (seeing that in Italy they change the napkins only when they change the table-cloths and the table-cloths only twice a week) we left the servants to board themselves and we ate at the hostelry at four giulios [5 sous] a day.

'Of holy relics and rare works and marbles wonderful for their rarity, size and workmanship, you find as many as in any other city of Italy. I was above all pleased with the cemetery building called the *Campo Santo*. In the middle of this building there is an uncovered place where they are constantly burying. They all say that bodies that are put here swell in eight hours to such a size that you can see the ground rising; in the next eight hours it subsides and in the next eight the flesh is so far consumed that there is nothing but bare bones. This miracle is similar to that other in the cemetery at Rome [since 1779 the German cemetery by St. Peter's] where if you put the body of a Roman the earth will immediately throw it out. They say that this earth was brought from Jerusalem [from Mount Calvary in both cases].'

Montaigne found Pisa unattractive and he was not well there. After three weeks he returned to Lucca and two weeks later to Villa where he rented the rooms he had had earlier. He received a warm welcome but the waters were no more effective than on the first visit and he 'began to find these baths a fatigue.' He had been four months without news from France and determined to leave as soon as he received some mail.

On 7 September Montaigne's long-awaited letters arrived and he learnt that he had been appointed Mayor of Bordeaux. 'They elected me when I was far from France and still farther from such a thought,' he wrote later, but none of his feelings about the invitation are recorded in the travel-diary. Nor was he in any hurry to take up the post. He returned to Rome and did not set out for home until 15 October.

When travelling to see the country, as on the trip from Rome to Loreto and back to Villa, Montaigne would ride between ten and fifteen miles a day and occasionally as much as twenty miles. He was now making for home and doubled this speed, often covering thirty miles or more in a day. At the outset, he experienced a severe drop in temperature.

'On the Monday morning I was astonished to feel so intense a cold that I thought I had never experienced so cold a season, and to see that the vintage has not yet ended in these parts. I came to dine at Viterbo where I put on my furs and all my winter trappings.'

Had he been travelling with these throughout? There is no mention of any such purchases although he seems to have recorded everything he bought in Rome and elsewhere. He was returning by the same route as far as Lucca and averaging thirty miles a day on good roads. 'All these roads have been repaired this year by order of the Duke of Tuscany: a very fine work and serves the public to great advantage. May God reward him for it for the most difficult roads have by this means become as easy and convenient as the streets of a city.'

At Siena he had a recurrence of his colic and thought he felt a stone falling so he consulted a Hebrew doctor who held forth at great length on the regimen he should follow for his kidneys and gravel. He then became aware, from the excessive pain, that the stone had fallen and continued his journey to Sarzana, the frontier town of Genoese territory, which he reached on 22 October.

'They were firing off artillery in their joy over the presence of Don Giovanni de' Medici, natural brother to the Duke of Florence, who was returning from Genoa where he had been to see the Empress [daughter of Charles V and widow of Maximilian II] and several other Italian princes had also been there. They were making a great cry over the sumptuousness of the Duke of Florence who had come to meet her with 400 carriages. He had asked permission of the Signoria of Venice to pass through their territory with 600 horses to which request they made answer that they allowed him to come with a certain somewhat smaller number: he put all his people into coaches and thus brought them all, but he diminished the number of horses.

'To go to Milan it makes very little difference whether you pass by Genoa or by the other way; I wished to see that city and the Empress, who was there. What put me off was that there are two roads leading thither: one, three days' journey from Sarzana, which is forty miles of very bad and very alpine road, of rocks and precipices and bad inns. This road is little frequented. The other is via Lerici, three miles from Sarzana, where you embark on the sea and in twelve hours cross over to Genoa. Since I cannot endure the water because of the weakness of my stomach, and fearing, even more than the discomforts of the voyage, the difficulty of obtaining lodgings in Genoa owing to the great crowd of people there, and moreover as the road from Genoa to Milan was said to be none too safe on account of *banditi* and having no idea in my head but getting home, I made up my mind to leave Genoa out and followed the road on the right through many mountains, keeping all the time to the bottom of the valley of the River Magra. And, keeping this river on our left, we passed now through the state of Genoa, now through that of the Duke of Florence, then through that of the lords of the Malespina house. In short, by a road that was good on the whole, with a few rugged and precipitous spots, we came by bed-time to Pontremoli, thirty miles.

'At table the first thing they gave me was cheese, as they do around Milan and Piacenza, and, according to the Genoese custom, olives without stones, dressed with oil and vinegar like a salad: very good.

'I left there on Monday in the morning and, on leaving the house, climbed the Apennines: very high but the road by no means difficult or dangerous. In the evening we came to sleep at Fornovo, in the state of the Count of San Secondo, thirty miles. It was a pleasure to be out of the hands of those rascals of the mountains who practise every kind of cruelty imaginable on travellers by their charges for food and horses.

'At table they served me with different kinds of savoury relishes [*intingoletti in forma di mostarda*]—excellent. One of them was made with quinces.

'You find in these parts an extreme scarcity of horses for hire. You are in the hands of lawless people who never keep their word with strangers. Every day it came to more than a crown for horse-hire because they also charged me for two stages when there was only one.'

Although it would have taken him only two stages out of his way to go to Parma, Montaigne decided to go straight ahead 'having dropped every other plan' but to get home. At Borgo San Donino he again had a *mostarda*, this time made with apples and oranges cut into slices, and after that he was on a very fine, level road 'changing horses at every stage; for two stages I went at a gallop, to try the strength of my loins, and I felt neither pain nor fatigue, the urine natural.' He arrived at Piacenza 'very early' and so walked all about the town for three hours seeing 'nothing worth seeing' except the beginnings of a new church. He then decided to go ten miles out of his way in order to see Pavia.

'I left early on Wednesday 25 October, going along a fine road, on which I urinated a small soft stone and a good deal of gravel. About the end of our journey we crossed the Po on a scaffolding placed on two boats, with a small cabin, conducted by means of a long rope supported at various places on little boats arranged in order on a river. Near this place the Ticino joins the Po.'

Numerous other rivers had to be crossed on the road to Turin, sometimes by boat, sometimes at fords, none by bridges. At Turin arrangements were made for crossing the Alps, for which horses were hired for six days as far as Lyons. Next morning they went on to Novelesa.

'Here I hired eight *marroni* [in French *marrons*, the men who make the way passable in deep snow] to carry me in a chair to the top of Mont Cenis and then to sledge me down on the other side.

'*Ici on parle Francès*; so I will quit that foreign language which I employ with great ease but with very little sureness for, having been all the time in the company of Frenchmen I have not had the opportunity of learning anything worth speaking of it.

'I crossed Mont Cenis, half-way on horseback, half-way in a litter carried by four men, with another four who relieved them. They carried me on their shoulders. The ascent takes two hours, stony and difficult for horses that are not accustomed to it, but otherwise without danger or difficulty; the mountain rises steadily and you see no precipices so there is no danger except of your mount stumbling.

'The descent is a league [Montaigne now reverts to French leagues for his distances], straight and steep, down which I was conveyed in a sledge by the same *marrons*, and for the whole service of the eight I gave them two crowns. It is a pleasant sport, but without any risk.'

It was still four days' journey to Chambéry, and Montaigne began to appreciate the excellence of the Italian oils which 'never rose again to the mouth' whereas in France they gave him stomach-ache. He had now made nineteen overnight stops and was not even half way in terms of travelling days. Three more days took him to Montluel which was only three leagues from Lyons, and here, in spite of his bargain to be taken to Lyons by the horses he had hired at Turin, he 'took the post after dinner and came on to sleep at Lyons,' arriving on Tuesday 7 November.

He was delighted to be there but in need of a rest and he settled down for a week.

'On the Friday I bought of Joseph de la Sione three unused curtals [small, cropped horses] for two hundred crowns and on the day before I had bought from Malesieu a pacing horse for fifty crowns and another curtal for thirty-three. On the Saturday I had a bad stomach-ache and remained in bed until after dinner, when I had diarrhoea; I did not dine at all and had very little supper. On the Monday I left Lyons after dinner and came to sleep at Bourdelliere, five leagues, a village where there are only two houses.'

Three days later he noted that 'the nearer I approached home the longer and more tedious did the way seem' and reflected on the fact that he had not been even half way at Chambéry. After two more days he reached Clermont-Ferrand where he stopped, although he had travelled only two leagues that day, 'for the sake of my young horses'. Here it came on to snow 'and the weather was so severe with cold winds, that one saw nothing of the country.' He passed a 'largish stone', the shape and texture of which he describes. Nevertheless, he now reverted to six- and seven-league travelling days and reached Pont-Charraud on 21 November.

'This road is lined with wretched hostelries as far as Limoges where, however, there is no lack of passable wines. My head was not right; and if storms and cold wind are bad for it, I gave it its fill of them on these roads where the winter is said to be more severe than in any other place in France.'

Two more days brought Montaigne to Limoges, 'where I stayed all the Saturday and there bought a mule for ninety *ecus-sol* [sun- or gold-crowns, also worth about six shillings sterling each] and paid for a mule-load from Lyons to here five crowns, having been cheated in this of four *livres* [there were three *livres* to a crown]: for all the other loads cost only three and two-thirds crowns.'

He was at last nearing home. On Tuesday 28 November he was at Périgueux and two days later he made the longed-for entry: 'Montaigne, five leagues, which I had left on 22 June 1580. Thus my travels had lasted seventeen months and eight days.'

It was 30 November, the anniversary of the day Montaigne had arrived in Rome the year before.

At the end of his two-year term of office Montaigne was re-elected for a second term. A second edition of the *Essays* was published in 1583, and in 1585, after his retirement from the mayoralty, he began work on a third book of longer, mainly autobiographical, essays which appeared in 1588. He now spent a considerable part of his time in Paris where he developed a close friendship with a young but scholarly girl called de Gourney whom he adopted as his daughter. He continued making lengthy additions to his own copy of the *Essays* until his death in 1592 at the age of fifty-nine. Three years later Mademoiselle de Gourney published these additions thus bringing Montaigne's lifework to completion.

The first English translation of the *Essays* was published by John Florio in 1602 and there is good reason to believe that Shakespeare owned a copy and came under its spell. Since then not less than half a dozen translators have felt impelled to do what they could to bring the ideas of this great Frenchman closer to the English reader. His travel diary, kept with no thought of publication, makes a small contribution to this worthy cause.

PART FOUR

Seventeenth-century Travellers

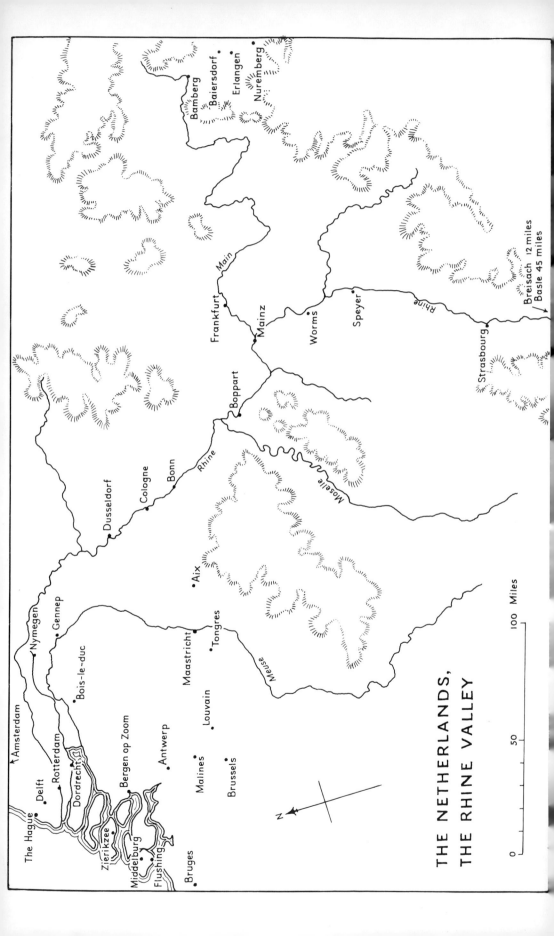

THE NETHERLANDS,
THE RHINE VALLEY

Amsterdam

Nymegen
Gennep

The Hague
Delft
Rotterdam
Dordrecht
Bois-le-duc
Bergen op Zoom
Antwerp
Zierikzee
Middelburg
Flushing
Bruges
Malines
Louvain
Brussels
Maastricht
Tongres
Aix

Dusseldorf
Cologne
Bonn
Boppart

Frankfurt
Mainz
Worms
Speyer
Strasbourg

Bamberg
Baiersdorf
Erlangen
Nuremberg

Main
Rhine
Moselle
Meuse

Breisach 12 miles
Basle 45 miles

N

0   50   100   Miles

19

Fynes Moryson

'I lit upon a coach'

London to Germany and Italy, 1591–5

(Map on p. 44)

A watershed separates the literature of travel before and after the turn of the sixteenth century. The pilgrims' records of their travels flowed for the most part into monastery libraries, those of the ambassadors into State archives, and the diaries of Montaigne and Dürer into cupboards from which they were much later retrieved. (Horace, de Comines and Benvenuto Cellini wrote for publication but travel played a small part in their writings.) After 1600 the words recorded by the European traveller flowed into publishers' offices where they were received with increasing eagerness. Many of the writers had publication in mind before they packed their baggage. Fynes Moryson was one of the very first of these: his journey began in 1591 but his book was not published until well into the seventeenth century.

The whole attitude to travel had changed by then. Apart from those who had to travel for their affairs, only religion, sickness or the attractions of a foreign university were likely to get a literate European on to the roads much before 1600. After that he was as likely to be drawn by what was known as 'curiosity', a desire to see what was going on in those so near, but so strange, lands across the border—the border being the Channel in the case of the English and those who visited England. Curiosity, not pleasure: it was to be many years before any but the most unusually sensitive or scholarly would expect to *enjoy* themselves more in a foreign country than at home, particularly the English who could find little recreation to their taste on the Continent but who were among the most ardent travellers. Meanwhile those who learnt by experience what was worth seeing and how best to see it were impelled to share their experience with as many others as possible. There were already plenty of so-called guide-books but they were road-books rather than accounts of personal experiences and few were published in English.

The English travellers of the period were, moreover, pioneers. It would have been extremely difficult for an Englishman under Elizabeth to travel, as did Montaigne, just because he wanted to do so. It was illegal for anyone, except a genuine sailor or merchant, to leave the country without the royal licence and such a licence would not normally be granted without good reason.

Fynes Moryson's reason for wanting to travel was good enough: he had resolved to write an account of Europe, and eventually he did so on a massive scale. He was reasonably well-connected and became a Fellow of Peterhouse, Cambridge, in 1586 when he was twenty years old. The College had the privilege of granting a licence to travel to two of its Fellows and Moryson obtained one of these in 1589. He still needed his father's permission to leave the country and he evidently felt that an Oxford degree would carry more weight abroad than one from Cambridge; these pre-liminaries, and the need for further study in London, took two more years and it was not until 1 May 1591 that he 'took ship at Leigh', at the mouth of the Thames, with a 'merchants' fleet of sixteen ships'. He was to be on the continent of Europe for four years, to leave again within six months, this time for the Holy Land, and finally, after three years' service in Ireland, to settle down to the writing of his book, *An Itinerary*, which was not published until 1617. By that time Elizabeth was dead, travel was more or less free for all who could afford to indulge in it, and the stream of travel books had begun its inexhaustible flow.

Fynes Moryson cannot compare with Montaigne for richness of mind, nor did he consort with princes and leaders, as did many of those whose tales have so far been told. He was a simple, rather poor scholar, intent on improving himself and in some need of improvement: his Cambridge and Oxford degrees may have testified to his knowledge of law but they seem to have left him without the ability to respond to the arts in any of their forms. Nevertheless, in spite of all his limitations, he was the first English traveller to provide a detailed account of what was involved in a protracted journey on the continent of Europe; how much everything cost, the means of conveyance, and how long everything took. We need scarcely follow him on every stage to Elsinore in the north, to Cracow in the east and to Naples in the south but there are points on his journey at which we would do well to join him.

The crossing of the North Sea was a trying one, the convoy of merchantmen being first dispersed by fog, then by tempest and finally by pirates—'that they were pirates was apparent since, as we for trial turned our sails, they like-wise fitted themselves to our course.' A few shots discouraged the pirates and on the ninth day of the voyage the convoy 'fell upon an island called Holy-land' (Heligoland). There was no room in the harbour, which held only six ships, so they struck sail and 'suffered their ship to be tossed to and fro by the waves all night.'

On the tenth day Moryson's ship entered the River Elbe and he landed at Stade. This was the rival port to Hamburg and was passing through a period of prosperity; it was in fact from Stade that one could best ensure finding a ship to take one to the Thames, and Moryson was to make use of it later on three occasions. He had prefaced his book with 'a brief table to understand the expenses in small coins most commonly spent' and his first report on landing was that he paid four Lübeck shillings and a half for his meal, the normal price in the 'Dutch' (German) inns, as opposed to 8d in the English inns which catered for the considerable English community. Moryson's references to money are here converted very approximately into the sterling equivalent of the time, $4\frac{1}{2}$ Lübeck shillings being about 5d—five pence, of which there were 240 to the pound sterling.

'From Stade to Hamburg are five [German] miles,' (about 22 English miles) and for this journey Moryson joined a party which hired a wagon, first to the Elbe for $6\frac{1}{4}$d each and thence, after crossing the river, by another wagon to complete the journey. At the very end of his long book Moryson dealt with 'the fit means to travel' and he gave details of the wheeled transport gradually becoming available throughout Europe. It is for such details, rather than for his descriptions of cities, that Moryson's work is so valuable.

'In the Low Countries [in which he included northern Germany] travellers pass most in narrow country wagons, the sides thereof being like racks for horses, and across them short and somewhat narrow boards being fastened for passengers to sit upon, two in a rank, so as they hold some eight or ten passengers; and they have goodly mares to draw these wagons. I never did see the means of passage so ready in any place as these wagons here at all times are before the door of the Wagoners' Inn. Neither did I ever

see travellers pass at so easy a rate (I mean for their passages, not for
the inns) so they have not heavy luggage: for in that case, the
wagons being left and taken at the gates of the city (as I think not to
wear the brick pavement with their wheels), and the wagons being
often changed in each day's journey, this carriage to his inn and
from it so often must needs be a great burden to his shoulders or
charge to his purse. The wagoners, being commonly drunken,
drive their mares like madmen, yet without danger of turning over
their wagons because the ways are most plain, fair and sandy.'

For his first journey, though, Moryson felt he had made a
mistake in travelling by wagon.

'The passage by water to Hamburg had been much easier,
especially for a stranger, and a boat daily passes from Stade thither
in some three hours space, if the wind be not contrary, wherein
each man pays 4½d for his passage: but all passengers without
difference of condition must help to row, or hire one [to do so] in
his stead, except the wind be good so as they need not use their
oars; besides that the annoyance of base companions will easily
offend one that is anything nice.'

Moryson was not taken with Hamburg, where the citizens
were 'unmeasurably ill affected to the English for removing
their traffic to Stade'. It was in fact 'unsafe to walk out of the gates
after noon, for when the common people are once warmed
with drink they are apt to do them injury.' Living was not
expensive, meals being the customary 5d each but beds only 1½ or
even free after a meal; Rhenish wine was 7½d a quart and sack the
same price. After a trip to Lübeck for which 'each of us paid for our
Coach twenty Lübeck shillings' (nearly three English shillings) he
went on to Lüneberg and then back to Hamburg by wagon. But, he
adds, 'let me admonish the Reader that if . . .' and he sets out a
cheaper way of accomplishing the journey if a party of six can be
made up. Once back in Hamburg, 'purposing to go up into
Meissen, because I had not the language I compounded with a
Merchant to carry me in his Coach and bear my charges to Leipzig
for ten gold Guldens.' This was more than £2 and it proved to be
another mistake since he could have hired a coach holding six, or
even perhaps eight, for just over £5 so that because of 'the
cheapness of victuals in these parts no doubt I gave the Merchant
too much.'

The journey to Leipzig took four days and on the following day
Moryson went on to Wittenberg. There he was shown an
inscription in Latin to the effect that 'here stood the bed in which

Luther gently died,' but he knew well enough that Luther had in fact died at 'Isleb' (Eisleben, his birthplace) 46 years before, 'yet they suffer not the least memory of him to be blotted out.' In spite of this deception Moryson liked Wittenberg. 'I lived at Wittenberg the rest of this summer, where I paid five shillings weekly for my diet and beer, which they account apart, and for my chamber at the rate of fifty shillings by the year. I hear that now all things are dearer; the Scholars used to pay each week four shillings and fourpence for their diet and the same for chamber and washing. Three of us hired a Coach all this journey for four shillings and fourpence each day, with condition that we should pay for the meat of the horses and of the coach-man, which cost as much more. And this we paid because we had freedom to leave the coach at our pleasure, though we returned with it to Leipzig, to which if we had tied ourselves we might have had the coach for half the price.'

Early in 1592 Moryson set out for Prague, joined by a friend as far as Torgau. There was an irritating incident after they had parted which Moryson described in a letter to his friend. 'By good hap, and beside my expectation, I lit upon a Coach going to Dresden, with which good hap, while I hasted to hire a place therein, I had forgot to pay for my Coach the day before. But when we were ready to go, remembering my error, and entreating my consorts to stay a while for me, I ran back to the Inn and, finding not the Coachman there, I gave the money to the servant of the house before witnesses, and so returned to the Coach all sweating with haste. There I found that dunghill rascal the Coachman, having my gown on his back. I laid hold of the garment and he held it fast as a pledge for his money. I being enraged that he should use me so, when I had dealt honestly with him, drew my sword and making known that I had paid the money, bade him lay down the gown upon his peril. I had almost drawn a rabble of Coachmen on my back, but they forbore in this heat, for you know they are not apt to quarrel in the morning; but if I had thus provoked them in the afternoon, being warmed with drink, sure they would have run upon me, though they had been naked.'

The journey by coach from Dresden to Prague, about 75 English miles, took three days. Prague, mostly built of timber and clay, was filthy and, although surrounded by walls, defenceless— 'except the stench of the streets drive back the Turks.' Moryson again stayed with a merchant who one day gave him pickled English oysters. A Bohemian, coming in by chance, so liked the

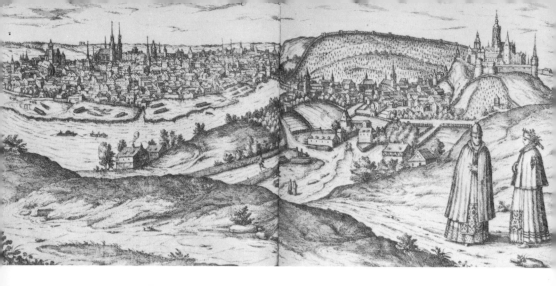

33. 'Defenceless, except the stench of the streets drive back the Turks'.
Prague in Fynes Moryson's time.

oysters that he ate five dishes of them, each containing twenty oysters. For this he had to pay over a pound sterling, 'the dearness no less displeasing his mind than the meat had pleased his taste.' Moryson stayed in Prague for two months and then left for a six-day journey to Nuremberg, still travelling by coach. At Nuremberg 'a merchant of noble family, well acquainted with me and my friends, arrived there and told me that my father had died some two months past.' Moryson, after a late night's drinking in Prague, had dreamt 'that a shadow passing by, told me that my father was dead,' and had written this down in a book which he had put into a barrel 'and sent it from Prague to Stade, thence to be conveyed to England.' It was to be four years before he opened the barrel in England in the presence of witnesses 'where myself and they were astonished to see my written dream answer the very day of my father's death.' Much the same had occurred when his mother had died while he was at Cambridge. A change of plan was now necessary.

'Being certified of my father's death, and thinking not fit to go on my journey into Italy, and yet being loath to return into England before I had finished my purposed voyage, I took the middle counsel, to return into the Low Countries, that in those near places I might dispose of my small patrimony (for in England gentlemen give their younger sons less than in foreign parts they give to their bastards) and so might leave the same in the hands of some trusty friend.'

Moryson no doubt feared that, were he to return to England, he would not be given another licence to travel abroad, but he was in no hurry to get to the Low Countries. He was in Nuremberg,

where Europe's first regular postal service had been organized
twenty years earlier, and there were 'City Carriers daily passing
between Nuremberg and Augsburg, paid by the merchants of the
two cities and allowed to charge for their services.' (It was in this
very year, 1592, that in England, by contrast, the private posts that
foreign merchants had been trying to organize were made illegal in
order to ensure that the Government could censor their correspondence.) Moryson hired a horse from one of these carriers
and went with the carrier to Augsburg in two and half days. From
there he rode to Ulm where he saw the River Danube. 'It hath a
most violent course so that boats carried down the stream used to
be sold at the place where they land, it being very difficult to bring
them back again; yet some Barkes of burthen are sometimes drawn
back by force of horses. Myself have seen ten horses drawing one
Barke but they use a greater number, some thirty or more, as they
report.'

Moryson continued his leisurely course through Europe, taking
in Holland, Denmark and Poland, until, at the end of October,
1593, he found himself in Padua. He had bought a horse in Cracow
which had cost him less than five pounds, including saddle, boots
and spurs, and was now able to sell it for more than he had paid,
although still less than he expected to get. This was a common
practice, as Felix Fabri had found in 1480 (page 67). In his essay on
'the fit means to travel' Moryson later wrote:

'He that travels for Italy cannot take a more frugal course than to
buy a horse in Germany which he may sell for gain in Italy,
especially if he sell him by the way, being within a few days of his
journey's end, whence he may pass by hired coach or horse to
Padua; for if he bring his horse thither [to Padua] those that are
there to buy him are such crafty knaves and will so conspire
together against him as he shall be forced to sell his horse under
hand, being made weary with the great charge of his meat: but this
frugality has some difficulties, if the passenger has no skill in the
tongue (in which case he must hire an interpreter) and if he have
not horsemen to accompany him, because they travel all by
coaches, yet if this horseman will follow the coach he may with a
small gift induce the Coachman to teach him the means to provide
for his horse.

'In Italy they use few or no coaches but only in the State of
Venice where, from Treviso to Padua, myself and my companion
hired a coach for eighteen Venetian lire. For other parts of Italy
travellers use horses or mares in hilly countries and in the plain

towards Naples they use mules and asses much more commonly than horses and the same beasts are used for all carriages.'

Moryson spent the winter in Padua, staying part of the time in Venice, and joined the university to perfect his Italian. He supplements Montaigne's account of the procedure at Fusina (called 'Lizzafusina' on maps up to the late eighteenth century) on the journey from Padua to Venice; this was the more generally used of the two mainland points for approaching Venice, the other being Mestre. 'Taking boat at Padua we were drawn by horses until we came to the village of Lizzafusina where there is a dam to stop the waters of the Brenta lest the marshes on that side of Venice should be filled with sand or earth and so a passage made on firm ground to the city; which they are careful to prevent, and not without just cause having found safety in their isles when Italy was often overflowed with barbarous peoples. Besides, they say that this dam was made lest this fresh water should be mingled with their salt waters, since all gentlemen of Venice fetch their fresh water by boats from thence, the poorer sort being content with well-water. Here, while our boat was drawn by an instrument out of the River Brenta into the marshes of Venice, we refreshed ourselves with meat and wine. Then we entered our boat again and passed five miles to Venice. We might have had coaches from Padua to Lizzafusina but most men use this passage as most convenient. For the boat is covered with arched hatches and there is very pleasant company.'

This boat was the forerunner of the *Burchiello* which, by the eighteenth century, had become the traditional way of travelling direct between Venice and Padua, or to the many villas on the banks of the Brenta.

Moryson worked his way conscientiously round Venice and its islands. 'The market place of Saint Mark is paved with brick,' he wrote (as it was to remain for another 130 years) and the new Rialto Bridge, begun only six years earlier, was, like so much else, the eighth miracle of the world. The prisons had been under the Doge's Palace 'but lately,' he noted, 'a new house is stately built of stone of Istria for that use near the bridge Della Paglia.' It was to be almost twenty years before this simple building was completed.

From Venice he 'went into the Barke which weekly passes to Ferrara', another journey on that complex canal system of northern Italy. After a long tour of Rome, the Campania and Tuscany he was at last able to write: 'On 3 March 1595 I turned my

Oriens

34. 'The market place of Saint Mark is paved with brick'. The Piazza San
Marco a few years before Fynes Moryson's visit in 1594.

face to journey towards my dear country.' Two months later he
landed at Dover after a fourteen-hour crossing and the next day he
was in London at his sister's house. After four years' travel he must
have been a sorry sight.

'And when I entered my sister's house in poor habit a servant
answered that my sister was at home, but when he did see me go up

the stairs too boldly (as he thought) without a guide, he not knowing me did furiously and with threatening words call me back and surely would have been rude with me had I not gone up faster than he could follow me, and he had taken hold of my old cloak, which I willingly flung off to be rid of him. Then by my sister's embraces he perceived who I was and stole back as if he had trodden upon a snake.'

Perhaps the most extraordinary thing about this extraordinary traveller was that within six months he was again off with his brother to Venice and the Holy Land. The expedition was financed by the equivalent of a life insurance policy in reverse—the traveller 'put out some four hundred pounds, to be repaid twelve hundred pounds upon his return, and to lose it if he died in the journey.' He could thus spend the greater part of his capital in buying the policy and going where he wished, knowing that if he returned safely he would have as much as, or more than, he began with. The terms sound generous but the writers of the policies doubtless knew the actuarial odds: Fynes's brother Henry died at Antioch, so in this case at any rate they made a profit.

After his solitary return Fynes Moryson resigned from Peterhouse and entered the service of Lord Mountjoy in Ireland, remaining there until Mountjoy's death in 1606. He then returned to England and spent his time writing up his notes. He wrote in Latin, perhaps in the hope that his work would be published in some of the countries he had visited, but he later translated the book into English. He did not find it easy to attract a publisher and after three years he destroyed the manuscript and began again; since the book ran to some three thousand pages and included much history and geography that he knew only by reading, as well as his own experiences, the hesitation of publishers is understandable. At last in 1617, seventeen years before his death, a publisher was found for three-quarters of the book. It was not until three hundred years later that his Part IV was published, to be followed in 1908 by the republication of the earlier parts.

It would be hard to find a more valuable source of information about the use of coaches in Europe at the end of the sixteenth century than Moryson provides in his 'fit means to travel'. References to wheeled transport have been gradually appearing in these pages after its virtual disappearance with the end of the Roman empire. Only Moryson tells us precisely what the ordinary traveller could expect to find just before the opening of the century in which coach travel would become a commonplace.

'The greatest part of Germany is a plain country with few hills and the soil is for the most part sandy and little subject to dirt, so they commonly use coaches for their journeys which are easily to be found in any city; neither shall a passenger long stay for companions to fill up the coach so as he shall not be put to any extraordinary charge. The ordinary coaches hold six consorts but those of Nuremberg receive eight, bearing two in each boot on the sides. [The boot on the front or back of the vehicle came much later.] But if companions be not readily found to fill the coach, the passengers shall do better in going forward with such company as they have, and the coachman will rather go for less, than stay in the inn and spend more in expecting the full number. The top of the coaches is made with round hoops (covered with leather, or with black cloth) which are buckled together in the middle when it rains, or if the weather is cold, for otherwise the hoops fastened with staples of iron to the body of the coach fall backwards.

'At the foot of the Alps, where the fall of waters makes the ways dirty, they usually ride on horseback. Switzerland consists of hills and mountains so they likewise travel on horseback. The horses in both places are to be hired for 18-20d by the day but the travellers' expense is doubled by paying for the days in which the horse returns empty; besides he must hire a footman to bring back his horse, and must bear his charges on the way, which greatly increases his expense in those countries yielding wine, the footmen being as good or better drinkers as the horsemen.'

After some advice on where, how and when (not the spring or autumn) to cross the Alps, Moryson returned to the coach. In Bohemia and Poland they were to be hired in most of the cities, and even slept in when necessary. In Denmark there were only wagons, as in the Low Countries. There remained only the France of Montaigne and the England of Shakespeare.

'The French seldom use coaches for journeys but in Paris he that will can hire a coach about the city. Likewise in Paris even notaries and ordinary men hire horses to ride about the city. The French also have long wagons covered with cloth (such as our English carriers use) wherein women, and such as can endure the slowness thereof, sometimes travel from city to city.

'In England coaches are not to be hired anywhere but only in London; howsoever England is for the most part plain, or consisting of little pleasant hills, yet the ways far from London are so dirty as hired coachmen do not ordinarily take any long journeys, but only for one or two days any way from London, the ways so far being sandy and fair and continually kept so by labour of hands. Sixty or seventy years ago, coaches were very rare in England but at this day pride is so far increased that there be few gentlemen of any account (I mean elder brothers) [Moryson could never forget the injustices of primogeniture] who have not their coaches, so as the streets of London are almost stopped up with them. But for the most part Englishmen, especially on long journeys, ride upon their own horses.

'Carriers let horses from city to city, with caution that the passenger must lodge in their inn, so that they may look to the feeding of their horse. Also, these carriers have long covered wagons in which they carry passengers from city to city: but this kind of journeying is so tedious, by reason they must take the wagon very early, and come late to their inns, as none but women and people of very inferior condition, or strangers (as Flemmings with their wives and servants) travel in this sort of thing.'

Morysons' *Precepts for Travellers* provided a model for all subsequent guide-books. His advice to 'young men to moderate their aptness to quarrel lest they perish with it' was echoed by Murray in his Hand-books 250 years later; Moryson went further and warned his reader just how far he could go with Italians, Germans, Swiss and Poles and precisely what would happen if he went too far. Indeed, everything that could befall the traveller was foreseen and the proper counsel given. The wise, practical, experienced, even though humdrum, Fynes Moryson may be left uttering a characteristic warning which all travellers might heed.

'In all inns, but especially in suspected places, let him take heed of his chamber fellows and always have his sword by his bedside. Let him lay his purse under his pillow, but always folded with his garters, or something he first uses in the morning, lest he forget to pick it up before he go out of his chamber. And to the end he may leave nothing behind him, let the visiting of his chamber, and gathering his things together, be the last thing he does before he puts his foot into the stirrup.'

20

Thomas Coryat

'I did eat fried frogs'

Venice and the Rhine, 1608

(Map on p. 92)

On 7 August 1620 a young Englishman called Peter Mundy found himself in Verona on the way back to England from Constantinople. He was to spend a great part of his life travelling outside Europe but on this occasion he was merely making a comfortable and leisurely return home in the company of a retiring ambassador with a large retinue and had chosen the long, overland route, probably to indulge his curiosity. Mundy had been studying the Verona amphitheatre with the aid of a travel book by George Sandys, which had been published in 1615, and had then copied into his diary much of Sandys's description and measurements. Even this was not enough and at the end of his notes he added: 'Read at large C.C.'.

There can be no doubt about the meaning of 'C.C.'. *Coryat's Crudities* had been published in 1611, before either Fynes Moryson's or Sandys's books, and had established itself as the travellers' companion of the period. Verbose as it was, it was almost compact in comparison with Moryson's *Itinerary*, and its popularity may be judged from the fact that Peter Mundy, who had been in Constantinople for three years, was in possession of a copy.

Thomas Coryat had travelled to Venice and back in 1608 and had covered enough of his 2,000-mile journey on foot to persuade him to hang up his shoes with pride in his parish church at Odcombe, Somerset, on returning after five months and to include an illustration of the shoes when, after great difficulty, he was able to find a publisher for his book. Had Moryson's book already appeared, Coryat might never have found a publisher since he provided very little in the way of practical information. Moryson spared his reader no detail on how best to get from A to B, the cost, and how long should be spent at B, if any time at all. Coryat was almost laconic. 'I departed from Montreuil in a cart,' he writes, 'according to the fashion of the country, which had three hoops over it, that were covered with a sheet of coarse canvas,' but, two days later, 'I took my journey from Amiens towards Paris in Coach.' No advice to the prospective follower in his footsteps as to which was more desirable, or available, or the relative cost. On the other hand his 'observations' on the cities he passed through were as prolix as those of Moryson and not a comma was cut from the *Latine Epistles* he addressed to those who had entertained him. But Coryat's mind was slightly—very slightly—less pedestrian than Moryson's and he made his own observations on the habits of foreigners and the food they ate.

'I observed a custom in all those Italian cities and towns through which I passed that is not used in any other country that I saw in my travels, neither do I think that any other nation of Christendom use it, but only Italy. The Italian, and also most strangers that are commorant [resident] in Italy do always at their meals use a little fork when they cut their meat. For while with their knife, which they hold in one hand, they cut the meat out of the dish, they fasten their fork, which they hold in their other hand, upon the same dish, so that should he who sit in company of any others at meals unadvisedly touch the dish of meat with his fingers from which all at the table do cut he will give occasion of offence unto the company as having transgressed the laws of good manners, in so much that for this his error he shall be at least brow-beaten, if not reprehended in words.'

Coryat 'thought it good to imitate the Italian fashion by this forked cutting of meat' even when he returned to England and in this he was among the pioneers: 'Then must you learn the use/And handling of your silver fork at meals', spoke a Ben Jonson character in *Volpone*, published in 1605, whereas Elizabeth I, who died in 1603, did not acquire the habit.

At Cremona Coryat noted: 'I did eat fried Frogs in this city, which is a dish much used in many cities of Italy: they were so curiously dressed that they did exceedingly delight my palate, the head and the forepart being cut off.' And at his inn at Mantua, 'there was such an exceeding abundance of flies that they had wooden flaps to beat them away. For no sooner would a dish of meat be laid on the table but there would incontinently be a thousand flies in it, were it not for those flaps. I told my fellow travellers at dinner that if the Emperor Domitian had been now alive and in that room with us he would have done us some pleasure in driving away those flies. For indeed Suetonius wrote that he would sometimes spend a whole hour alone by himself every day in some private room of his Palace in catching of flies.'

From Mantua Coryat rode to Padua and then 'in a Barke down the River Brenta', passing 'many palaces of pleasure' until he reached 'Lucie Fesina' where 'the fresh and salt water would meet and be confounded together were it not kept asunder by a sluice over which the Barkes are lifted up by a certain crane.' So by gondola to Venice where he spent six weeks.

35. 'Many palaces of pleasure'. One of Veronese's frescoes at Villa Maser, built by Palladio about 1560. Several of the travellers describe passing these villas which Tom Coryat in 1608 called 'delectable houses of retreat wherein the Venetians solace themselves in the Summer'.

Like Fynes Moryson, Coryat was disappointed that the Piazza should be paved with brick: 'had it been paved with stone it would have made the whole Piazza much more glorious and resplendent than it is.' The Doge's Palace 'hath been five times consumed with fire, yet so sumptuously re-edified that it never was so fair as at this present.' The easiness of the ascent of the Campanile impressed him and, like most travellers, he was told that a horse could climb its stairs. 'I confess I saw no horse ascend it, but I heard it much reported in Venice, both by many of our countrymen and by the Venetians themselves; neither is it unlikely to be true.' But he did see a horse, 'a little bay nag feeding in the churchyard of St. John and St. Paul, whereat I did not a little wonder, because I could not devise what they should do with a horse in such a city where they have no use for him. For you must consider that neither the

36. 'It hath been five times consumed with fire'. The burning of the Doge's
Palace in 1577, the last before Coryat's visit.

37. 'I have here inserted a picture of one of their nobler Cortezans . . . as we saluted each other'. Engraving from Coryat's *Crudities*.

Venetian gentlemen nor any others can ride horses in the streets of Venice, their streets being so narrow and slippery the horse would quickly fall into the river and so drown both himself and his rider.'

Horses had indeed been used in Venice in the past, although this bay nag would have been one of the few survivors. By 1291 they were enough of a nuisance to demand an order forbidding anyone to ride in the Merceria, the main shopping street, in the day-time.

Coryat was as impressed by the number, and quality, of the courtesans as any of his predecessors had been. He wrote eight pages about them and paid one of them a gallant compliment. 'I have here inserted a picture of one of their nobler Cortezans, according to her Venetian habits, with my own near unto her, made in that form as we saluted each other.' It was, he insisted, the melodious notes that she warbled out on her lute, and her elegant discourse as a rhetorician, that most delighted him.

At last Coryat left Venice on 8 August, taking the barge to Padua from the city itself rather than from Fusina. He studied Palladio's work at Vicenza with care and interest and then passed on to Verona where he prepared the description of the Amphitheatre which Peter Mundy found so useful a few years later (page 167). After noting that Verona had four bridges across the Adige (compared with London, which was to remain with only one across the Thames for another 150 years), Coryat followed the Milan road as far as Bergamo where he turned north, crossed the Splügen Pass and worked his way through Chur to Zurich and Basle. Once in Switzerland he explained to his reader, unlike Fynes Moryson, what he meant by a 'mile'—'I reduce their miles to our English computation, one of theirs being five of ours' (in fact, about three).

At Basle Coryat embarked on the Rhine and reached Strasbourg the next morning. Then he went on to Heidelberg where he saw a 'stupendious mass' in the form of a cask holding 50,000 gallons of wine. 'As it was the strangest spectacle that I saw in my travels I have inserted a true figure thereof in this place, though in a small form. Also I have added an imaginary kind of representation of myself upon the top of the same, in that manner as I stood there with a cup of Rhenish wine in my hand.'

The journey down the Rhine has already been described by Dürer. Coryat was equally struck by the constant stopping to pay tolls, and between Mainz and the Netherlands he reports 'a very strange custom': 'Every man, whatsoever he be poor or rich, shall labour hard when it comes to his turn except, either by friendship or some small sum of money, he redeem his labour. For the passengers must exercise themselves with oars and rowing a couple together. This exercise, both for recreation and health sake, I confess is very convenient. But to be tied to it by way of strict

38. 'A stupendious mass . . . myself upon the top of the same'. Engraving from Coryat's *Crudities*.

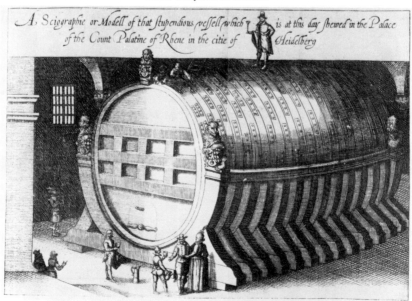

A Sciographie or Modell of that stupendious vessell which is at this day shewed in the Palace of the Count Palatine of Rhene in the citie of Heidelberg

necessity when one payeth well for his passage was a thing that did not a little distaste my humour.' But however well he may have paid for his passage, it was, he notes later, 'but a small price' since he was travelling downstream. Going upstream their vessels are drawn by horses with great might and main. For this cause, all passengers that ascend into the higher parts of Germany pay much more for their carriage than those that descend.'

Coryat liked Holland, although he ate too much there and complained of not getting his supper before seven o'clock, and then having to sit at least an hour and a half over it. After a day in Middelburg he walked to Flushing whence 'a pleasant and prosperous gale of wind' took him to the Custom House in London in only two days.

Before Coryat could persuade a publisher to take his *Crudities* he had to solicit 'panegyrick verses' from almost every member of London's literary society, including Ben Jonson, John Donne and Inigo Jones. These occupied more than a hundred pages of the first volume. The book was then a great success and, a year after its publication in 1611, Coryat set off again, this time for the East. In 1616 he was known to be in the ancient city of Ajmer in India. He remained there for eight months and sent home a number of letters which were later published. From Ajmer he went to Surat, north of Bombay where, according to a later traveller, he suffered from a flux. Unhappily some English friends gave him sack. He drank it, according to the same traveller, 'moderately, for he was a temperate man, but it increased his flux and this caused him within a few days, after his very tedious and troublesome travels (for he went most on foot) to come to his journey's end in December 1617.'

With the publication of Fynes Moryson's and Coryat's books travel was never again to be quite the same. The flow of guide-books had been set in motion and it was to be fed by many tributaries. Every guide-book leans to a varying extent on its predecessors but unhappily every traveller leans on his guide-book. So, into the river of travel-writing flowed also the streams of error, each one perpetuated, and sometimes inflated, by later travellers. Travellers had always been prone to see what they expected to see, from the tales told by others: from now on they were to see what they had read about and it was only to be expected that their powers of observation should degenerate, except in the cases of those few capable of original thought. Fortunately, the attraction of European travel (stimulated, of course, by these very guide-books) increasingly drew men of education and talent to leave home and see for themselves. So, while the average standard of travel-writing fell, the pool from which selection could be made vastly increased, until the time was to come when the reader would be embarrassed, not by the scarcity of fine travel-writing, but by a surfeit.

21

John Evelyn

'I had set my affections on a daughter'

The Netherlands, France and Italy, 1641–47

(Map on p. 92)

One evening in 1814 the sub-librarian of the London Institution, named William Upcott, was sitting with the widow of Sir Frederick Evelyn whose library at Wotton, near Dorking in Surrey, he had catalogued the previous year. The talk turned to hobbies and Upcott said that, having collected many things in a modest way, he was now interested in autographs. 'Oh,' cried Lady Evelyn, 'if you care for old papers you shall have plenty, for Sylva Evelyn kept all his correspondence, which has furnished the kitchen with abundance of waste paper.' Upcott was duly given the run of the cupboards and next day found a diary in the handwriting of John Evelyn, who had died in 1706 at the age of eighty-six. 'Bless me,' exclaimed Lady Evelyn when she was told, 'if here isn't old Sylva's diary; why, I haven't seen it for years. It was suggested once that I print it, but I don't think it would interest the public enough to repay the expense.' Upcott disagreed and the outcome was that much of the diary was published in 1818.

Upcott ends his story with the sequel. 'John Evelyn's intimate friend Samuel Pepys also kept a diary, which is preserved. The success which *Evelyn's Diary* met with induced Lord Braybrooke to have transcribed Pepys's very difficult shorthand manuscript, comprising ten years only of his active life, and this was printed uniform in size and type with that of *Evelyn's Diary*.' Upcott's chat with Lady Evelyn had borne considerable fruit. He implies that, had it not taken place, neither Evelyn nor Pepys would ever have been heard of and, whereas this may be an exaggeration, one must pardon his pride at having been the indirect begetter of no less than two of the classics of English literature.

'Old Sylva' was the name by which Lady Evelyn remembered her husband's ancestor and, had the diary never been published, John Evelyn might have retained some small fame as the author of *Sylva, or a Discourse of Forest-trees*. Intended for estate-owners, this discursive book had considerable success in Evelyn's lifetime and was still being printed 150 years after his death. Apart from *Sylva*, Evelyn covered a wide range of subjects in his literary work but spread his ink a little too thin for lasting fame. He held a number of official posts in his lifetime but none of much consequence, and he achieved no success comparable with that of his socially inferior, but far more competent, acquaintance (Upcott was scarcely justified in calling him an intimate friend) Samuel Pepys. Evelyn's biographers generally describe him as a *virtuoso*, a species which the expansion of knowledge and pursuit of specialization have rendered almost extinct, and he would not have quarrelled with the description.

However, there is no need to speculate on Evelyn's place in history without his diary: the diary exists and his place is secure. For this, much of the credit is due, not only to Upcott, but to William Bray, an eighty-year-old solicitor who was entrusted by the family with the task of preparing some extracts of the diary for publication, with Upcott's help. Bray set about the work in his own way, not only deciding what should be included, but 'editing' his selections with a freedom which could only shock modern scholars. In doing so he produced what the greatest Evelyn scholar, Dr. E. S. de Beer, described, after chastising its editor as he deserved to be chastised, as 'one of the best-loved books of the nineteenth century', and which has for the most part been used in the extracts that follow.

Evelyn began keeping a diary, or at any rate notes for a diary, at a very early age. Hardly any of these notes have survived but when he was in his forties he used them to write up what purported to be a diary but was not one in the ordinary sense of the word. The process continued for a very long time, new notes being made all the while, and it was not until 1684 that the diary became a contemporary record, being continued as one until a few months before Evelyn's death in 1706. This explains the fact that, in his account of the two continental tours he made when still a young man, Evelyn includes descriptions taken from books which were not published until several years after his return. He also relied on books which he probably took with him, such as *Coryat's Crudities* for his account of Venice, and George Sandys's *Relation of a Journey* which we know Peter Mundy was reading at Verona (page

167). All travellers of the period who published notes on their journeys followed descriptions of monuments to a greater or less extent from those of earlier writers. There is therefore little worth reading in any of them. Evelyn's curiosity, on the other hand, was sufficiently wide-ranging to provide much of interest in his record of his own experiences, as opposed to descriptions of well-known objects.

John Evelyn was born in 1620, second of three sons of Richard Evelyn of Wotton in Surrey, a man of wealth and standing. On his mother's death in 1635, John went to live with her mother. After three years at Oxford he took a chamber in the Middle Temple, although he never studied law; he was under no necessity to earn his own living. At the beginning of 1640 his father became seriously ill and died at the end of the year. 'London, and especially the Court', wrote Evelyn, 'was at this period often in disorder, and great insolences were committed by the abused and too happy people.' The difficulties of Charles I were mounting; two Parliaments were dissolved and the Scots threatened invasion. In 1641 Evelyn was present at part of the trial of Lord Strafford and in May of that year he 'saw the fatal stroke on Tower Hill which severed the wisest head in England' from his shoulders. 'The ill and ominous face of the public at home' made Evelyn resolve to spend some time abroad and, as a first step, he 'procured a pass at the Custom-house.' In fact, according to a proclamation of 1635, a licence from a secretary of state was needed before anyone could travel abroad but the power seems to have been delegated; Peter Mundy had also found a 'Custom-house pass' sufficient in 1640.

Evelyn spent less than three months abroad, most of the time in the United Provinces, but also in the Spanish Netherlands; the United Provinces had been fighting the Spaniards since 1621 and it was to be another eight years before the Netherlands were to become united.

He set off on 15 July 1641 with 'one Mr Caryll and our servants' for Gravesend, to await the essential favourable wind. It was six days before it came so they embarked on 21 July. 'We were in a Dutch frigate bound for Flushing, convoyed and accompanied by five other stout vessels, whereof one was a man-of-war whose assistance we might have needed if the two ships we discovered making towards us at midnight had proved to be the enemy, which we apprehended.' However, they were only Norwegian merchant-men and by noon the next day 'with a fresh gale (which made it the most pleasant passage that could be wished)' they landed safely at Flushing.

The scene, as Evelyn wrote, had already 'infinitely changed' with the 'pretty and neat town' of Flushing and that evening they went on to Middelburg, 'another sweet town in this island of Walcheren', from whence they embarked for Dordrecht. But it was evidently not upon a boat, along the River Waal, that they 'embarked' from what follows.

'I may not forget that being insufferably tormented with the stitch in my side, caused through the impetuous motion of the wagon which, running very swiftly upon the paved causeways, gives a wonderful concussion to such as are unacquainted with that manner of travelling. The Foreman [*voerman*, carter or wagoner], perceiving me ready to drop from my seat, immediately cured and eased me of my pain by unbuttoning my doublet and applying a handful of couchgrass to my side, having gathered it from a ditch. We passed over many towns, houses and ruins of demolished suburbs which have formerly been swallowed up by the sea; at what time no less than eight of these islands have been irrecoverably lost.' A comparison of any old map of the Netherlands, such as those of the Blaeu family, with a modern one will confirm how the roads and waterways of the area have been changed by constant inundation.

Uncomfortable though they must have been, the wagons were fast. From Dordrecht Evelyn 'took wagon to Rotterdam, whither we were hurried in less than an hour, though it be ten miles distant, so furiously do these Foremen drive.' After a quick look at Rotterdam Evelyn went by canal-boat, through Delft, to The Hague and, 'by the like passage', to Leyden and Utrecht where there was a 'Kermas, or fair, the streets swarming with boors and rudeness'. Here Evelyn quickly satisfied his curiosity till his 'return and better leisure' and passed on to Nijmegen and Gennep which was being besieged by the Dutch in their war against Spain. Here he was received as a volunteer, and it is more than probable that the idea of obtaining some military experience was in his mind when he decided to leave England. It took Evelyn a very short time to realise how unsuited he was for camp life and he managed to extricate himself, so that by 13 August he was back in Rotterdam.

Turbulent though the times still were in Holland, the country had entered its golden age of painting and almost every Dutchman seemed to be either an artist or a patron of the arts. Evelyn explained why. 'We arrived late at Rotterdam where there was at that time their annual mart or fair, so furnished with pictures (especially landscapes and drolleries, as they call these clownish representations) that I was amazed. The reason of this store of pictures, and their cheapness, proceeds from their want of land to employ their stock, so that it is an ordinary thing to find a common farmer lay out two or three thousand pounds in this commodity. Their houses are full of them, and they vend them at their fairs to very great gains.'

When, a few days later, he found himself in Amsterdam, Evelyn soon 'went amongst the booksellers,' and modern collectors will read with envy how he 'went to Hondius's shop to buy some maps, greatly pleased with the designs of that indefatigable person.' 'Mr Bleaw [Blaeu],' he added, 'the setter forth of atlases and other works of that kind, is worthy seeing.'

39. 'I went to Hondius's shop to buy some maps'. Jocondus Hondius, founder of the firm, who died in 1612, shown here with his partner, Mercator, in an engraving from one of his atlases, of which a new edition was published by Henricus Hondius in 1641.

Evelyn was determined to return home through the Spanish Netherlands and did so, in spite of the difficulties. He was fascinated to find the wagons drawn by dogs, 'harnessed like so many coach-horses', and in Bruges he saw the *Waterhalle* and aqueduct that had so impressed Tafur two hundred years earlier. The usual delays occurred over the crossing to England, with a twelve-hour wait outside Dover harbour, but on 14 October he was able to write, 'I retired to my lodgings in the Middle Temple being about two in the morning.'

Six months later the Civil War broke out. Part of Evelyn's family were royalists, another part parliamentarians. Evelyn, a sincere churchman, sympathized with the King's cause but his nature was far from heroic and his short experience at Gennep was enough to discourage him from joining the King's army, even had he been willing to risk the consequences of being on the losing side. He decided to remove himself from the uncomfortable scene, and the King, evidently satisfied that he could manage without the young man's support, gave him a licence to travel again. On 6 November 1643 he left his home at Wotton for London; it was to be four years before he would return, to find the first Civil War over and the King a prisoner at Hampton Court.

'I arrived at London on the 7th and two days after took boat at the Tower-Wharf, which carried me as far as Sittingbourne, though not without danger, I being only in a pair of oars, exposed to a hideous storm: but it pleased God that we got in before the peril was considerable. From thence, I went by post to Dover, accompanied with one Mr Thicknesse, a very dear friend.'

There was nothing unusual in beginning the journey to Dover by water but it seems extraordinary to go down as far as Sittingbourne instead of taking to the road at, say, Gravesend or earlier. One would indeed wonder whether the hideous storm had blurred the traveller's memory were it not for the fact that some fifty years later Evelyn spelled out the details of his journey. He had set out, as an old man, to rewrite the transcription of his original notes and diary. In this revision, which he completed only as far as the year 1644, he substituted for the words 'we got in before the peril was considerable' the words 'we got into the Medway before the weather grew worse as soon after it did.' There can therefore be no doubt that these two men were rowed by a single oarsman down to Sheerness, into the River Medway and then the Swale, to land at Sittingbourne—all, it must be presumed, to avoid the perils of the

Dover Road. But there were still perils in store.

'On the 11th, having a reasonable good passage, though the weather was snowy and untoward enough, we came before Calais when, the master of our vessel mistaking the tide, we were fain to get into a shallop [probably a dinghy, rather than a sloop] which struck with no small danger on the sands, but at length we got off.

'Next day after dinner we took horse with the *messagers* [couriers who contracted to provide food, lodging and carriage] hoping to arrive that night at Boulogne; but there fell so great a snow, accompanied with hail, and a sudden darkness, that we had much ado to gain the next village; and in this passage, being obliged to cross a valley where a narrow causeway and a bridge were built over a small river, the rain that had fallen making it an impetuous stream for near a quarter of a mile, my horse slipping had almost been the occasion of my perishing. Conducted by the *messagers* we got to a miserable hovel, wet as we were, but we none of us went to bed. For the soldiers in those parts leaving little in the villages, we had with difficulty got ourselves dry between the fire and the fresh straw by the next morning. [This may have been a village called La Chaussée on the Boulogne road from Calais.] So we came early to Boulogne where we were willing to recover some repose, though to the loss of a day. Boulogne is a double town, one part situated on a steep rock, like the Downs by Dover and perhaps rent from thence by some earthquake ages since (as many think).'

Evelyn was at last on the road to Paris, and the rest of the journey, through Montreuil, Abbeville, Beauvais and St. Denis, was uneventful. In Paris he stayed at the *Hotel Ville de Venise*, known to the guide-books and described by several travellers between 1595 and 1687. He settled down for the whole winter and early spring with only the usual excursions to divert him.

'The summer now drawing near, and determining to pass the rest of it in some of the towns upon the Seine and Loire, on 19 April I took leave of Paris, we agreeing with the messenger [the *messager*, or courier] for our journey to Orleans. The way from Paris to this city (as indeed are most of the roads of France) is paved with a small, square sort of freestone, so that the country does not much molest the traveller with dust and dirt, as ours in England does. Only it is somewhat hard to the poor horses' feet, which causes them to ride more temperately, seldom going out of the trot, or *grand pas* as they call it (for here are few amblers) and seldom or never galloping, the saddles likewise hard and uneasy, rising high and heavy.'

40. 'We had a most delicious journey'. Detail from Melchior Tauernier's *Post roads of France, 1632*, showing Evelyn's journey from Orleans to Genoa.

The paved roads of France, and of some parts of Italy, as noted by Montaigne, were the envy of many English travellers. The first passenger coach service from London had begun in 1605 and stage coaches, started in 1637, were by 1643 extending to many areas. The effect on the roads, built, where they were built at all, for horse traffic, was deplorable and wheeled traffic was regarded by everyone except the relatively few who used it, as a thorough nuisance.

After Orleans Evelyn left the roads in favour of the River Loire. It must have been a delightful trip.

'On 28 April, taking a boat on the Loire, I went towards Blois, the passage and river being both very divertissant. Passing Mehun, we dined at Beaugency, thence to a little town called St. Dieu where we reposed that night. Thence quitting our bark we hired horses to carry us to Blois by the way of Chambord, a famous house of the King's. Blois is a town where the French spoken is the best in

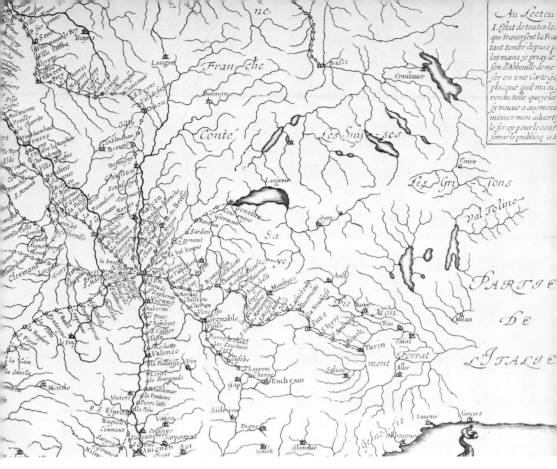

France; the inhabitants are very courteous and the pastures about the river rich and pleasant.

'The 2 May we took boat again, passing Chaumont, a proud castle on the left hand; before it a sweet island, deliciously shaded with tall trees. A little distance from hence at Amboise, we went on shore; this is a very agreeable village, built of stone and covered with blue slate, as all the towns generally are upon the Loire, but the castle was that which chiefly invited us. We entered by the drawbridge which has an invention to let one fall unhappily if not premonished.

'And now we came within sight of Tours where we were designed for the rest of the time I resolved to spend in France, the sojourn being so absolutely agreeable.'

Evelyn stayed in Tours, perfecting his French, for nineteen weeks and then, still with 'my friend Mr Thicknesse and our guide', 'went towards the more southern parts of France minding now to shape our course so as I might winter in Italy.' The journey continued to be enjoyable. They rode post to Lyons whence, 'we bargained with a waterman to transport us as far as Avignon upon the river and got the first night to Vienne. Here we lay and supped,

(183)

having (amongst other dainties) a dish of truffles, which is a certain earthnut, found out by a hog trained up to it and for which those creatures are sold at a great price. It is in truth an incomparable meat.

'The next morning we swam (for the river runs so exceeding rapid that we were only steered) to a small village called Thein, where we dined. After we had eaten we came to Valence, then, leaving our bark, we took horse and, lodging one night on the way, arrived by noon at Avignon. Entering the gates of this town the soldiers at the guard took our pistols and carbines from us and examined us very strictly; after that, having obtained the Governor's leave to tarry three days, we were civilly conducted to our lodging. We then took mules and a guide for Marseilles and the next morning came to Aix, having passed over that most dangerous and extremely rapid river of Durance. In this track all the heaths, or commons, are covered with rosemary, lavender, lentiscus and the like sweet shrubs for many miles together, which to me was a very pleasant sight. [All travellers had been impressed by this— and still are.]

'From hence we had a most delicious journey to Marseilles through a country sweetly declining to the south and Mediterranean coasts, full of vineyards and olive-yards, orange trees, myrtles, pomegranites and the like sweet plantations, to which belong innumerable pleasantly situated villas, built all of freestone and most of them in prospect showing as if they were so many heaps of snow dropped out of the clouds amongst those perennial greens.

'At Marseilles we bought umbrellas against the heat and consulted of our journey to Cannes by land, for fear of the Picaroon [pirate] Turks who make prize of many small vessels about these parts, finding never a galley bound for Genoa whither we were designed. So on 9 October we took our mules and proceeded on our way.

'On the 11th we lay at Cannes, which is a small port on the Mediterranean; here we agreed with a seaman to transport us to Genoa, so, having procured a bill of health (without which there is no admission to any town in Italy) we embarked on 12 October. Touching the islands of St. Margaret and St. Honoré, where we bought trifles offered us by the soldiers without going on land, we coasted within two leagues of Antibes, which is the utmost town of France. Thence by Nice, a city in Savoy, built all of brick, which gives it a very pleasant aspect towards the sea, we also sailed by

Morgus, now called Monaco [the principality had been called Morgues or Mourguez] having passed Villa Franca [Villefranche] where, arriving after the gates were shut, we were forced to abide in our bark all night, which was put in the haven, the wind coming contrary. In the morning we were hastened away, having no time permitted us (by our avaricious master, with whom we had made a bargain) to go up to see this strong and considerable place; it now belongs to a prince of the family of Grimaldi of Genoa, who has put both it and himself under protection of the French.

'Next we sailed by Menton and Ventimiglia, being the first city of the republic of Genoa, and supped at Oneglia where we anchored and lay on shore. The next morning we coasted in view of the Isle of Corsica, all whose rivage is incomparably furnished with evergreens, oranges, citrons and even date-trees. Then by Alassio, famous for the best coral fishing, which grows in abundance upon the rocks, deep and continuously covered by the sea. By Albenga and Finale, a very fair and strong town belonging to the King of Spain, for which reason a monsieur in our vessel was extremely afraid, as likewise the patron of our bark for they frequently catch French prizes as they creep by these shores to go into Italy; he therefore plied both sails and oars to get under the protection of a Genoese galley that passed not far before us and in whose company we sailed as far as the Cape of Savona; for all this coast (except a little at St. Remo) is a high and steep mountainous ground, consisting all of rock-marble, without any grass, tree or rivage, most terrible to look on.

'Here on the 15th, forsaking our galley, we encountered a little foul weather which made us creep terra, terra as they call it. But our patron, striving to double the point of Savona, making out into the wind, put us all into an incredible hazard; for blowing very hard from land betwixt those horrid gaps of the mountains, it set so violently as raised on a sudden an overgrown sea, so as we could not then by any means recover the weather-shore for many hours, insomuch that, what with the water already entered, and the confusion of fearful passengers, we were almost utterly abandoned to despair, our pilot himself giving us up for gone. But so it pleased God on the sudden, just as we were almost sinking down, right wearied with pumping and laving out the water, to appease the wind, and with much ado and great peril we recovered the shore, which we now kept within less than half a league in view and sight of those pleasant villas and fragrant orchards which are situated on this coast, full of princely retirements for the sumptuousness of their buildings, and nobleness of the plantations, especially those at St. Pietro d'Arena; from whence, the wind breathing as it did, might perfectly be smelt the peculiar joys of Italy in the perfumes of orange, citron and jasmin flowers, for divers leagues to seaward. October 16, we got to anchor under the Pharos, or watch-tower, erected on a high rock at the mouth of the Mole of Genoa.'

Undeterred by this alarming experience, Evelyn, after two days sight-seeing at Genoa, put to sea again, this time in a *felucca* bound for Leghorn. Another high sea made them put in at Porto Venere and take post-horses to Pisa, stopping for the night at Viareggio. At Pisa he duly visited the Campo Santo, 'made of divers galley ladings of earth brought formerly from Jerusalem which consumes dead bodies in the space of forty hours' (for Montaigne it had been eight hours swelling, eight hours subsiding and another eight for consumption to 'nothing but bare bones'). There was an hourly coach service between Pisa and Leghorn and Evelyn took advantage of this, arriving on 21 October. There was another coach service to Florence and, after five days there, he 'took horse for Siena' and was at last close to the principal object of his travels.

'I came to ROME on 4 November 1644 about 5 at night, and, being greatly perplexed for a convenient lodging, wandered up and down on horseback till one conducted us to one Monsieur Petit, a Frenchman who entertained strangers, being the very utmost house on the left hand as one ascends Monte Trinità near the Piazza di Spagna. Here I alighted, delivered my horse to the *vetturino*, and, having bargained with mine host for 20 crowns a month [£5:6:8d], I caused a good fire to be made in my chamber and so went to bed, being very wet.'

The very next morning Evelyn was out with his sights-man— 'for so they name certain persons in Rome who get their living only by leading strangers about to see the city.' He spent the next ten weeks seeing all the usual monuments and some sights which, since Montaigne had also recorded them, were evidently an accepted part of the tourist's round: a circumcision, the German cemetery where, also, the earth from Jerusalem had 'the virtue to consume a carcass in 24 hours', and an execution—'a Gent in his cloak and hat; for murder: they struck the malefactor with a club that first stunned him and then cut his throat.' Towards the end of January he set out for an excursion to Naples with a party which included 'two courtesans in man's apparel, who rode astride, booted, sworded and spurred, and whereof one was marvellous pretty'.

Naples had a far larger population than Rome at the time—

250,000 against 110,000—but there were no antiquities of any consequence to be seen, Tourists went for the beauty of its situation and the ever-attractive mysteries of Vesuvius, and the whole party duly ascended the volcano which had erupted in 1631 after a century of quiescence. Evelyn spent 'some whole hours' contemplating the 'stupendous curiosity which made the learned and inquisitive Pliny adventure his life and to lose it in too desperate an approach'. After a few days he returned to Rome and stayed there until 18 May when he 'took coach with two courteous Italian gentlemen.'

Evelyn was now bound for Padua and Venice and made his way by road to Bologna where he took to the water. He was towed along the River Reno, with many interruptions from sluices and locks, towards Ferrara, stopping to eat at 'an ugly inn called *Mal Albergo*, agreeable to its name'. The 'ill lodging', Fynes Moryson had called it.

'After we had supped we embarked and passed that night through the Fens, where we were so pestered with those flying glow-worms, called *Luccioli*, that one who had never heard of them would think the country full of sparks of fire, in so much as, beating some of them down and applying them to a book, I could read in the dark by the light they afforded.

'Quitting now our boat, we took coach and by morning got to Ferrara. We parted from hence about 3 in the afternoon and went some of our way on the canal and then embarked upon the Po, or Padus. We supped this night at a place called Corbola. After 3 miles we embarked in a stout vessel (having made 30 on the Po) and, through an artificial canal, very straight, entered the Adige which carried us by break of day into the Adriatic, and so sailing prosperously by Chioggia and Pellestrina we came over against Malamocco (the chief port and anchorage where our English merchantmen lie that trade to Venice) where we arrived at 7 at night after we had stayed at least two hours for permission to land. So soon as we came on shore we were conducted to the Dogana [on the site of the present Dogana del Mare which was not begun until 1677] where our portmanteaus were visited and we got to our lodging, which was the *Black Eagle* near the Rialto and one of the best quarters of the town. This journey from Rome to Venice cost me 7 pistoles and 13 julios [£6].

'The next morning, finding myself extremely weary and beaten with my journey, I went to one of their bagnios which are made, and treat, after the eastern manner, washing one with hot and cold water, with oils, rubbing with a kind of strigil [scraper] which a naked youth ['operator' in Bray's edition] puts on his hand, fetching off a world of dirt and stretching out one's limbs. This bath did so open my pores that it cost me one of the greatest colds that ever I had in my whole life, by reason of my coming out without that caution necessary of keeping myself warm for some time after. For I immediately began to visit the famous places of the city. And travellers that come into Italy do nothing else but run up and down to see the sights.

'The first thing I went to see of public building was the Rialto. It was evening and the Canal (which is their Hyde Park, where the Noblesse go to take the air) was full of ladies and gentlemen. There are many times very dangerous stops by reason of the multitude of gondolas ready to sink one another, and indeed they affect to lean them so on one side that one who is not accustomed to it would be afraid of oversetting. Here they were singing, playing on harpsicords and other music and serenading their mistresses. I went next day to their Exchange [Campo S. Giacomo di Rialto] but nothing so magnificent; from thence my guide had me to the Fondaco dei Tedeschi and here the merchants have their lodging, especially Germans; the outside of this stately fabric is painted by Giorgione del Castelfranco and Titian himself. Hence I passed through the Merceria, one of the most delicious streets in the world for the sweetness of it, being all the way on both sides continually tapestried as it were with cloth of gold, rich damasks and other silks, which the shops expose and hang before their houses from the first floor. To this add the perfumers' and apothecaries' shops, and the innumerable cages of nightingales which they keep, so as shutting your eyes you would imagine yourself in the country when indeed you are in the middle of the sea; besides, there being neither rattling of coaches nor trampling of horses, 'tis almost as silent as the field.'

It is a far more engaging description of the city than any that has gone before. The Fondaco dei Tedeschi of Felix Fabri's time had been burnt down in 1505 and its replacement had indeed been frescoed by Giorgione and Titian; their work must have been already fading when Evelyn saw it and within less than a century it was gone. The building was still the resort of Germans and one wonders whether the dog that barked at all but Germans (p. 64) had a successor.

After his share of running up and down to see the sights Evelyn

41. 'Fusina, being only an inn'. From G. F. Costa's *Delle Delicie del Fiume Brenta*.

decided to go to Padua to study anatomy and he paid his first visit there in June.

'The first terra firma we landed at was Fusina, being only an inn [familiar words] where we changed our barge and were then drawn up with horses through the River Brenta, a straight canal, as even as a line for 20 miles, the country on both sides deliciously planted with country villas and gentlemen's retirements, gardens planted with oranges, figs and other fruit. Observable in this passage was their buying water of those who farm the sluices, for this artificial river is in places so shallow that reserves of water are kept with sluices, which they open and shut with a most ingenious invention, or engine, so as to be governed even by a child. Thus they keep up the water or dismiss it, till the next channel be either filled by the stop or abated to the level of the other; for which every boat pays a certain duty.' After returning to Venice for a short spell, during which he found that the oysters of Murano were the first he had been able to eat in his life, Evelyn returned to Padua for the whole winter.

He was never certain of the date when he began the journey home but it was some time in April 1646. He travelled with friends to Milan where there was a little sight-seeing and there they arranged for a coach to carry them to the foot of the Alps, leaving it at Sesto Calende and crossing Lake Maggiore to the village of Mergozzo.

'In this wretched place I lay on a bed stuffed with leaves which made such a crackling, and did so prick my skin through the tick, that I could not sleep. The next morning I was furnished with an ass (for we could not get horses) but without stirrups, but we had ropes tied with a loop to put our feet in. At Duomo we exchanged our asses for mules, sure footed on the hills and precipices, and with a guide which now we hired, we were brought that night to a village called Vedra, being the last of the King of Spain's dominion in the Duchy of Milan, a very infamous wretched lodging.'

They had chosen to cross by the Simplon, the most dangerous of the passes in ordinary use, over which a post-service had only recently been established. The weather was bad; they were concerned at the risk of assault by bears and wolves, and they 'frequently alighted, freezing in the snow and anon frying by the reverberation of the sun against the cliffs' when they began a descent. To add to their discomforts, a 'water spaniel, a huge filthy cur who had followed' one of Evelyn's companions out of England hunted a herd of goats and, when they tried to leave their inn the following morning, they were surrounded by Swiss peasants demanding compensation. Rather than 'expostulate it among such brutes' they laid down the money and now began the major ascent, over ground which was said to 'have been covered with snow since the Creation, for that never man remembered it to be without'. The horse carrying their baggage 'slid down a fearful precipice' but was reached lower down and the rest of the journey to Brig was completed on foot. They now followed the easy valley of the Rhone for the seventy miles to the Lake of Geneva and, almost at the end of this journey, arrived at Le Bouveret.

'Here, being extremely weary and complaining of my head, and little accommodation in the house, I caused one of our hostess's daughters to be removed out of her bed and went immediately into it, whilst it was yet warm, being so heavy with pain and drowsiness that I would not stay to have the sheets changed; but I shortly after paid dearly for my impatience, falling sick of the smallpox so soon as I came to Geneva, for, by the smell of frankincense and the tale the good woman told me of her daughter having had an ague, I afterwards concluded she had been newly recovered of the smallpox. Notwithstanding this, I went with my company the next day, hiring a bark to carry us over the lake, and indeed, sick as I was, the weather was so serene and bright, the water so calm and air temperate, that never had travellers a sweeter passage.'

Evelyn went straight to bed and stayed in Geneva until July to recuperate. When he was fully recovered he moved on to Paris where he stayed for a year. On 22 May 1647 he was robbed of clothes and plate by his valet and he tells the sequel in three touching entries.

'Through the diligence of Sir Richard Browne, His Majesty's Resident at the Court of France, and with whose lady and family I had contracted a great friendship (and particularly set my affections on a daughter) I recovered most of them.

'10 June: We concluded about my marriage, in order to which I went to St. Germain, where his Majesty, then Prince of Wales, had his court [the future Charles II had been in France for the past year] to desire of Dr. Earle, then one of his chaplains, to come with me to Paris.

'So, on Thursday 27 June 1647, the Doctor married us in Sir Richard Browne's chapel, some few select friends being present. And this being Corpus Christus feast, the streets were sumptuously hung with tapestry and strewn with flowers.'

Mary Browne, now Mary Evelyn, was twelve years old at the time. After a few weeks her husband at long last returned to England, leaving her with her parents. He stayed there until after the execution of Charles I in January 1649. A few months later he went back to Paris, returning to England in 1652.

Evelyn then succeeded in obtaining possession of his father-in-law's house, Sayes Court, Deptford, which had been sequestered and sold by the parliamentarians. His wife and her mother joined him there and it remained his home for forty years.

22

Bulstrode Whitelocke

'I shall surprise you with something'

London to Uppsala, Stockholm and Hamburg, 1653–4

(Map on p. 44)

By no means an heroic man in temperament, Bulstrode Whitelocke found himself on a journey of heroic proportions at the age of forty-eight, and he accomplished his task with perhaps more honour than attended most of his career. Born in 1605, a lawyer and the son of a lawyer, he spent many years in Parliament and played a leading part in the impeachment of the Earl of Strafford in 1640; in this affair he was chairman of a committee which included some of the most influential men in the country. By 1648 he was sufficiently regarded as a supporter of Oliver Cromwell to be named as a member of the committee to draw up the charges against Charles I. He found it convenient, wisely as events turned out, to stay out of the way while the committee was sitting and never attended. He held high office under Cromwell, becoming one of the four Commissioners of the Great Seal, and in 1653 he was persuaded by Cromwell, in spite of a genuine reluctance on his part, to become the first ambassador to be appointed by the Commonwealth.

Whitelocke's reluctance to accept the post was due partly to his age and to the fact that his third wife was on the point of presenting him with his twelfth child; it was not lessened by a suspicion that Cromwell might have a course of action in mind for which he would prefer Whitelocke's absence from England (and this suspicion proved justified in the event). The embassy which Whitelocke finally agreed to accept was to the twenty-seven-year old Queen Christina of Sweden whose father, Gustavus II, had made their country the most powerful, and the most mistrusted, of the northern powers. Whitelocke's task was to conclude an alliance with Sweden to the disadvantage of Denmark and of the Dutch who had for a year been at war with England. These two countries controlled the Sound, between Denmark and what is now the southern tip of Sweden, and it was hoped that passage through this vital channel would be made free to all as a result of Whitelocke's efforts. He was not successful in this part of his charge (the Swedes proved to be already suffering much less than the English from the restrictions) but he did conclude a commercial treaty and both Whitelocke and Cromwell seem to have been well satisfied with the outcome. Meanwhile Cromwell had dismissed Parliament and assumed supreme power, an act which troubled Whitelocke in distant Sweden but which he accepted on his return. Cromwell's plans may well have been laid when he sent Whitelocke out of the country and it has even been suggested that Whitelock himself knew of them and again chose to stay out of the way; his journal certainly does not give any support to this view but the fact that it could be suggested at all is some indication of the repute in which he was held.

Whitelocke was a prolific writer and seems never to have thrown away a letter, legal document or page of his many diaries. Much of his archive was burnt or destroyed by others, but much survived; perhaps, indeed, too much, to judge by the seven volumes of his *Annals* which were published soon after his death. This led to Carlyle calling him 'Dry-as-dust' and dismissing him as dull.

Carlyle can scarcely have read the *Journal of the Swedish Embassy* which was published in one volume in 1772 and again, in two volumes, in 1855. Everything that Whitelocke wrote about his extraordinary journey, and he recorded each day's events as they occurred, has a freshness and narrative skill at strange variance with the verbosity of his speeches and letters. The pages that follow represent less than a tenth of the *Journal* as published and follow the orthography of the 1855 edition with occasional corrections from the original manuscript as transcribed by Miss Ruth Spalding in *The Improbable Puritan* (London, 1975). Whitelocke wrote both his diaries and the present *Journal* in the third person; this is here transposed to the first person.

Much of the first hundred pages of Whitelocke's published *Journal* consist of verbatim accounts of discussions with his wife, friends and Cromwell himself as to the advisability of his going to Sweden. His wife, Mary, distrusted Cromwell and did her utmost to dissuade him: two others sent on missions abroad had been murdered and Cromwell might 'take this occasion to lay' her husband aside, that he 'might be no hindrance to his further designs.' William Cooke, a former servant and now tenant farmer on Whitelocke's family estate, was also consulted and suggested there might be as much danger in refusing as accepting the offer. 'What can he do to me?' asked Whitelocke, 'I am not under his command.' 'What can he not do!' replied Cooke. 'Don't we all see he does what he list? It is an easy thing to find a staff to beat a dog.' Three days later Cromwell himself uttered a veiled warning. 'If you should decline it,' he said, 'the Commonwealth would suffer extremely by it, your own profession perhaps might suffer likewise. Indeed, you cannot be excused.' This was final, and Whitelocke began his preparations. He demanded £1,500 a month, an enormous sum in terms of travelling costs noted earlier in these pages, but he was determined to travel in state and Cromwell's own words had been that Queen Christina 'stands much upon ceremonies.' Whitelocke therefore chose a retinue of 'about one hundred persons', including two chaplains, a physician and an apothecary, a clerk of the stable and sewer and a second sewer (these were 'seaters', responsible for arranging the table and tasting the dishes). Eleven 'gentlemen admitted to his table' included two of Whitelocke's sons, and these gentlemen 'had of their servants about twenty-five, and all their lackeys in Whitelocke's livery'. There were four cooks, a barber, two 'trumpets' in addition to two others 'chiefly for music', and 'for the laundry' there were three women.

Whitelocke was granted £1,000 a month instead of the £1,500 he hoped for but his ceremonial coach was provided and a single extra payment of £500. 'I know your allowance is but small,' said Cromwell at their final dinner; 'I wish it had been more, yet, if I live, I will see that you shall be no loser by this employment.' Two merchant ships were hired for baggage, provisions and horses, and two frigates were placed at Whitelocke's disposal. At the last moment Mary Whitelocke became hysterical and threatened that he might well find her 'gone out of this vale of tears' when he returned—if he returned.

'With that word, floods of tears stopped her further speaking and the company called upon me to hasten away, telling me the wind and tide would stay for no man; that all was ready and they now stayed only for me: I was therefore forced to break away.'

He went to the Tower wharf and boarded one of the state barges which took him to the *Phoenix* frigate in which he sailed down to Gravesend. He then did something rather touching.

'Two of my ships not being yet fallen down, I returned to London and had a dark and dangerous passage. I came about eight o'clock at night to my brother's house to see my sad wife once more, and to comfort her, who was much surprised and pleased. I kept my return as private as I could, that the Council might not have notice of it. My wife was now in less passion than before but tears again concluded our discourse, nor was I without my share of anxiety.'

Whitelocke returned to Gravesend on the afternoon of 5 November 1653 and from now on tells of his Swedish Embassy in his own words.

6 November 1653. The Lord's Day. The wind was fair and all things ready, and no opportunity must be lost; therefore about two hours before high water, I ordered all my people to go on board. I then desired Captain Foster to send for the captains and officers of the other ships and spake to them to this effect:

'Having been entrusted by the Council of State with the command of these ships, I take the liberty to tell you that I expect the same obedience to orders as if your generals gave them; but withal, I shall let you know that my commands will not be rigid or supercilious, but with love and kindness, as to my countrymen, friends and fellow-seamen.

'I confess to my want of knowledge of sea affairs, yet this is not my first voyage, and I shall be glad to have my lack of experience supplied by yours, and be willing to be informed by the meanest mariner; and shall give a due regard to the advice of you who are officers, and of so much ability and experience as you have.

'Our voyage, my noble countrymen, is not like to be without dangers. The perils of this season, of storms and tempests, are no strangers to you; no more are those of our enemies, the Dutch and Danes. I shall freely adventure my life with you and pray that God will bring us back again in safety to our native country.'

I then led the officers into my cabin and gave them my orders. I gave orders about the sailing of the ships, their firing and the like; prayers to be constantly twice a day; none to take tobacco but behind the mainmast, where a tub of water was set to blow their coals into it, and to prevent the danger of fire; divers other orders for regulating the seamen.

By the evening we had sailed as far as the buoy in the Nore in the Thames mouth; here the wind chopped about to the north so that I caused them there to let fall their anchors. God was pleased to commend my stay here, to make me partaker of a great mercy, the earlier notice of my wife's being brought to bed who, the same day that her husband set sail to go from her, was delivered of a son: a hard time to be hurried away from her. Her friends had procured two bold watermen to undertake to carry letters of this good news, hoping to overtake us; they rowed all night by the shore side till they came over against the ships, but, by reason of the roughness of the water, could not come to them with their wherry; therefore the watermen made fires on the shore, the custom of giving notice that an express was come: the mariners, used to such fires, sent out a boat and fetched the watermen on board. I acknowledged that God was pleased to cause the wind to change whereby I was forced to stay my course that night, otherwise I had gone too far for the watermen to have come with the letters, and I could not have heard the news for a month afterwards. Moreover, as soon as I had written answers to these letters and rewarded the watermen, the wind instantly came about again. Whereupon we weighed anchor and bade adieu to the coast of England.

8 November. The wind blew high and the night was very tempestuous; yet I slept soundly until about midnight. Notwithstanding the hindrances [one of the ships being towed had broken away] and the foul weather, we ran a course this night of about thirty leagues.

By sunrising we espied some sails afar off. I spread all my sails to fetch them up. When I came within distance I fired to warn them to strike sail. One struck, but while my boat was hoisting out to fetch the Dutch skipper on board to me, the wind changed, he hoisted his sails and got clear away. The other made away as fast as she could but I overtook her and shot through her tackle; seeing which torn, and that I was in earnest, the Dutchman came to leeward and struck. The Dutch skipper was brought on board and I examined him.

w. Skipper, whence art thou?
s. A Flushinger.
w. What brought you to sea this weather?
s. My trade; though the weather be foul, we must fish, or our wives and children must starve.
w. What right have you to fish in these seas?
s. I thought anyone might fish in the broad sea.
w. Not without leave of those who have the dominion of those seas.

s. I know not who have the dominion of the sea, but they who have the best fleet. I have been thirty years a fisherman and never yet asked leave.

w. Though you never asked leave to fish on the seas of our Commonwealth, your predecessors have.

s. My father and grandfather were fishers on these seas but I never heard them say they asked leave.

w. It may be so but others have.

s. I must not contradict you.

w. Thou mayest freely speak to me.

s. No, I thank you; I know to whom I speak. I think you are the English Ambassador for Sweden.

w. What do they say in your country of my going to Sweden?

s. Our lords don't like it but their subjects think you do wisely to get the Swedes for friends.

w. We must seek new friends when our old ones forsake us and make war upon us as your lords do.

s. We poor men give our lords no thanks for it; it is their pleasure but they are sufficiently cursed for it.

w. God says you must not speak evil of your rulers.

s. And God says our rulers must not do evil.

w. God will punish them if they do evil.

s. And man will punish them also; I am sure you have done it.

w. And what did you do when you revolted from your king?

s. These things are too high for me; I will not speak of them. But I may tink [Whitelocke's spelling].

w. What do your people say of the English Ambassador? Tell me truly.

s. They say he is a very honest gentleman, and a fit man for such a business, and one that loves peace and is likely to do his work.

w. Now I see you know to whom you speak.

s. I should say the same behind your back, for I have often heard it said by others.

w. It seems then that your people are not pleased with the war against England.

s. They are much displeased at it and their losses by it are very great and our trade decays; so that it will be the wisest way for our lords to make a peace with you; if they do not, few will fight for them in this quarrel.

w. My masters have not been backward for a peace with you.

s Our lords understand not the business so well as you.

w. Prithee tell me what convoys you have abroad this way?

s. Three or four of our men-of-war lie not far off, which were sent to guard us, and you see how well they do it.

w. Why do they not keep nearer to you?

s. They have no great mind to come near you where they know they can get nothing but blows.

w. But their duty and honour bind them to guard you.

s. Honour and duty will buy no butter; and they hold it no duty of theirs to hazard themselves and their ships against you.

w. Why did you not come in sooner to me, but stood out so many shots?

s. Because I hoped to have got away from you; my ship was never before outsailed.

w. Well, Skipper, thou seemest to be an honest man, and thou sayest thou hast a wife and seven children; therefore I shall do more for thee than thou expectest. Thou shalt have thy ship again. Captain Foster, give order that the ship be restored to the poor man.

s. What did you say, Sir? Shall I have my ship and all my goods again too?

w. Thou shalt have them all again: thou mayest be sure of it.

s. What, have all again, when I expected not a pennyworth of them? Now I pray God bless thee and bless the business thou goest about. There never was such an ambassador upon these seas.

The skipper went away a joyful man and had his ship and all his goods to a pennyworth; and in token of his thankfulness he sent back by my men a Holland cheese and a great bottle of brandy-wine for a present to me. But I, believing the poor man to have more need of it than myself, and being no lover of that meat or drink, sent them back again with hearty thanks to the skipper for his love.

Most of my men were very sea-sick. The wind came into the north-east so that I could make no way in my course, but was forced to steer back towards the coast of England.

9 November. All last night the sea continued extreme rough so that the ships, especially the merchantmen, were in great danger of being foundered in the sea. By the advice of the officers I ordered to direct our course to Yarmouth for fear of being driven upon the coast of Holland; then the wind veered to west-south-west whereupon we stood on again in our course for Gothenburg. From four o'clock in the afternoon the wind blew large and fair and we began to come somewhat near to the Continent, towards the coast of Denmark. [Five days of storm, calm, adverse and favourable wind followed, with much seasickness, and a momentary running aground off Jutland Head.]

14 November. The Lord was pleased to preserve me and my company from immediate dangers of the sands and, hoping that we were near the coast, I promised a bottle of sack to the mariner who should first descry land, which carried many of them to the topgallant. About eight o'clock in the morning there were so many descriers of land that all my bottles would not suffice to keep my word. About nine o'clock I saw land myself, being the coast of Jutland in Denmark. With this good news I went to the sick people to comfort them; I drolled with them and cheered them the best way I could as having now but a little while longer to be in their sick cabins and with their bad entertainment.

About three in the afternoon we came to the head of the Skaw and I cast anchor. I then learnt that one of my ships had chased a Dutch ship and taken her; from her skipper they understood that the late great storm drove eighteen of the Dutch men-of-war on shore and split most of them and that four thousand dead carcasses of their men floated to the Holland shore.

15 November. After I had cast anchor, within two hours the wind grew to a very raging storm but about midnight it began to cease and blow fair for Gothenburg. I cheered my company and had got much into their affection by my kindness and familiarity and by being much on the decks, and drolling with them, especially by affording them now and then a douse in the neck or a kick in jest, seeing them play, and then giving them some of my own tobacco and wine and strong waters, which demeanours please those kind of people. The wind being fair and large I hasted and came by twelve o'clock noon in safety to the port of Gothenburg.

I sent some of my people who spoke Dutch to salute the Governor and let him know that I was come thither Ambassador from England to the Queen of Sweden. He replied that he was glad of my safe arrival, and if I pleased to come to the town the next day he would send boats to attend me and be ready to give me entertainment with all due respect. I was earnestly entreated by my people to go on shore that night, and to dispense with the ceremonies, and I yielded to their request. As we passed by, the castle saluted me with two guns and no more whereof I, enquiring the reason, was informed that their constant custom was to give but two guns on any occasion, which they call a Swede's leasing, for saving of powder.

16 November. About nine o'clock came an officer from the magistrates of the city to know if I were at leisure to give them leave to wait upon me and was answered that they should be welcome. The ceremonies duly took place, the speeches made in Latin. My trunks and goods could not be brought on shore by reason of the ill weather. In the evening about twenty men and boys, with lanterns and candles, came to my lodging and sang in parts, with indifferent good skill and voices.

17 November. The rest of my goods were brought on shore to the town, being but three miles from the ship, and my horses were lifted on shore; and, which was wondered at, after so long and tempestuous a voyage, not one of the thirty-two horses was spoiled, lame or hurt. I intended to have the provisions sent by sea to Stockholm but, by advice of the magistrates that, the frost being come, if it should hold, the goods could not be brought by sea to Stockholm till next spring, I ordered them also to be brought on shore.

The house where I lay was a common *cruise*, or inn, greatly inferior to our ordinary inns in England. The house was meanly furnished—not any hangings or wainscot, but bare walls in the best chambers. I found the stoves close and suffocating and not so sweet as the chimneys; these are built high and are broad and sloping on either side; where the tunnel grows narrow is set a plate of iron so as the chimney may be shut or opened by a string on the outside. When the fire is burnt to coals, and no smoke left, they thrust the iron plate in across the tunnel so that no air can come down nor heat ascend, but strikes the heat out into the room, which much increaseth the warmth. Their provision of diet is plentiful enough but of no great variety; their beef and mutton is very lean in the winter, which was now begun, but it was made the better by my cook's dressing of it; and the best entertainment that I found was what I brought with me—good English beer, butter, cheese, baked meats, Spanish and French wine and divers good provisions.

[The Queen had left Stockholm because of the plague and Whitelocke was still in Göteborg on 27 November.]

I began to grow weary of my stay in this place and being now certainly informed that the Queen was at Uppsala, and purposed to reside there all this winter, I resolved to begin my journey from hence the next Wednesday.

30 November. Early in the morning were come to my door a hundred waggons out of the country; they were with four wheels, very small, and drawn by one horse apiece, or by two cows abreast. They will not hold above one large trunk, or two little ones; they drive slowly, and the more slowly because many of their waggoners be women. There were also brought in by the country a hundred saddle-horses, which are small, hard trotters. As soon as the waggons were loaded I appointed them to be sent away, with some of the servants to attend them whom I ordered to be constantly with them, and the gentlemen of my horse to bring up the rear of this train. My quartermaster, cooks and butlers were sent before to make provision at the *dorf* where I intended to lodge this night.

This company being gone it was time to get on horseback. I mounted my best horse, of excellent shape and mettle; my other horse, being also very beautiful, and with a rich saddle and pistols, was led leer [in hand]: the rest of my English horses were mounted by my gentlemen, as many as there were horses for; the rest of my gentlemen and people rode upon the Swedish horses and all had swords and pistols.

After the horsemen came my travelling-coach, being of blue velvet and richly gilded; it would hold eight persons and was drawn by six bay English horses, very handsome; and two more of the same set of coach-horses were led by leer for a supply if there should be an occasion. In this coach I ordered Mr. Ingelo to ride, being sickly, and Colonel Potley, who was too unwieldy to ride on horseback.

Last of all came the best coach, of crimson velvet, very richly embroidered with silk, and gilded, which cost above £400; it was large enough to hold ten persons. It was drawn by six black English horses. This coach I ordered to be drawn empty, and in the way they covered it. With the coaches went the grooms who did not wait on my person, and my lackeys went by my horse's side.

The citizens drew up in several divisions in the market-place and, as I rode through them, they saluted me with great civility and with loud volleys of their shot. From the bulwarks the cannoneers bade me adieu with discharging all their great guns; and some of their complimental bullets came very near to me as I rode but, I supposed, not directed at me.

When I was come about an English mile from Gothenburg, the Governor and other officers took their leave of me, and they parted with many compliments. After these gentlemen were gone, I took to my coach for travel. The way was rough and stony and in some places were deep precipices from the rocks; the bridges and roads had been newly repaired, by the Queen's commands to the governors through whose precincts I was to pass. The country is very stony, uneven and barren.

When we were come one Swedish mile [seven English miles] which is a stage, there were fresh horses and waggons ready, summoned by warrants. When we had changed our horses and waggons we went on our journey and travelled this day about fourteen English miles; and was a great journey at this time of the year, the days being but about four hours in length of daylight. I came not to my quarters till above an hour after it was dark and my waggons two hours after me. My lodging was taken up at a little *dorf*, or village, which was very mean; myself lay in my field-bed, most of my people in straw. The meat was not good, the beer worse—exceeding strong and thick; our best refreshment was lusty fires and our own cheerfulness which I increased what I could.

Mr. Berkman [he had come from England with Whitelocke and been to Uppsala to see the Queen] made great speed to return from the Court to meet me and to conduct me to the Queen according to her commands. He told me that as soon as he came to the Court he was admitted to her presence, who longed to discourse with him about the English Ambassador. She thought herself much honoured by the Parliament of England sending such an ambassador to her. She had heard much commendation of his quality and favour with the General Cromwell and she took it kindly from me to undertake such a long and dangerous voyage to see her; she was only sorry she could not receive me at Uppsala with that respect which she intended, and as at Stockholm where she could have given me better entertainment; but wheresoever she was, she said, the Ambassador should be welcome to her.

1 December. There being much trouble in the taking of horses and the unloading and loading of waggons and payment of the boors at every stage, I entreated Mr. Berkman and the Syndic of Gothenburg to take upon them the care of that business, and to appoint some Swede to see to it, which they readily undertook and thereby saved me much trouble.

2 December. Our quarter this night was at a *dorf* called Shifda, their provisions here little else but lean beef, boiled roasted, broiled and stewed; it was whispered this beef was of a rotten cow that died in a ditch. I charged them not to speak of it, and to those who knew it not it went down savoury to good stomachs in cold weather after a long journey; I ate of it as well as the rest and made mirth of it afterwards.

3 December. We had a very long journey of above twenty English miles, and daylight very short. The weather was extreme cold, and hard frosts so that one of my pages did break his arm, as seldom any in the frosty weather had a fall without the breach of some limb. The quarter this night was extreme bad, and more beef (suspected of kin to the last); and whether that diet, or the hard and cold journey might occasion it, I was exceeding ill and feverish but took something that did me good.

4 December. Dr. Whistler's man, with a fall from his horse, broke his leg. The doctor saw it well set by the apothecary and I offered to leave the apothecary and a servant to attend to him if he would stay till he were well again to travel. But the man would by no means be persuaded to stay behind in this strange country, but chose rather to endure the greatest pain to go along with the company. Whereupon the doctor directed a carriage to be made of deal boards, in the fashion of a horse-litter, and the man was laid upon a bed and straw in this litter, which was carried between two horses, and in this posture the poor man, in great torment, was carried above three hundred miles and recovered very well.

7 December. This day's journey was about thirty-five English miles; the country marvelled at so long a journey taken by strangers when the days were so short and the company so great. We met with one extreme bad piece of way on the side of a rock cut out by men's hands, not two foot broader than the track of my coach: on the right hand was nothing but craggy huge rocks hanging over us, and on the left was a steep precipice, fifty or sixty fathoms down to the lake which was at the foot of it. I caused my people to alight and walk on foot, leading their horses till they were past it. Had not my coachman and postilions been their art's masters, and of mettle, they could hardly have been able to drive a coach that way.

(203)

9 December. About half a mile before the end of this day's journey, came a gentleman of the Queen's chamber, well habited and fashioned, who spoke French to the effect that he was sent by the Queen to inquire of my health in this journey and to attend me to Uppsala and to take care that I should want no accommodations in my journey. Also that Prince Adolphus presented his service to me with letters which I opened and read.

10 December. I invited the Queen's gentleman to take a room in my coach but he excused it and rode on horseback. One of my gentlemen received a dangerous hurt in his forehead, by the kick of a horse, to the great danger of breaking his skull. I saw him dressed with medicaments out of my own cabinet. Here [Orebro] I received the first packet of letters from England, about five weeks after the date of the letters.

12 December. This day's journey was to a place called Fitzborough where was a very bad quarter; and it was a hard duty, after long travel upon such horses and furniture as is before described, in bitter cold weather, and for the most part in the night-time, the days being not above four hours long, to come to bad diet and a bed of straw; but we were contented because better could not be had in those places.

Upon the way there fell out a kind of mutiny among my people; some of them, tired and sore with their hard horses and saddles, grumbled at their bad accommodations. To appease them I alighted from my coach, caused the gentleman who first began the disturbance to alight and go in my place into my coach and I mounted on the Swedish horse and rode along with the rest of my company, drolling and partaking in their hardships, which gave more satisfaction than severity at such a time would have done.

[They continued thus until 20 December, each day becoming icier and shorter, but until now the snow had held off. Approaching Uppsala it began to fall in great abundance. The Queen's representatives met Whitelocke and his company with her own carriages, two senators, and her master of ceremonies; Whitelocke transferred to the Queen's carriage.]

The coach was of green velvet inside and outside, richly laced with broad silver laces and fringed; the horses studded and gilded. Six handsome white horses drew it and about twenty of the Queen's lackeys in trunk-hose of yellow attended it. There were in all eighteen coaches with six horses apiece and about six other

42. 'In this equipage they brought me to Uppsala'. The Queen's castle at Uppsala. Engraving by Willem Swidde, published in 1690, after a drawing by Erik Dahlberg (1625-1703).

coaches, with many of the Queen's gentlemen on horseback.

In this equipage they brought me to Uppsala, multitudes of people by the way, and through the town they brought me to a fair brick house provided and furnished by the Queen; none besides the Queen's castle a fairer house than this was.

[After a series of ceremonial dinners (at which Whitelocke's known disapproval of the drinking of healths was respected), he was received in public audience by the Queen.]

23 December. The master of the ceremonies and two of the senators came to my lodging with two of the Queen's rich coaches and about twelve of her lackeys to conduct me to my audience. At my gate stood my porter in a gown laced with blue velvet between edges of gold and silver lace. The liveries of my coachmen and postilions were buff doublets laced with the same lace, also of my twelve lackeys. My four pages wore blue satin doublets, the cloaks up to the cape, and lined with blue plush, their long stockings of blue silk. My two trumpets in the like liveries. My gentlemen were nobly and richly habited and spared for no cost. I myself was plain, but extraordinarily rich in my habit, my suit of English cloth of an exceedingly fine sort set with very fair rich diamond buttons: my hatband of diamonds answerable [suitable]; and all of the value of £1,000.

[The company was received in the courtyard of the castle, conducted into the presence of many notabilities and eventually into that of the Queen herself.]

I perceived the Queen sitting upon her chair of state of crimson velvet, with a canopy of the same over it. As soon as I came within the room I put off my hat, and then the Queen put off her cap, after the fashion of men, and came two or three steps forward. This, and her being covered and rising from her seat, caused me to know her to be the Queen, which otherwise had not been easy to be discerned, her habit being of plain grey stuff; her petticoat reached to the ground, over that a jacket such as men wear, of the same stuff, reaching to her knees, no gorget [ornamental collar] or band, but a black scarf about her neck, tied before with a black ribbon, as soldiers and mariners sometimes use to wear; her hair was braided and hung loose upon her head; she wore a black velvet cap lined with sables, and turned up after the fashion of the country, which she used to put off and on as men do their hats.

Her countenance was sprightly, but somewhat pale; she had much of majesty in her demeanour, and though her person were of the smaller size, yet her mien and carriage was very noble.

[Speeches were made.]

The Queen was very attentive whilst I spake, and coming up close to me, by her looks and gestures (as was supposed) would have daunted me; but those who have been conversant in the late great affairs in England are not so soon as others appalled with the presence of a young lady and her servants.

[At the end of the ceremonies] I took my leave and was conducted back to my lodgings with more ceremonies. The Marshal and senators supped with me and they excused their not beginning an health to me and my superiors because they understood my judgment to be against it. I acknowledged my judgment to be so and thanked them for their civility of not offering what was so contrary to it.

After a long supper, which was the less tedious because the Queen's music played and sang excellently well all the time of it, they took their leave of me.

[Whitelocke now made a series of visits to other ambassadors and was advised by the Spanish envoy to request private audiences with the Queen, rather than going through the Secretary of State. On 26 December he procured such an audience and even the Queen's favourite, Count Tott, left them alone together behind closed doors. They discussed the possibility of an alliance between their two countries, the situation in England, and the state of the war between England and the Dutch.]

This audience lasted above two hours, not any person coming in or knocking all that time. We stood and walked up and down the room all the while, which made me very weary, being lame; yet at the time of a discourse with such a Princess, and upon such high matters (like a wounded man when he is hot) I felt not the pain, but felt it afterwards.

[Whitelocke had another private audience on 29 December and discussed which countries should be included or excluded from an alliance. The Queen enjoined Whitelocke to acquaint nobody with their discourse 'but only General Cromwell, whose word I shall rely on', nor was he to speak of it to any of her own ministers. They then turned from State matters.]

QUEEN. Have you not heard in England that I was to marry the King of Scots? [Charles II, in exile in the Netherlands; he had been crowned King of Scots after the execution of Charles I].

WHITELOCKE. It has been reported so in England, and that letters have passed between your Majesty and him for that purpose.

Q. I confess that letters have passed between us; but this I will assure you, that I will not marry that King; he is a young man [twenty-three; four years younger than Christina], and in a condition sad enough; though I respect him very much, yet I shall never marry him, you may be well assured. But I shall tell you under secrecy that he lately sent a letter to the Prince Palatine, my cousin [the Elector Charles Louis] and with it the order of the Garter; but the messenger had the wit to bring it first to me and when I saw it, and had read the letter, I threw it on the fire and would not suffer the George [the order of the Garter] to be delivered to my cousin.

W. Your Majesty did very judiciously. I met in your Court one of my countrymen, no friend to our Commonwealth, whom I suspect might be the messenger.

Q. Who was that?

W. Sir William Balendine [a Scottish royalist].

Q. He was indeed the messenger; but do not communicate this to any but your General.

[Next day Whitelocke had another audience with the Queen

who, he was beginning to learn, was apt suddenly to change the subject of discussion. Whitelocke had been giving her a dissertation on religion.]

Q. How do you contrive to write to your superiors in case your letters should be intercepted? Do you write by ciphers? [She had offered to send his letters to London by her own messenger, which he had naturally refused.]

w. That is a way that may easily be unciphered. I write to my General by such a way as no flesh can ever find out but by agreement beforehand.

Q. How is that, I pray?

w. I leave with my General two glasses of water which I make: with one of the waters I write my letters, having two like glasses of water myself. The letter thus written no man can possibly read, but wash over this letter with the water in the other glass, and it turns to black, just as if it had been written with ink.

Q. That is a curious way indeed; and have you these waters here?

w. Yes, Madam, I make them myself so that no creature can read his or my letters without them.

Q. What huge dog is this?

w. It is an English mastiff which I brought with me and it seems is broke loose and followed me even to this place.

Q. Is it your dog?

w. I cannot tell; some of my people told me that one Mr Peter sent it for a present to the Queen. [Hugh Peter, executed after the Restoration, was Chaplain to the Council of State.]

Q. Who is that Mr. Peter?

w. A minister and a great servant to the Parliament.

Q. That Mr. Peter sent me a letter.

w. He is a great admirer of your Majesty; but to presume to send a letter or a dog for a present to a Queen, I thought above him.

Q I have many letters from private persons. His letter and the dog do belong to me and I will have them.

w. Your Majesty commands in chief and I will obey you, not only as to the letter and dog, but likewise as to another part of his present, a great English cheese of his country making.

Q. I do kindly accept them from him, and see that you send my goods to me.

And so we parted in much drollery. On 5 January I had a private audience above two hours together. The Queen was pleased first to discourse of private matters.

Q. Hath your General a wife and children?

W. He hath a wife and five children.

Q. I believe your General will be King of England in conclusion.

W. Pardon me, Madam, that cannot be, because England is resolved into a Commonwealth; and my General hath already sufficient power and greatness.

Q. Resolve what you will, I believe he resolves to be king; and hardly can any power or greatness be called sufficient when the nature of man is so prone, as in these days, to all ambition.

W. I find no such nature in my General.

Q. It may easily be concealed till an opportunity serve and then it will show itself. How many wives have you had?

W. I have had three wives.

Q. Have you had children by all of them?

W. Yes, by every one of them.

Q. Pardieu, vous êtes incorrigible.

W. Madame, I have been a true servant to your sex; and as it was my duty to be kind to my wives, so I count it my happiness to have many children.

Q. You have done well; and if children do prove well it is no small or usual blessing.

[On 11 January 1654 the Queen told Whitelocke she was going away for eight days and that her Chancellor, Axel Oxenstierna, would continue the negotiations. Two days later Whitelocke was embarrassed to learn that Cromwell had dismissed Parliament and made himself Lord Protector. The Queen, who had had the news before Whitelocke himself, approved of the change and assured Whitelocke that the next step would be that Cromwell would become King.]

15 January. This Lord's Day, early in the morning, the Queen took her journey to see her mother. Her conveyance was by sledges, the easiest and most speedy way for a journey in the winter-time. They wrap themselves warm with furs and the snow is so hard frozen over as ice that it bears horse and sledge, and they pass over rivers, lakes and arms of the sea the nearest way to their journey's end.

[Whitelock's sons and others now tried to persuade him that he should not support Cromwell's illegal assumption of supreme power but he could not contemplate stranding himself and all those with him so far from home. He felt justified in continuing his negotiations which were now being deliberately delayed by the Swedes until more news was received from England. The Queen returned on 20 January and sent for Whitelocke the following day.]

I was admitted into her bedchamber where two stools were set. The Queen sat down and caused me to sit by her. Many compliments passed touching her journey and the like. After this she drew her stool close to me and this discourse passed:

Q. I shall surprise you with something which I intend to communicate to you; but it must be under secrecy.

W. Whatsoever your Majesty may think fit to impart. . .

Q. I have great confidence of your honour and judgment and, though you are a stranger, I shall acquaint you with a business which I have not communicated to any creature. I have it in my thoughts and resolution to quit the Crown of Sweden and to retire unto a private life. What think you of this resolution?

W. I am sorry to hear your Majesty call it a resolution. But I suppose your Majesty is pleased only to droll with your humble servant.

Q. I speak to you the truth; and had it not been for your coming hither, which caused me to defer that resolution, probably it might have been done before this time. The reasons are, because I am a woman, and therefore the more unfit to govern, and subject to the greater inconveniences; that the heavy cares of government do outweigh the glories and pleasures of it, and are not to be embraced in comparison of that contentment which a private retirement brings with it.

W. But, Madam, you enjoy the kingdom by right of descent, you have the full affection and obedience of all sorts of your subjects; why should you be discouraged to continue the reins in your own hands? How can you forsake those who testify so much love for you?

Q. It is my love of the people which causeth me to think of providing a better governor for them than a poor woman can be; and it is somewhat of love to myself, to please my own fancy by private retirement.

W. What your Majesty likes best is best to you; but do you not think that Charles V had as great hopes of contentment by his abdication as your Majesty hath, and yet repented it the same day he did it?

Q. That was by reason of his son's unworthyness; but many other princes have happily and with all contentment retired themselves to a private condition; and I am confident that my

43. 'I am a woman, and therefore the more unfit to govern'. Queen
Christina in 1653, by S. Bourdon.

cousin the Prince [Charles Gustavus, the heir apparent] will see that I shall be duly paid what I reserve for my own maintenance. I can content myself with very little; and for servants, with a lackey and a chambermaid.

[The negotiations over the treaty made little progress and Whitelocke found his expenses exceeding his allowance; he was buying thirty loads of firewood a day, had 'five tables furnished for every meal' for the 'grandees' he felt obliged to entertain, and considered it essential to bestow 'gratuities' on a large scale. He could do nothing to hasten the business in hand, but his personal relations with the Queen continued to grow closer. On 8 February he met his rival for her affections.]

The Queen sent Count Tott to invite me to the audience of the Envoy from Moscow. Later he brought me word that the audience was put off because the Russ had sent word that, the notice of his audience not being given him till about ten o'clock this morning, he had before that time drunk so much aquavitae that he was already drunk, and not in a condition to have his audience that day.

In the evening I went again to Court, as the Queen had invited me, and was brought into her bedchamber with my gentlemen to hear her Majesty's music, which was very rare. The Queen was in a very good humour and, taking me by the hand, she led me to a lady in the room whom they called La Belle Comtesse, the wife of Count Jacob de la Garide. The Queen said to me, 'Discourse with this lady, my bedfellow, and tell me if her inside be not as beautiful as her outside.' I, discoursing with her, found it so, and great modesty, virtue and wit accompanying her excellent beauty and behaviour. The Queen pulled off the Countess's gloves and gave one of them to me for a favour; the other she tore in four pieces and distributed them to others. In recompense of the glove I sent to the 'belle Comtesse' a dozen pairs of English white gloves, which are in much esteem in this country.

[This was Ebba Sparre, regarded as the most beautiful woman in Sweden. As lady-in-waiting she served as bed-warmer to the Queen but the relationship was rumoured to be more intimate.

The Queen's intention to abdicate gradually leaked out, although Whitelocke feigned astonishment when told of it. The treaty negotiations grew increasingly complex and at one time it seemed that the mission would fail. Eventually, after 'long and intricate and, it might be said, vexatious transactions', on 28 April 1654, the treaty was signed. Whitelocke arranged a celebration.]

w. Will your Majesty be pleased on Monday next to go into England?

q. Hardly so soon; yet perhaps I may one day see England. But what is your meaning in this?

w. Madam, Monday next is the first of May, a great day in England when gentlemen wait upon their mistresses to bid the Spring welcome and have some collation for them. Now your Majesty being my mistress, if you will do me the honour, I may wait on you on May-day and have a little treatment for you after the manner of England; this I call going into England.

q. I shall be very willing, as your mistress, to go with you and to see the English mode.

1 May 1654. This being May-day, I put the Queen in mind of it that, as she was my mistress, I was to wait upon her and treat her with some little collation. The Queen said the weather was very cold, yet she was very willing to bear me company after the English mode.

The meat I gave the Queen and her ladies was such fowl as could be gotten, dressed after the English fashion and with English sauces, creams, puddings, custards, tarts, tansies, English apples, pears, cheese, butter, tongues, potted venison, and sweetmeats brought out of England, as my sack and claret also was. My beer was also brewed and my bread made by my own servants in my house, after the English manner; and the Queen and her company seemed highly pleased with this treatment. Some of her company said she did eat and drink more at it than she used to do in three or four days at her own table. The Queen was pleased so far to play the good housewife as to inquire how the butter could be so fresh and sweet, and yet be brought out of England. I, from my cooks, satisfied her Majesty that they put salt butter into milk, where it lay all night, and the next day it would eat fresh and sweet as this did, and any butter new made.

[The ship by which Whitelocke was to return home was not yet ready and he remained at Uppsala, entertaining and frequently seeing the Queen. She invited him, through Vanderlin, her Master of Ceremonies, to attend the meeting of the Riksdag at which her abdication would be announced. Representatives of the four Estates, boors (peasants), citizens, nobility and clergy, were present and the Queen made her entrance.]

After the Queen had sat a little, she rose, and beckoned to the Chancellor [Oxenstierna] to come to her, who came with great

44. 'With good grace and confidence spake to the Assembly'. The
abdication, engraving by W. Swidde.

ceremony and respect; and after a little speaking together he
returned to his place and the Queen sat down again a little time;
then rising up with mettle she came forward and with a good grace
and confidence spake to the Assembly.

[A hitch had occurred, although Whitelocke did not know it at
the time. After the Queen had announced her intentions, leaders of
the three Estates spoke of their regret.]

In the last place stepped forth the Marshal of the Boors, a plain
country fellow, in his clouted shoon, and spake to her Majesty
without any ceremony at all.

'Oh, Lord God, Madam, what do you mean to do? It troubles us
to hear you speak of forsaking those that love you as well as we do.
Can you be better than you are? You are Queen of all these
countries and if you leave this kingdom where will you get such
another? If you should do it (as I hope you won't for all this), both
you and we shall have cause, when it is too late, to be sorry for it.
Therefore my fellows and I pray you to think better on't, and do
keep your crown on your head, then you will keep your own
honour and our peace; but if you lay it down, in my conscience you
will endanger all. Continue in your gears [harness], good Madam,

and be the fore-horse as long as you live, and we will help you the best we can to bear your burden.'

When the boor had ended his speech he waddled up to the Queen, took her hand and shook it heartily; then turning his back on her, he pulled out of his pocket a foul handkerchief and wiped the tears from his eyes, and returned back to his own place again.

[Four days later, on 15 May, Whitelocke saw the Queen alone in her bedchamber and thanked her for allowing him to be present.]

Q. How did you like the manner of it when you were there?
w. It was with the greatest gravity and solemnity that I ever saw in any public assembly, but, Madam, I expected that your Chancellor, after he spake with your Majesty, should have declared the causes of the Council's being summoned.
Q. It belongs to his office and when I called him to me it was to desire him to do it.
w. How then came it to pass that he did not?
Q. He desired to be excused and said that he had taken an oath to my father to keep the Crown on my head, and that if he made the proposition for me to quit the Crown it would be contrary to the oath and he could not do it.
w. Did not your Majesty expect this answer?
Q. Not at all, but was wholly surprised by it; but rather than the Assembly should be put off, and nothing done, I plucked up my spirits the best I could and spoke to them on the sudden as you heard, although much to my disadvantage.
w. Madam, you spoke and acted like yourself and were highly complimented by the several Marshals, but above all the rest by the honest boor.
Q. Were you so taken with his clownery?
w. It seemed to me as pure and clear natural eloquence as could be expected.
Q. I think he spoke from his heart.
w. I believe he did, and acted so too, especially when he wiped his eyes.
Q. He showed his affection to me in that posture more than greater men did in their spheres.

[After further conversation they made their final farewells and Whitelocke offered the Queen his black English horses for her coach in return for the loan of horses to take him to Stockholm (she had hinted that such a present would be welcome), and they parted.

The exchange of presents had proved troublesome. Whitelocke had been offered copper, valued at £2,500, by the Queen in addition to her portrait and small gifts. This was highly acceptable since it could be sold in England and his own presents were, he judged, going to cost him at least £3,000, in addition to the horses for the Queen, worth another £2,000. Four of Whitelocke's gentlemen were given chains of gold of four links, with a gold medal at the end of the chain. Three others, though, were given chains of only three links and some of only two, all with the same gold medal attached. Several were discontented 'because their chains were not so good and valuable as those given to others—so seditious a thing is gold', wrote Whitelocke, and he was much displeased by their behaviour. To avoid the same difficulties with his own presents to the Queen's staff he tried to vary them and in two cases adopted a subtle ruse.]

To Secretary Canterstein I sent my secretary Earle with a silver inkstand, curiously wrought; at sight of which Canterstein seemed much discontented, till Earle showed him the manner of opening the inkstand, and in it forty pieces of English gold, which made the present very acceptable. In like manner I sent to Vanderlin, the Master of Ceremonies, an English beaver hat, with a gold hatband, and a pair of rich English gloves; at which the Master seemed offended, saying that ambassadors used to send better presents to the master of ceremonies; but being desired to try if the gloves would fit him, he found therein forty pieces of gold and thereby much satisfaction in the present.

[At last, on 20 May, the long round of farewell visits was finished and Whitelocke set off for Stockholm, the first lap of his 'longed-for journey of return to England'.]

I had taken leave of the Queen and all my friends in Uppsala. My business was successfully despatched; myself and all my people in good health and exceeding joyful to be on our return homewards. I left not a penny of debt, nor any unrewarded who had done me service. The greater part of my baggage, and most of my inferior servants, were on board a great hoy [barge] of the Queen's to go by water to Stockholm; I and the rest of my people went by land. The Queen's Master of Horse had sent six coach-horses to be ready in the midway from Uppsala to Stockholm [the total distance was forty English miles] and this morning he sent six other horses with my blue coach to my lodging, to carry me the first half of the day's journey, driven by the Queen's coachman. He had also provided a sufficient number of saddle-horses, if they might be so called, he having forgotten to cause saddles to be brought with them, so that most of my people were forced to make shift with straw and cushions instead of saddles.

We arrived in the evening at Stockholm and were conducted to a lodging in the suburbs. This being post-night, I made up my despatches for England, which I had prepared at Uppsala but dated them from Stockholm, that my friends in England might perceive that I was on my journey homewards.

[After ten days at Stockholm, during which Whitelocke heard and recorded details of the abdication and coronation ceremonies at Uppsala, they set off for Lübeck. There they left the Swedish ship which had been placed at their disposal by the Queen and went by road to Hamburg where two English frigates were awaiting them in the Elbe. After attending a banquet in Hamburg, Whitelocke was taken ill as a result, both he and his doctor believed, of an attempt to poison him. He was well enough to sail by 24 June and the voyage began with four days of alternating storm and calm.]

Wednesday 28 June was the day of my greatest deliverance. About five o'clock in the evening rose a very great fog and thick mist so that we could not see our way a ship's length before us. I came upon the deck and, seeing night coming on and that all the sails were spread, I did not like it. I asked the master and the pilot why they spread their sails and they said because the wind favoured them and they might safely run as they did, notwithstanding the bad weather. I asked them if they knew whereabouts they were. They confessed they did not because the sun had not shined whereby they might take the elevation. They continued earnest to hold on their course, saying they would warrant it that there was running enough for all night but I was little satisfied with their reasons, and less with their warranties, which among them are not of binding force. My own reason showed me that to run on as they did with all sails spread might be dangerous and upon a strange earnestness in my own mind and judgment I gave a positive command to the captain to cause all sails to be taken down except a half-furled mainsail. After the sails were taken down I also ordered them to sound and try what water and bottom they had. They found eighteen fathom water; the next sounding they had but fifteen fathom and so lessened every sounding till they came to eight fathom, which startled them and made them endeavour to tack about. But it was too late, for the ship struck upon a bank of sand and there stuck fast. I was sitting with some of the gentlemen in the steerage-room when this happened, and felt a strange motion of the frigate, as if she had leaped, not unlike the curveting of a great horse; and the violence of the striking threw several of the gentlemen from off their seats into the midst of the room. The condition we were in was quickly understood both by seamen and landsmen, more by the seamen than others, who knew less of the danger.

Since nothing would be done but what I in person ordered in this frightful confusion, I ordered the master-gunner to fire some pieces of ordnance, to signify our being in distress. But he was so amazed with the danger that he forgot to unbrace [run out] the guns, and shot away the main-sheet; had not the ship been strong and staunch, the guns had broke the sides of her. I then ordered the sails of the ship to be reversed, that the wind, being high, might so help us off; but no help was it, nor by all the people's coming together to the stern, then to head, then to the sides of the ship, all in a heap together; nothing would help us. Then I ordered the mariners to hoist out one of the boats, in which some would have persuaded me to put out myself and to leave the rest, and seek to preserve my own life, but I knew that if I should go into the boat, besides the dishonour of leaving my people in this distress, so many would strive to enter into the boat with me (a life knows no ceremony) that probably the boat would be sunk by the crowding. [The captain was sent out in the boat to take soundings.]

The captain found it very shallow to windward and very deep to leeward, but no hopes of help. At his return I held it best to begin to lighten the ship by casting overboard the ordnance [guns] and gave orders for it. Walking on the decks to see my orders executed, the boatswain met me and spake thus:

Boatswain. My Lord, what do you mean to do?
w. Why dost thou ask my meaning? It is for our preservation.
b. If it be done, we are all destroyed. It may do well to lighten the ship, but not by throwing overboard the ordnance; you can but drop them close to the ship's side, and where the water is shallow they will lie up against the side of the ship and fret it, and with the working of the sea make her to spring leaks presently.

w. I think thou speak good reason and I will try a little longer before it be done.

Upon this discourse with the honest boatswain I forbade the throwing of the ordnance overboard and as I was sitting on the deck, Mr. Ingelo, one of my chaplains, came to me and said:

Ing. Since there is little hope of continuance in this life, it is good to prepare ourselves for a better life, and therefore it will be good to call the company together in your cabin and recommend our souls to Him. I believe they are not to remain long in these bodies of clay.

w. I pray send and call the people into my cabin to prayer.

Whilst Mr. Ingelo was gone to call the people together, a mariner came from the head of the ship, crying out to me, which caused me to suspect that the ship had sprung a leak and was sinking. He called out:

Mariner. My Lord! My Lord!

w. What's the matter, mariner?

m. She wags! She wags! Upon my life the ship did wag; I saw her move.

w. Mr. Ingelo, I pray stay awhile before you call the people. Fellow-seaman, show me where thou sawest her move.

m. My Lord, here, at the head of the frigate. I saw her move and she moves now,—now she moves! You may see it.

w. My old eyes cannot discern it.

Whilst we were thus speaking and looking the ship herself came off from the sand and miraculously floated on the water. The ship being thus, by the hand of God, again floating on the sea, the mariners would have been hoisting of their sails, but I forbade it and said I would sail no more that night. I spent this night in discourses with my people and went not to bed at all. To express cheerfulness to the seamen, I promised that as soon as light did appear if they would up to the shrouds and top he that could first descry land should have a bottle of good sack.

29 June. As soon as day appeared the mariners claimed many bottles of sack and I endeavoured to give them all content on this day of rejoicing.

Next day they sailed up the Thames and Whitelocke's 'long, most difficult, and most dangerous journey' was over.

Whitelocke was warmly received by Cromwell on his return. He was granted £2,500 in cash and was re-appointed First Commissioner of the Great Seal, a post he later resigned on a matter of principle. He became a member of Parliament again and managed to preserve a relationship with Cromwell and even, after the Protector's death in 1658, with Richard Cromwell, the new Protector.

The Restoration naturally provided an anxious period for Whitelocke who might have found himself on the list of Regicides to be hanged; he had also in 1657 been chairman of the committee to urge Cromwell to become King, which can hardly have endeared him to Charles II. However, Whitelocke had always been adept at keeping out of trouble and the time came when he obtained an audience. The King went so far as to smile at him— but his last words were said to have been: 'Mr. Whitelocke, go into the country; do not trouble yourself any more about state affairs, and take care of your wife and your sixteen children.'

This was not advice to be ignored, and Whitelocke accepted it. He lived another fifteen years, long enough to see the Queen who had told him of her intention to abdicate try to recover the throne of Sweden, then that of Poland, then of Naples. When Whitelocke died in 1675 she still had fourteen years of her outrageous life to endure in poverty in Rome.

23

Samuel Pepys

'He called me Pepys by name'

London to Scheveningen and back, 1660

'Gifford [editor of the *Quarterly Review*] told me he had lately seen a curious journal, kept by a person named Pepys, who had been Secretary to the Admiralty in Charles II's time. Pepys was in the habit of noting down all the occurrences of his life with the most singular minuteness. He employed shorthand for the purpose, the key to which it appears that some friend or other inquisitive person had discovered. Part of it will probably be published by Murray.' Thus wrote Stratford Canning, the diplomatist, in his diary for 3 June 1820. A hundred years earlier, Magdalene College, Cambridge, had inherited Samuel Pepys's library and, just as William Upcott later stated (p. 175), the publication of Evelyn's diary in 1818 had led to the realization that Pepys's library also contained a diary. These six bound volumes, with 'Journal' and the dates stamped on the spine, had been looked at twice and quoted from once, but no one had had time to try to transcribe the apparently obscure shorthand in which they were written. A nineteen-year old undergraduate named John Smith was offered the task and, since he already had a wife and child and no money, he accepted it. No one told him that in the very library itself was also Pepys's copy of Shelton's *Tutor*, which described the shorthand system which Pepys had used: no one knew which of several systems had been used and some believed that it was in fact a private cipher devised by the diarist himself. However, Smith did find a longhand manuscript together with the shorthand from which it had been transcribed and, presumably using the method later used for deciphering the Rosetta Stone, he managed to produce a complete transcription of the diary. It took him three years, working, he said, for twelve to fourteen hours a day. This was two years after

Canning had heard about the project, and in fact John Murray declined to publish the manuscript when it was offered to him. Henry Colburn, the publisher of Evelyn's diary, was more optimistic and about one quarter of the fifty-four volumes of transcript which Smith had prepared was published in 1825 under the so-called editorship of Lord Braybrooke, elder brother of the Master of Magdalene College. Smith was paid £200 for his trouble. The book was enthusiastically received and Sir Walter Scott, reviewing it in *The Quarterly*, observed that, although 'in its tone of sentiment and feeling' it was inferior to Evelyn, it was superior 'in variety and general amusement'; for the review containing this sublime understatement, Scott was paid just half as much as Smith for his three years at the grindstone.

Such is the briefest summary of how Pepys's *Diary* came to be published. The edition over which Lord Braybrooke had presided as editor was perfunctory and misleading, even by the low standards of its day, but nothing could mask the magic of Pepys's writing, however bowdlerized. Reprints were quickly called for and produced and a new, and rather expanded, edition was published in 1848–9. This was also 'edited' by Braybrooke, who had never himself read the diary but only Smith's transcript—which, it was true, was accurate enough to make it hardly necessary for the original to be re-read. Braybrooke, however, did not know this and in the new edition removed all mention of Smith's name. Further editions followed and after Braybrooke's death at the age of seventy-five a new editor was allowed to make a new transcription. Astonishingly enough, this, too, was offered to John Murray II who again declined the book, as his father had done, and another publisher had to be found. The new edition contained four fifths of the whole but the transcript was less accurate than Smith's. In 1893–6 H. B. Wheatley's edition was published, containing almost the whole diary, and this remained the standard edition for nearly eighty years. Even this had little to be said in its favour in terms of scholarship and, when Arthur Bryant published his life of Samuel Pepys in 1933, he was able to foreshadow a definitive edition. Forty-three years later this was completed and published as far as the diary itself was concerned; a final volume of commentary and the index only remain at the time of writing. It may safely be said that, due to the labour and understanding of Mr. Robert Latham and the late Professor William Matthews, and their contributing editors, the *Diary of Samuel Pepys* is available to the world as nearly in its original form as it ever can be, bearing in mind that the greater part of it was originally written, not in longhand at all, but in shorthand with an admixture of longhand words and, for some passages, foreign words and phrases.

Samuel Pepys is said to have been a great naval administrator by those learned in naval administration and his diary provides historians with one of their greatest source-books for the history of seventeenth-century England. Neither description would have dismayed the diarist, who was not a particularly modest man and who was well aware that he was recording a memorable ten years. He had seen Charles I executed and his diary begins with a description of the restoration of Charles II; later, he was able to describe both the Great Plague and the Fire of London. But it is as a matchless piece of literature that the work remains imperishable and it is very unlikely that its writer saw it thus. He was concerned only with describing what was going on, but this included what was going on within his mind as well as the outside events. Unlike Montaigne who, however willing he might be to lay himself bare to his readers, was nevertheless writing for his readers, Pepys was writing exclusively for himself. The fact that he never destroyed his diary, and that he left it in the library he bequeathed to his old college, is strong evidence that he expected it to be read by scholars after his death. But no one was allowed to see it during his lifetime—and he lived for thirty-three years after abandoning the diary in the mistaken belief that he was going blind. Even had anyone been able to penetrate the locked cases in which the diary was kept, he would not have been able to understand what was written unless he happened to have been a student of Shelton's shorthand system and privy to Pepys's own mixture of languages for his erotic entries.

It was of course this exclusion of all living people from knowledge of what Pepys was writing that enabled him to write with an honesty unknown in the case of any other self-revelations. Perhaps, moreover, the consciousness that his words would ultimately be read, although not in his own lifetime, gave an extra dimension to his attitude; there is something between writing for a waiting public and writing merely for the consuming flames. Whatever the explanation, no man before him, not even Montaigne and certainly not Evelyn, has left his readers with such a sense of intimacy with their writer, and the claims of those who came after, such as Boswell or Rousseau, are given short shrift by lovers of Pepys. 'Which, among writers of the past would you most like to have known?' goes the rhetorical question. 'Samuel Pepys,' comes the reply '—but I know him already.'

He was born in 1633, the son of a London tailor, but his family had good connections without which it is hard to see what would have become of him. With the aid of exhibitions, or scholarships, he was educated at St. Paul's School and Magdalene College, Cambridge, where he studied law, Latin, mathematics—and shorthand. A fairly distant relative, Edward Montagu (or Mountagu, later first Earl of Sandwich), then took Pepys into his service as a kind of steward; Montagu, who was intimate with Oliver Cromwell, was at the time spending long periods abroad on naval affairs and needed someone to look after his household in his absence. He increasingly relied on his young cousin, and Pepys felt sufficiently secure in December 1655 to marry the fifteen-year-old daughter of a penniless Huguenot exile. He was then able, with Montagu's help, to get an additional appointment in the Exchequer Office under George Downing (after whom the street was later named). Pepys, and many others, regarded Downing as a perfidious rogue and the post provided little pay; it did however introduce its holder to the system of 'fees' and presents which could provide an excellent substitute. In 1658 Pepys and his wife left Montagu's house in Whitehall, where they had been living, and set up in Axe Yard close by. In the same year he had an operation for the removal of a kidney stone, a formidable ordeal before the advent of chloroform, and one which he repeatedly referred to later in his diary.

With the death of Oliver Cromwell in September 1658 the country was left without an effective leader. The army took over and dismissed the Rump, those fifty odd survivors of what had once been a national parliament of five hundred, but one of its most powerful officers, General Monck, demurred. He marched down from Scotland and gave his support to the fleet and the City of London in declaring for a restoration of parliament, with its inevitable sequel of a restoration of the monarchy. Unknown to Pepys, Montagu was already corresponding with Charles II in May 1659 and, soon after, he resigned his office and went into semi-retirement.

On 1 January 1660 Pepys began his diary with the words: 'Blessed be God, at the end of the last year I was in very good health, without any sense of my old pain but upon taking of cold. I lived in Axe-yard, having my wife and servant Jane, and no more in family than us three.' He was to continue writing it for ten years, at the end of which he would have written a million and a quarter words (Evelyn wrote less than half as much in his diary over a period of sixty years). Like Evelyn, Pepys went abroad soon after beginning his diary but, unlike Evelyn's, his journey was a brief one, culminating in one of the most dramatic episodes in English history.

Montagu was soon persuaded to return from retirement and was appointed General-at-Sea and a member of the Council of State. By now, Pepys wrote, 'everybody drinks the King's health without any fear, whereas before it was very private that a man dare do it.' For Pepys himself it had been a difficult period financially, in spite of the two nominal posts he held. 'Presents' had not been coming in as they should and he had had to borrow from a friend in order to square his accounts. It was therefore with delight that he received from Montagu an invitation to go to sea as his secretary. His luck had turned and, perhaps as an omen, a seaman appeared immediately afterwards and promised ten pounds if a purser's place could be found for him. Pepys closed his entry for the day happily: 'My mind, I must needs remember, hath been very much eased and joyed in my Lord's [Pepys's usual way of referring to Montagu, although he did not become Earl of Sandwich until later in the year] great expression of kindness this day; and in discourse thereupon, my wife and I lay awake an hour or two in our bed.'

After a great deal of preparation, on his own behalf and Montagu's, everything was ready for embarkation. Already a glimpse of the life that lay before him had been afforded: 'Strange how these people do now promise me anything; one a rapier, the other a vessel of wine or a gown, and offered me his silver hatband to do him a courtesy. I pray God keep me from being proud or too much lifted up hereby.'

On 23 March they went aboard the *Swiftsure* which lay at anchor close by the Tower of London. Two days later, among the letters which arrived daily, was one addressed 'to Samuel Pepys Esquire' of which Pepys was 'not a little proud'; he had always counted himself a 'gentleman', now he was a rank higher and but one rank below a knight. The following day he celebrated the second anniversary of his operation, in as good health as ever he was in his life. Commissions began to flow in: £4 from the captain of the *Wexford*, for whom he had got that post from Montagu, thirty shillings from the commander of the *Bearer*, presumably a smaller ship, for the same service.

On 2 April the *Naseby* arrived at Gravesend, where they now 'were, and Montagu and his attendants, including Pepys, transferred themselves. After dinner they went ashore but could not stay for fear of not getting back again, owing to the low water. There was one cloud in the otherwise blue sky of Pepys's spirits: 'My heart exceeding heavy for not hearing of my dear wife; and indeed I do not remember that ever my heart was so apprehensive of her absence as at this very time.' The intention was to join the rest of the fleet in the Downs, that part of the English Channel off Deal, between the North and South Foreland, but the pressure of business and, later, bad weather, prevented their anchoring at their destination until the 10th. When at last they did arrive there was a great welcome. 'Great was the shot of guns from the castles [on shore] and ships and our answers, that I never heard yet so great a rattling of guns.'

Pepys now settled down to a month of work, visits to and from the officers of other ships, and play, which consisted generally of ninepins, music and, occasionally, getting drunk. 'It comes in my mind', he observed on 11 April, 'that I have been a little too free to make mirth with the Minister of our ship, he being a sober and an upright man.' Mysterious visitors arrived on their way to Flanders and duly had their passages smoothed by the great Montagu's secretary. But by 27 April there was no longer any mystery. 'All the world know that they [two recently departed knights] go where the rest of the many gentlemen everyday flock, to the King at Breda.' On 4 May Pepys's cup almost overflowed when Montagu called him to read his letter to the King, 'to see whether I could find any slips in it or no'. Two days later he wrote: 'I went up to my cabin and looked over my accounts and found that all my debts paid and my preparation to sea paid for, I have above £40 clear in my purse.'

The next day he was ordered to write for silk flags and scarlet waistcloths to decorate the ship and also 'for a rich barge, a noise of trumpeters and a set of Fiddlers'. Two days later the secret was out.

'My Lord called me into his cabin and told me how he was commanded to set sail presently for the King, and was very glad thereof; and so put me to writing of letters and other work that night till it was very late.

'11. [May] Up very early in the morning, And so about a great deal of business, in order to our going hence to-day. This morning we begun to pull down all the State's arms in the fleet—having first sent to Dover for painters and others to come to set up the King's.

'After dinner we set sail from the Downs.

'12. In our way in the morning, coming in the midway between Dover and Callis, we could see both places very easily, and very pleasant it was to me but the farther we went the more we lost sight of both lands.'

The next day they 'came within sight of Middelburg shore' and on the following morning Pepys was told that he was looking out on to The Hague. A party was made up to go ashore and kiss the hand of the nine-year old Prince of Orange, the King's nephew (and future William II), and Pepys was given permission by Montagu to join them.

'The weather bad; we were soundly washed when we came near the shore, it being very hard to land there. The shore is, as all the country between that and The Hague, all sand. The rest of the company got a coach by themselves. Mr Creed [Montagu's servant] and I went in the fore-part of a coach, wherein there was two very pretty ladies, very fashionable and with black patches, who very merrily sang all the way and that very well. And were very free to kiss the two blades that were with them.

'I took out my Flagelette and piped, but in piping I dropped my rapier stick; but when I came to The Hague, I sent my boy back again for it and he found it, for which I gave him 6d. but some horse had gone over it and broke the scabberd. The Hague is a most neat place in all respects.

'Here we walked up and down a great while, the town being now very full of Englishmen. By the help of a stranger, an Englishman, we saw a great many placces and were made to understand many things, as the intention of the Maypoles which we saw there standing at every great man's door, of different greatness according to the Quality of the person. About 10 at night the Prince comes home, and we found easy admission. His attendance very inconsiderable for a prince. But yet handsome, and his tutor a fine man and himself a pretty boy. It was bright Moonshine tonight. This done, we went to a place we had taken up to sup in—where a sallet and two or three bones of mutton were provided for a matter of ten of us, which was very strange.'

The next morning the King arrived in The Hague but Pepys makes no mention of the fact: perhaps he did not know. He was up at three in the morning and found a schoolmaster who spoke good English and French and who showed him round—but 'everybody of fashion speak French or Latin, or both.' He then took the schoolmaster back to his lodging for a drink and, after he had gone,

45. 'I and my boy by coach to Scheveningen again'. Detail from *The Shore at Scheveningen* by Willem van de Velde, probably painted in the year Pepys was at Scheveningen.

went off with the Judge Advocate who was sharing the lodging. They then bought some books 'for the love of the binding'.

'After that, the Judge and I and my boy by coach to Scheveningen again—where we went into a house of entertainment and drank there, the wind being very high; and we saw two boats overset there and the gallants forced to be pulled on shore by the heels while their trunks, portmanteaus, hats, and feathers were swimming in the sea.

'In the afternoon my Lord called me on purpose to show me his fine clothes which are now come hither; and indeed are very rich— as gold and silver can make them. Only his sword he and I do not like.'

Pepys stayed on board for supper and was asked to play cards with Montagu, 'but I not knowing Cribbige, we fell into discourse of many things, till it was so rough sea and the ship lurched so much that I was not able to stand; and so he bid me go to bed.'

'As soon as I was up, I went down to be trimmed [shaved] below in the great cabin, and while I was doing of it, in comes Mr. North very sea-sick from shore, and to bed he go.

'My Lord in his best suit, this the first day, in expectation to wait upon the King. But word was brought that the King would not put my Lord to the trouble of coming to him— but that he would come to the shore to look upon the fleet to-day; which we expected, and had our guns ready to fire and our scarlet waistcloths out and silk pennants, but he did not come.

'This afternoon Mr. Pickering [a relative by marriage of Montagu's] told me in what a sad, poor condition for clothes and money the King was, and all his attendants, when he came to him first from my Lord—their clothes not being worth 40s, the best of them. And how overjoyed the King was when he was brought some money; so joyful that he called the Princess Royal [his sister] and Duke of York [his brother, later James II] to look upon it as it lay in the portmanteau before it was taken out.'

The next day Pepys and some others went on shore and by coach to The Hague in the hope of 'finding one that might show us the King incognito'. They found a friend who promised to do so. 'But first we went and dined—at a French house, but paid 16s for our part of the club. At dinner in came Dr. Cade, a merry mad parson of the King's. And they two after dinner got the child [Montagu's eldest son, Edward] and me, the others not being able to crowd in, to see the King, who kissed the child very affectionately. There we kissed his and the Duke of York's and the Princess Royal's hands. The King seems to be a very sober man; and a very splendid Court he has in the number of persons of quality that are about him; English, very rich in habit. From the King to the Lord Chancellor [Sir Edward Hyde who had been given the title by the King and was staying with him at the Mauritzhuis] who did lie bed-rid of the gout; he spoke very merrily to the child and me. Then to see the Queen of Bohemia [the King's aunt] who used us very respectfully. She seems a very debonaire, but plain lady.'

After that they went to see 'the house in the woods' (*Huis ten Bosch*), the home of the widow of Prince Frederick of Orange, and here they fell among friends from England and 'had two or three fine songs which was very pleasant. . . The more so because in a haven of pleasure and in a strange country—that I never was taken up more with a sense of pleasure in my life. After that we parted and back to The Hague and took a tour or two about the Forehault [Voorhout, the principal street] where the ladies in the evening do as our ladies do in Hidepark. But for my life I could not find one handsome; but their coaches very rich and themselves so too.'

Next morning, very early, Pepys and Pickering went by wagon to Scheveningen, intending to re-embark and greet the Duke of York who was expected to go on board. High winds made this impossible so they returned to The Hague and found that young Edward Montagu, who had been left behind with Mr. Pierce, the *Naseby*'s surgeon, had gone off to see Delft. 'So we all took a schuit [a canal barge] and went after them, but met them by the way. But,

46. 'A haven of pleasure'. The 'Huis ten Bosch' at The Hague, by Jan van
der Heyden, painted shortly after Pepys was in The Hague.

however, we went forward, making no stop—where when we were
come, we got a smith's boy of the town to go along with us (but
could speak nothing but Dutch) and he showed us the church
where Van Tromp [the Dutch admiral] lies intombed. It is a most
sweet town, with bridges and a river in every street. After we had
seen all, we light by chance of an English house to drink in, where
we were very merry discoursing of the town. Back by water, where
a pretty sober Dutch lass sat reading all the way, and I could not
fasten any discourse upon her.'

On landing at The Hague again they met more friends and went
off for another visit to the *Huis ten Bosch*. 'Besides, we went into the
garden wherein is gallant knots [flowerbeds], better than ever I
saw, and a fine echo under the house in a vault made on purpose
with pillars, where I played on my flagelette to great advantage.
Ater that to our lodging where I was exceeding troubled not to
know what is become of our young gentleman [Edward Montagu].

'19. Up early hearing nothing of the child, and went to
Scheveningen, where I found no getting on board, though the
Duke of York sent every day to know whether he could do it or no.
At The Hague we went to buy some pictures and while we were
here we saw Mr. Edward and his company land—who told me they

had been at Leyden all night, at which I was very angry with Mr. Pierce and shall not be friends, I believe, a good while. To our lodging for dinner. After that out to buy some linen to wear against tomorrow, and so to the barber's. We went into a little drinking-house, where there was a great many Dutch boores eating of fish in a boorish manner, but very merry in their way. From hence to The Hague again where I met my old chamber fellow Mr. Ch. Anderson and a friend who took me to a Dutch house where there was an exceeding pretty lass and right for the sport; but it being Saturday we could not have much of her company. However I stayed with them till 12 at night; by that time Charles was almost drunk; and then broke up, he resolving to go thither again and lie with the girl, which he told me he had done in the morning.

'20. Up early and with Mr. Pickering and the child by waggon to Scheveningen, where it not yet being fit to go off, I went to lie down in a chamber in the house, where in another bed there was a pretty Dutch woman in bed alone; but though I had a month's-mind to her, I had not the boldness to go to her. So there I sleep an hour or two. At last she rise; and then I rise and walked up and down the chamber and saw her dress herself after the Dutch dress and talked to her as much as I could; and took occasion to kiss her hand but had not the face to offer anything more. So at last I left her and went to my company.

'[Navy] Commissioner Pett at last comes to our lodging and caused the boats to go off, so we all bid adieu to the shore. But through badness of weather we were in great danger, and a great while before we could get the ship; so that of all the company not one but myself that was not sick. This has not been known, four days together such weather at this time of year, a great while— indeed our fleet was thought to be in great danger, but we found all well. Being not very well settled, partly through last night's drinking and want of sleep, I lay down in my gown upon my bed and sleep till the 4 o'clock gun the next morning waked me, which I took for 8 that night; and rising to piss, mistook the sun-rising for the sun-setting on Sunday night.'

Pepys's week of sightseeing and pleasure, with all its temptations was at last over. On 22 May the storm abated and the Dukes of York and Gloucester went on board, to a salute of guns 'round the fleet'. They seemed to be 'both very fine Gentlemen' and the Duke of York joined Montagu and Pepys for an hour 'allotting to every ship their service in their return to England'. Dinner followed, to which Pepys was not invited, and then the Dukes went ashore in the Dutch boat which had brought them. 'The shore was so full of people to expect their coming as that it was as black (which otherwise is white sand) as everyone would stand by another.' Pepys and Montagu followed. 'By the time we came on board again, news is sent us that the King is on shore; so my Lord fired all his guns round twice, and all the fleet after him. The gun over against my cabin I fired myself to the King, which was the first time that he hath been saluted by his own ships since this change. But holding my head too much over the gun, I have almost spoiled my right eye.

'Nothing in the world but going of guns almost all this day. Many of the King's servants came on board to-night; and so many Dutch of all sorts came to see the ship till it was quite dark that we could not pass one by another, which was a great trouble to us all.

'23. The Doctor and I waked very merry, only my eye was very red and ill in the morning from yesterday's hurt. In the morning came infinity of people on board from the King, to go along with him.

'My Lord and others go on shore to meet the King as he comes off from shore, where I hear that His Majesty did with a great deal of affection kiss my Lord upon his first meeting.

'The King, with the two Dukes, the Queen of Bohemia, the Princess Royal and the Prince of Orange came on board; where I in their coming in kissed the King's, Queen's and Princess's hands, having done the other before. Infinite shooting off of guns, and that in a disorder on purpose, which was better than if it had been otherwise.

'All day nothing but Lords and persons of Honour on board, that we were exceeding full.

'Dined in a great deal of state, the Royal company by themselves in the coach [captain's state-room], which was a blessed sight to see.

'After dinner, the King and Duke altered the name of some of the ships, viz, the *Naseby* into *Charles*. That done, the Queen and others took leave of the King, which done, we weighed anchor and, with a fresh gale and most happy weather, we set sail for England— all the afternoon the King walking here and there, up and down (quite contrary to what I thought him to have been), very active and stirring.

'Upon the Quarter-deck he fell in discourse of his escape from Worcester [in 1651]. Where it made me ready to weep to hear the

47. 'Infinite shooting of guns'. The departure of Charles II, engraved by
Nicolaus Visscher after P. H. Schut.

stories he told of his difficulties he had passed through. As his
travelling four days and three nights on foot, every step up to the
knees in dirt, with nothing but a green coat and a pair of country
breeches on and a pair of country shoes, that made him so sore all
over his feet that he could scarce stir. Yet he was forced to run away
from a miller and other company that took them for rogues. His
sitting at table at one place, where the master of the house, that had
not seen him in eight years, did know him but kept it private; when
at the same table there was one that had been of his own Regiment
at Worcester, could not know him but made him drink the King's
health and said that the King was at least four fingers higher than
he. Another place he was by some servants of the house made to
drink, that they might know him not to be a Roundhead, which
they swore he was. In another place, at his inn [the *George* at
Brighton], the master of the house, as the King was standing with
his hands upon the back of a chair by the fireside, he kneeled down
and kissed his hand privately, saying that he would not ask him
who he was, but bid God bless him whither he was going. Then the
difficulty of getting a boat to get into France, where he was fain to
plot with the master thereof to keep his design from the four men
and a boy (which was all his ship's company), and so got to Fécamp
in France [having sailed from Shoreham]. At Rouen he looked so

poorly that the people went into the rooms before he went away to see whether he had not stole something or other.'[1]

After the privilege of being perhaps the first to hear the King's own account of his experiences (he could not speak openly before without risk to those who had helped him), the next day was bound to be something of an anticlimax for Pepys. He made himself as fine as he could with the linen stockings and wide boot ornaments ('canons') he had bought in The Hague and spent most of the day in conversation with the King's attendants. At the end of it came another moment of excitement. He was called upon to write a pass for Lord Mandeville to take horses up to London which he wrote 'in the King's name and carried it to him to sign, the first and only one that ever he signed in the ship *Charles*.' They came in sight of land a little before dark.

'25. By the morning we were come close to the land and everybody made ready to get on shore.

'The King and the two Dukes did eat their breakfast before they went, and there being set some ship's diet before them, only to show them the manner of the ship's diet, they eat of nothing else but pease and pork and boiled beef.

'I spoke with the Duke of York about business, who called me Pepys by name, and upon my desire did promise me his future favour. Great expectations of the King's making some Knights, but there was none. About noon (though a brigantine was there ready to carry him) yet he would go in my Lord's barge with the two Dukes; our captain steered and my Lord went along bare with him. I, with two others, went in a boat by ourselves with a dog that the King loved (which shit in the boat, which made us laugh and think that a King and all that belong to him are but just as others are) and so got on shore when the King did, who was received [by General Monck] with all imaginable love and respect at his entrance upon the land at Dover. Infinite the crowd of people and the gallantry of the horsemen, citizens and noblemen of all sorts. And so [after reception by the Mayor] away straight through the town towards Canterbury without making any stay at Dover.

'I, seeing that my Lord did not stir out of his barge, got into a boat and so into his barge and so returned. My Lord almost transported with joy that he hath done all this without the least blur and obstruction in the world that would give an offence to any, and with the great honour that he thought it would be to him.

'26. All the great company being gone, I find myself very uncouth [at a loss] all this day for want thereof.'

It was understandable, but the rewards were still to come. For Pepys there was £30 out of the £500 the King had given to the ship's officers and another £7 as one of Montagu's staff. For Montagu himself there was the Order of the Garter, brought by Garter King of Arms from London on the King's command. There was much work to be done and Pepys and Montagu, now Sir Edward, did not leave the *Charles* finally until 8 June. By 2 June, though, Pepys could discern his future:

'Being with my Lord in the morning about business in his cabin, I took occasion to give him thanks for his love to me in the share he had given me of His Majesty's money and the Duke's. He told me that he hoped to do me a more lasting kindness, if all things stand as they are now between him and the King—but says "We must have a little patience and we will rise together. In the meantime I will do you all the good jobs I can." Which was great content for me to hear from my Lord.'

[1]Twenty years later, in October 1680, the King dictated this story in fuller detail to Pepys who later transcribed the shorthand in which he had taken it down. It was these two manuscripts, later found in Pepys's library, that enabled John Smith, unaware of the existence of Shelton's *Tutor* in the same library, to make the first transcription of Pepys's diary (see p. 221).

24

Samuel Pepys

'My condition doth require it'

An Epilogue on the acquisition of a coach, 1665–8

'At this day,' wrote Fynes Moryson of the beginning of the seventeenth century, 'pride is so far increased that there be few gentlemen of any account who have not their coaches.' And, lest there be any doubt as to what constituted a gentleman of account, he added 'I mean elder brothers.' Younger brothers, minor officials, lawyers, priests, did not keep their own coach. Outside England it was not very different, although the coach had made its appearance earlier. Erasmus found no difficulty in hiring a vehicle of some sort in 1518 although he found the pace slow and the smell of the horses disagreeable (it was their *pedor*, breaking wind, that he minded); even Montaigne occasionally hired a coach, although he could not long endure any other transport than horseback. Neither, it is true, thought of owning his own coach. In Germany, Moryson 'compounded with a merchant' to carry him in his coach from Hamburg to Leipzig, and a merchant was not a gentlemen of account. A coach to such a man, though, was a tool of his trade, probably used to accompany goods being carried by wagon, or even to carry small merchandise itself: 'pride' played but a small part in its acquisition. In short, the ordinary traveller did not yet own a coach.

By 1665, five years after Pepys had brought the King back from Holland, the number of coaches had increased to an extent that made them a thorough nuisance, at any rate in the narrow streets of London. They were, though, still the coaches of the gentlemen of account and the hackney-coaches, often a gentleman's coach that had seen better days; the 'younger brother's' day of ownership had still not arrived. There were arguments against private ownership.

None of the coaches had glass windows, and instead of springs they had leather straps which did little to allay the jolting of the occupants over the cobbled roads of London and nothing to avoid the swaying of the vehicle over the mud tracks which still passed for roads out in the country. There was a feeling in the air that improvements were not far away.

One day, on 1 May 1665, Pepys was on his way to the Royal Exchange when he ran into some friends.

'They were going by coach to Colonel Blunt's to dinner. So they stopped and took me with them. Landed at the Tower-wharf, and thence by water to Greenwich; and there coaches met us; and to his house, a very stately sight for situation and brave plantations; and among others a vineyard, the first that ever I did see. No extraordinary dinner, nor any other entertainment good; but only after dinner to the trial of some experiments about making of coaches easy. And several we tried; but one did prove mighty easy (not here for me to describe, but the whole body of the coach lies upon one long spring), and we all, one after another, rid in it; and it is very fine and likely to take. These experiments were the intent of their coming, and pretty they are. Thence back by coach to Greenwich, and in his pleasure boat to Deptford, and there stopped and into Mr. Evelyn's, which is a most beautiful place; but it being dark and late, I staid not.'

This was Pepys's first meeting with John Evelyn who was thirteen years his senior and had been settled at Sayes Court, the house given him by his father-in-law, since 1652. Evelyn had bought himself a coach in the year he took possession of Sayes Court and replaced it two years later. He notes the purchase of a new one in 1666 and again in 1669 but it may be presumed that he did not keep his second coach for twelve years: the arrival of a replacement was scarcely worth recording.

Evelyn had been one of the original Fellows of the Royal Society on its foundation in 1652. It was the Royal Society that had supported the efforts of Colonel Blunt to find a better form of suspension for coaches than the leather strap, and the friends whom Pepys joined to visit the Colonel's house were members of a committee appointed to study Blunt's proposals and report at the next meeting of the Society. The results were evidently encouraging and on 5 September Pepys was dining with a friend when Colonel Blunt appeared again.

'He was in his new chariot made with springs; as that was of wicker, wherein a while since we rode at his house. And he hath rode, he says, now this journey, many miles in it with one horse, and out-drives any coach, and out-goes any horse, and so easy he says. So for curiosity I went into it to try it, and up the hill to the heath [they were at Shooter's Hill, Blackheath] and over the cartruts and found it pretty well, but not so easy as he pretends.'

On 22 January 1666 the committee again went to Colonel Blunt's house and one of them rode back in the new chariot. Pepys wrote: 'The coachman sits astride upon a pole over the horse, which is a pretty odd thing; but it seems it is most easy for the horse, and, as they say, for the man also.'

In spite of Colonel Blunt's persistence it seems probable that Pepys's doubts were shared by other members of the Royal Society. At any rate, Blunt retired from the Society the following year and no other significant development in carriage suspension is recorded for the period.

Pepys would have been less than human had an idea not entered his mind which he did not confide, even to the diary from which he had no secrets, until more than a year later. Why should he not keep a coach? He may not have been a gentleman of account such as Evelyn who, although also a younger son, had inherited both from a wealthy father and a distinguished father-in-law and had enjoyed Court favour since the Restoration. Pepys was the younger son of a tailor, connected with the nobility only by earlier family marriages, with a penniless wife, and dependent for his living on what he could earn. But the years since Montagu had promised him they would rise together had been good years. He had himself been elected to the Royal Society in February 1665. Worth £40, with all debts paid, when he sailed to Holland on the *Naseby*, he was worth £1,300 ('for which God be praised!') when he first met Evelyn, and £5,000 by the beginning of 1666. The Duke of Albemarle had told him he was 'the right hand of the Navy'; gifts and prizes which were a recognized part of the posts he held were an unfailing source of income. He passed unscathed, and with some credit, through the plague of 1665 and the fire of 1666. News of the war with Holland seemed encouraging. On 21 April 1667 Pepys at last confided his thoughts to his diary.

'(Lords day) Up, and John, a hackney-coachman whom of late I have much used, coming to me by direction to see whether I would use him today or no, I took him to our back-gate to look upon the ground which is to be let there, where I have a mind to buy enough to build a coach-house and stable; for I have had it much in my

48. 'I am almost ashamed to be seen in a hackney'. Hackney coaches waiting outside the palace of Westminster in 1647, by W. Hollar.

thoughts lately that it is not too much for me now, in degree or cost, to keep a coach; but contrarily, that I am almost ashamed to be seen in a hackney; and therefore, if I can have the conveniency, I will secure the ground at least till peace comes, that I do receive encouragement to keep a coach or else that I may part with the ground again. The place I like very well, being close by my own house, and so resolve to go about it.'

Five days later he had to confess: 'My mind is mightily of late upon a coach' and the following month, on 8 May, he chanced to meet Mr. Andrews, his neighbour, and spoke to him about the ground. He added: '. . . for I do see that my condition doth require it, as well as that it is more charge to my purse to live as I do than to keep one; and therefore I resolved before winter to have one, unless some extraordinary thing happens to hinder me. He [Mr. Andrews] promises to look after it for me.'

Pepys had no diffidence in admitting to himself that he had reached a position where 'honour' demanded that he keep his own coach, yet there was still sufficient doubt in his mind to spur him to find another justification. It was really an economy, he told himself, again and again. He took his lawyer to the site on 11 May.

'My condition doth require it'. Samuel Pepys in 1666, by J. Hayls.

'He and I out to the ground where I am resolved to take a lease of some of it for a stable and coach, and so keep a coach, unless some change come before I can do it; for I do see it is a greater charge to me now in hackneys and I am a little dishonoured by going in them.'

Again, on 1 June, the theme recurred: 'I do find it necessary for me, both in respect to honour and the profit of it also (my expense in hackney-coaches being now so great) to keep a coach, and therefore will do it.'

But resolution was not enough. Circumstance intervened in the form of a flaw in the title of the ground and the whole plan had to be deferred 'till a suit in the law be ended'. 'I am a little sorry that I cannot presently have it,' Pepys wrote philosophically, 'because I am pretty full in my mind of keeping a coach; but yet, when I think on it again. . .' The Dutch and the French were still at sea against England and England was poor; there was no knowing what turns there might be and he was about to lose one of his posts. 'I ought to be well contented to hope awhile, and therefore am contented,' he wrote, and then, to underline the sacrifice he was making, he crossed out 'hope' and substituted 'forbear'.

He forbore for two days and then, after a trying morning at the office where his accounts were being examined by unfriendly auditors, he confessed that he was not wholly content. 'Home and to sing and pipe with my wife; and then to supper and to bed—my head full of thoughts how to keep, if I can, some part of my wages as Surveyor of the Victualling, which I see must now come to be taken away, among the other places which have been occasioned by this war—and the rather because I have of late an inclination to keep a coach.'

These and, with one exception, all other thoughts were driven out of Pepys's mind when, on 12 June, the Dutch fleet sailed up the Medway, raided Chatham dockyard and finally escaped, towing one of the Navy's principal ships with it. Invasion or at least a rising of the people against those responsible for the disgrace, including Pepys himself, were talked of. There was time for nothing except business—and the dispersal of such gold as he could lay his hands on, together with 'my journals, which I value much'.

There was no invasion and gradually hope began to spread that the representatives of England, France and Holland, who had been discussing peace at Breda, might be successful at last. On 24

August Pepys took his wife to Mile End to drink the ale of Alderman Bides, a Shoreditch brewer. 'And so home, most of our discourse about keeping a coach the next year, which pleases my wife mightily; and if I continue as able [wealthy] as now it will save us money.'

'All afternoon talking in my chamber with my wife about keeping a coach the next year,' he wrote in September and, as the time grew nearer, he told himself that it was expected of him. On 3 June 1688 he went into the Park, where there were many fine ladies. 'And in so handsome a hackney I was, that I believe Sir W. Coventry and others, who looked on me, did take me to be in one of my own, which I was a little troubled for.'

On 20 October a new girl was taken into the house, but 'to stay only till we have a boy, which I intend to keep when I have a coach, which I am now about'. That afternoon he went 'to look out for a coach, and saw many; and did light on one' for which he bid £50 and which pleased him mightily. The bid was accepted, the 'finishing' agreed and the coachmaker promised to fit Pepys with a coachman. His wife was taken to Cow Lane to see the coach and was 'out of herself for joy almost'.

And then a bitter blow. Thomas Povey, a colleague for whose competence Pepys had nothing but contempt, but whose taste he admired, was told of the purchase. 'And I got him to see it, where he finds the most infinite fault with it, both as to being out of fashion and heavy, with so good reason that I am mightily glad of his having corrected me in it; and so I do resolve to have one of his build, and with his advice, both in coach and horses, he being the fittest man in the world for it. And so he carried me home, and said the same to my wife.'

There was a delay of just over a month, but on 28 November the coach approved by Povey was delivered at the Navy Office, and the coachman's clothes at home in the afternoon. Two days later Elizabeth Pepys 'went for the first time abroad to take the maidenhead of her coach' and her husband was able to reflect. Less than five weeks earlier he had been discovered by Elizabeth *in flagrante delicto* with her servant, Deb Willet. Now he wrote: 'Thus ended this month with very good content, that hath been the most sad to my heart and the most expenseful to my purse on things of pleasure, having furnished my wife's closet and the best chamber, and a coach and horses, that ever I yet knew in the world; and doth put me into the greatest condition of outward state that ever I was in, or hoped ever to be, or desired.'

50. 'Out of fashion and heavy'. Detail of W. Hollar's engraving of Covent Garden, 1640.

Only in the admittance of later readers to the secret processes that moved him was Pepys's purchase of a coach unusual. All over Europe roads were being prepared to receive the wheeled transport that was no longer the prerogative of princes, ambassadors and elder sons. The horse would dominate those roads for another two centuries or so, but as a mere beast of burden, despised as the ass, mule or ox. His long reign as the closest companion of the European traveller was ended.

SOURCES
AND BIBLIOGRAPHY

Translations and transcriptions are based on the following sources, the first in each case being the principal, or only, one used. All published in London unless otherwise stated.

HORACE Translation based on C. Smart's literal translation, 1858, and those of Lonsdale and Lee, 1887, and E. C. Wickham, 1903. For commentaries, see Arthur Palmer, 1899, and *The Satires of Horace*, Nial Rudd, 1966. Illustrations suggested by *Roman Colonization under the Republic*, E. T. Salmon, 1969.

PLINY Reprinted by permission of Penguin Books Ltd. from Book 2, letter 17 and Book 6, letter 20 of Betty Radice's translation of *The Letters of the Younger Pliny*, 1963.

SIDONIUS *Letters of Sidonius*, trs. O. M. Dalton, Oxford, 1915; *Sidonius, Poems and Letters*, trs. W. B. Anderson, 1963.

ROBERT OF CLARI *The Conquest of Constantinople*, trs. Edgar Holmes McNeal, Columbia U.P., 1936; *La Conquête de Constantinople*, ed. Philippe Lauer, Paris, 1924; *Villehardouin: La Conquête de Constantinople*, ed. and trs. into modern French, with original text alongside, Edmond Faral, Paris, 1938 (also trs. into English, T. Smith, London, 1829).

TAFUR *Pero Tafur: Travels and adventures*, trs. and ed. Malcolm Letts, London, 1926; *Andanças è Viajes*, ed. with voluminous biographies by M. Jimenez de la Espada, Madrid, 1874. (Also an article by Otto Cartellieri in *Festschrift to Alexander Cartellieri*, Weimar, 1927.)

BRASCA AND FABRI *The Wanderings of Santo Brasca and Felix Fabri*, trs. Aubrey Stewart, Palestine Pilgrims Text Society, 1892–7; *Jerusalem Journey*, 1954 and *Once to Sinai*, 1957, by H. F. M. Prescott.

CASOLA *Canon Pietro Casola's Pilgrimage to Jerusalem* by M. Margaret Newett, Manchester, 1907.

COMINES *Memoirs of Philip de Comines*, ed. and trs. Andrew R. Scobie, 1901.

TREVISANO, BADOER AND GIUSTINIAN *Calendar of State Papers and Manuscripts relating to English Affairs (Venice)*, vol. I, 1202–1509, 1864 and vol. II, 1509–1519, 1867, ed. Rawdon Brown; *Four Years at the Court of Henry VIII* by Rawdon Brown, 1854.

ERASMUS *Life and Letters of Erasmus* by J. A. Froude, 1894.

DÜRER *The Writings of Albrecht Dürer* by William Martin Conway, 1958; *Albrecht Dürer, Sketchbook of his journey to the Netherlands*, trs. with a commentary by Philip Troutman, 1971; *Albrecht Dürers Niederländische Reise* by J. Veth, S. Muller, 2 vols., Berlin and Utrecht, 1918.

CELLINI *The Life of Benvenuto Cellini*, trs. John Addington Symonds, 1889; trs. R. H. Hobart Cust, 1910; trs. George Bull, Penguin Classics, 1956.

NUCIUS *A Relation of the Island of England* by Charlotte Augusta Sneyd, Camden Society, 1847

MONTAIGNE *The Diary of Montaigne's Journey to Italy*, trs. E. J. Trechmann, Hogarth Press, 1929; *Complete Works of Montaigne*, trs. Donald M. Frame, Hamish Hamilton, 1958; *Oeuvres complètes de M. de Montaigne*, vols. 7 and 8, Dr. Armaingaud, Paris, 1928: *Giornale del viaggio di Michele de Montaigne*, ed. Alexandre d'Ancona, Città di Castello, 1889 (containing an exhaustive bibliography of the writings of foreign visitors to Italy).

MORYSON *An Itinerary*, Fynes Moryson, 1617 reprinted Glasgow, 1908; *Shakespeare's Europe*, unpublished chapters of Fynes Moryson's *Itinerary*, Charles Hughes, London, 1903.

CORYAT *Coryat's Crudities*, Thomas Coryat, 1611, reprinted, Glasgow, 1905.

EVELYN *The Diary of John Evelyn*, ed. John Bray, 1818 and many subsequent editions; ed. E. S. de Beer, Oxford 1955.

WHITELOCKE *A Journal of the Swedish Embassy in the years 1653 and 1654, impartially written by the Ambassador Bulstrode Whitelocke, first published from the original manuscript by Dr. Charles Morton; a new edition revised by Henry Reeve*, 1855.

PEPYS *The Diary of Samuel Pepys*, transcribed by Mynors Bright, ed. Henry B. Wheatley, 1893–9 and many subsequent editions; new and complete transcription ed. Robert Latham and William Matthews, 1970–

In addition to the above, and to sources already acknowledged in the text and notes, material not available from usual sources has been used from the following:

BABEAU, ALBERT: *Les Voyageurs en France depuis la Renaissance jusqu'à la Révolution*, Paris, 1885.

BRAUDEL, FERNAND: *The Mediterranean and the Mediterranean World in the Age of Philip II*, trans. Sian Reynolds, London, 1972.

HAY, DENIS: *Europe in the Fourteenth and Fifteenth centuries*, London, 1966.

MOLMENTI, P.: *La storia di Venezia nella vita privata*, Turin, 1880.

ORIGO, IRIS: *The Domestic Enemy*, Speculum, 30 (1955); *The Merchant of Prato*, 1957.

PINE-COFFIN, R. S.: *Bibliography of British and American Travel in Italy to 1860*, Florence, 1974.

RUNCIMAN, STEVEN: *A History of the Crusades*, vol. III, book II, chap. 1, Cambridge, 1954.

SINGER, CHARLES and others (ed.); *A History of Technology*, Oxford, 1957.

STOYE, J. W.: *English Travellers Abroad, 1604–1667*, 1952.

INDEX